ALLISON TRANSMISSIONS

HOW TO REBUILD & MODIFY

Steve Garrett

S-A DESIGN

CarTech®

CarTech®

CarTech®, Inc.
6118 Main Street
North Branch, MN 55056
Phone: 651-277-1200 or 800-551-4754
Fax: 651-277-1203
www.cartechbooks.com

Edit by Wes Eisenschenk
Layout by Monica Seiberlich

ISBN 978-1-61325-779-1
Item No. SA540

Library of Congress Cataloging-in-Publication Data Available

Written, edited, and designed in the U.S.A.
Printed in China
10 9 8 7 6 5 4 3 2 1

Author note: A special thanks to Tom Hess for being my hand model and for help with the photos for this book.

DISTRIBUTION BY:

Europe
PGUK
63 Hatton Garden
London EC1N 8LE, England
Phone: 020 7061 1980 • Fax: 020 7242 3725
www.pguk.co.uk

Australia
Renniks Publications Ltd.
3/37-39 Green Street
Banksmeadow, NSW 2109, Australia
Phone: 2 9695 7055 • Fax: 2 9695 7355
www.renniks.com

Canada
Login Canada
300 Saulteaux Crescent
Winnipeg, MB, R3J 3T2 Canada
Phone: 800 665 1148 • Fax: 800 665 0103
www.lb.ca

CONTENTS

LCT 1000 and 2000 Allison Operation and Service

Allison Transmission is the world's largest producer of medium- and heavy-duty transmissions. It was part of General Motors until 2007, when the division was sold to the Carlyle Group and Onex Corporation.

The Allison 1000- and 2000-series transmissions were introduced in 1999 on non-GM applications and in 2001 on GM applications. Production continued for GM applications through the 2019 model year, at which time the transmission was replaced by a 10-speed (10L1000) for 2020-and-later applications. Non-GM applications are still being produced.

General Motors refers to the transmissions as the Light Commercial Truck (LCT) 1000 or 2000, while non-GM applications refer to the transmissions as the A1000 or the A2000. The primary differences between the 1000 and the 2000 is component size, gear ratios, and unit torque capacity. The 2000 uses larger components, which means it can be used in larger vehicles.

General Motors uses the 1000 and 2000 in pickup, van, and medium-duty truck applications equipped with a 6.6L Duramax diesel or an 8.1L Vortec gas engine, although not all van applications with the Duramax use the Allison. Non-GM applications use the 1000 and 2000 transmissions in Peterbilt, Kenworth, Ford, Freightliner, Hino, Isuzu, Sterling, and International truck and bus applications to name a few. Multiple 1000- and 2000-series transmissions are available, depending on the application. The differences between models can be anything from clutch count to whether or not the transmission is equipped with a parking pawl. There are some differences between the General Motors and non-GM applications, so some parts are interchangeable while other components are not.

Since there are differences between the various applications, it is important to properly identify which one is on the lift before ordering parts or a remanufactured unit. Allison units are referred to by the model and a use designation. Allison 1000 models include the 1000, 1350, 1700, and 1750. The 2000 models include the 2100, 2200, 2300, 2350, 2400, 2500, 2650, 2700, and 2750.

The model-use designator further breaks down the model into its vehicle

Multiple versions of the 1000- and 2000-series units were used, such as this Allison 2400. Make sure to find out which transmission you are working on. This information is located on the tag. The service process is the same for all versions, but the parts vary greatly and many are not interchangeable.

type and application. Each Allison uses a two- or three-digit designator to identify the type of use for which the transmission was designed. The model designation looks like this: A2200MH, A2350PTS, or A2300RDS. Designators can include abbreviations in the following table.

Abbreviation	Designation
EVS	Emergency vehicle service
HS	Highway service
MH	Motor home
MIL	Military
PTS	Pupil transportation service (school bus)
RDS	Rugged duty service
SP	Specialty
PK	Pickup

GM Allison units are available as 5-speed or 6-speed applications, while non-GM applications are available as 5-, 6-, or 7-speed versions. The 6-speed 1000- and 2000-series applications were introduced in the 2006 model year. More than 100 update changes have occurred with the 1000- and 2000-series units. Several of the changes will not back service earlier-model applications.

Generations

Six generations of Allison 1000- and 2000-series applications have been produced. Generations 1 through 3 were used from 1999 to 2005. Generation 4 ran from 2006 to 2012 on non-GM applications and from 2006 to 2014 on GM applications. Generation 5 was used for 2013 to 2021 non-GM applications and from 2015 to 2019 on GM applications. Generation 6 was introduced in 2022.

Keep in mind that GM applications never ran the Generation-6 units, as it is now using the 10L1000 that replaced the LCT 1000. Multiple changes occurred with each generation, so always rely on the unit serial number to access the correct parts and service information for your application.

Transmission Identification

Years ago, the GM numbering system for transmissions was significantly different than it is today. Everything except the Allison 5- and 6-speed applications and some units developed by Aisin Warner and Jatco are numbered using the GM numbering system.

Early Years

Allison's numbering systems included A, B, S, and M, which designated the application for which the transmission was used (automotive, bus, or marine). Truck applications included units such as the AT542, AT543, and AT545. All of those units were 4-speed applications.

Hydra-Matic and Allison were the GM divisions that provided the transmission engineering and manufacturing for General Motors. Allison quickly became the dominant heavy-duty automatic transmission in the heavy-truck market worldwide.

1991

Allison introduced its fully computer-controlled units in the 1990s. Allison introduced its "world transmissions" as it expanded its lineup into more trucks and buses worldwide. The world transmission led the way for all manufacturers with technology changes that had never been seen before in the automotive and heavy-truck markets.

With the advent of the new transmission designs, Allison changed the designations of the world transmission to include multiple-series units, such as the 1000-, 2000-, 3000-, 4000-, 5000-, 6000-, 8000-, and 9000-series units. Typically, as the series number increases, so does the torque capacity and the physical size of the unit. Generally, the 1000- and 2000-series applications include light- and medium-duty trucks, vans, and buses; 3000- and 4000-series applications include medium- and heavy-duty trucks and buses; and the 5000-, 6000-, 8000-, and 9000-series applications are generally used for off-highway applications, such as mining trucks.

2006 and Later

The years 2006 and later have seen major introductions of GM 6-, 8-, 9-, and 10-speed applications for both rear-wheel-drive and front-wheel-drive vehicles. Again, the designations changed. The "E" designation is no longer used by General Motors, as all of the 6-, 8-, 9-, and 10-speed applications use fully integrated electronic control systems. The updated transmission designs are now used by GM as well as sold to other manufacturers.

The LCT 1000- and 2000-series applications changed in 2006 from a 5-speed to a 6-speed application. The designation remained the same, but the RPO code for the transmission changed.

2012–2020

Allison introduced a 10-speed version for the heavy-truck market known as the TC10 in 2012. The TC10 was dropped from production in 2020. A new 9-speed unit was introduced in 2022 as a replacement for many of the 2000-series applications. The new unit has some hybrid features, such as start/stop and two-mode hybrid operation.

GM Non-Hybrid Transmission Applications

GM's non-hybrid transmission options include the 6L45, 6L50, 6L80, 6L90, 6T30, 6T35, 6T40, 6T45, 6T50, 6T70, 6T75, 6T80, 8L45, 8L90, 9T45, 9T50, 9T60, 9T65, 10L60, 10L80, 10L90, 10L1000, LCT 1000, LCT 2000, A1000, A1350, A1700, A1750, A2100, A2200, A2300, A2350, A2400, A2500, A2650, A2700, and A2750.

GM LCT 1000 and 2000 North America Usage

The GM LCT 1000 and 2000 were used in the following vehicles in North America:

- Silverado, Sierra (C/K Trucks, C = 2WD, K = 4WD)
- Express, Savana (G/H Vans, G = 2WD, H = AWD)
- Topkick, Kodiak (3500/4500/5500/6500 medium-duty truck)

Car/truck and model/body designations refer to the fourth or fifth digit of the vehicle identification number (VIN) code. The fourth digit is used on cars, and the fifth digit is used on trucks for the body-type designation.

RPO Identification

General Motors has always used a process known as regular production option (RPO) codes to identify the component content for its vehicles. When a dealership orders a vehicle, every option on that vehicle (engine, transmission, axle ratio, radio, brake system, suspension system, air-conditioning system, and all other component options) is given a three-digit alpha numeric designation. That three-digit designation (RPO) is used by the assembly plant to ensure the vehicle is built with the options the dealership ordered. For example, a Chevrolet or a GMC truck may have a Z71 decal on the truck bed, and Z71 is the RPO code for an off-road suspension package.

All RPO codes are three digits. Engine RPOs typically start with the letter L (LT1, LT4, and L88). Rear-wheel-drive axle options typically start with the letter G (GT4 and G80), and transmission RPO codes start with the letter M (MT1 and M30). The RPO codes are found on a label known as a service parts identification (SPID) label. The codes are positioned in alpha-numeric order on the label. The SPID label is typically located in one of four locations, depending on the year and vehicle model. Locations include: the glove box, center console, rear decklid (trunk of cars), and on the spare tire cover (cars).

During the transition from Generation 4 to Generation 5 Allison applications, vehicles were constructed using components and wiring from both generations. On those transitional applications, RPO AVF was used to designate which transmission control module (TCM) was used, which also determines if the TCM connector is a 66-pin or an 80-pin connector. If the RPO AVF is used, the unit uses the 66-pin connector and its appropriate schematics, and it is configured with Generation 5 components.

GM 2018 and Later

Up to the 2018 model year, the RPO/SPID label was located in one of

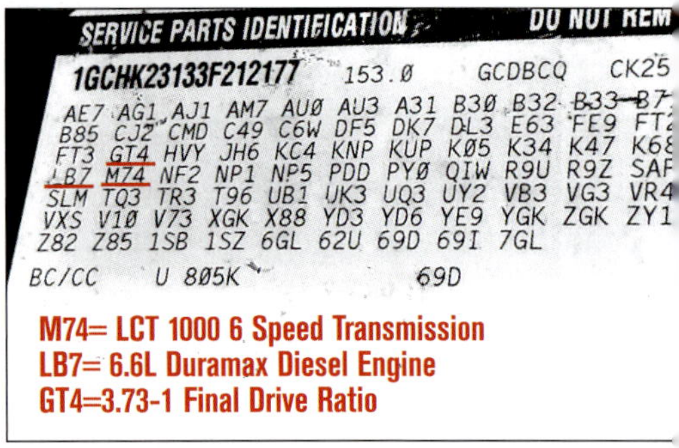

The RPO codes are listed on the RPO tag, which is typically located in the glove box, center console, spare tire cover, or trunk lid for 2018-and-earlier applications. Transmission RPOs start with the letter M, engine RPOs start with the letter L, and rear-wheel-drive final-drive information starts with the letter G. The 5-speed and 6-speed GM LCT 1000 uses either RPO code MW7 or M74. The RPO is often required for parts ordering and to access the correct service information.

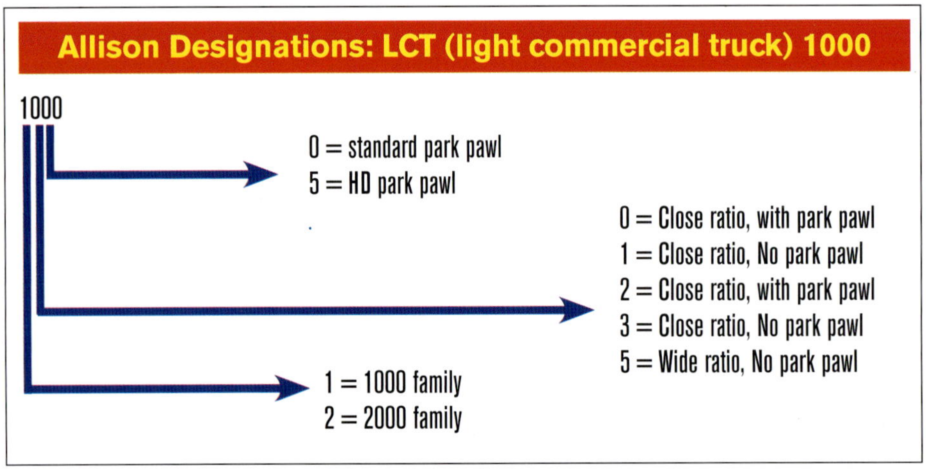

the positions previously mentioned. Starting with the 2018 model year, General Motors began to transition the label information to a different location and format with new body-styles and vehicle redesigns. The new label requires a smart phone to read a quick-response (QR) code image to access the three-digit codes. The label is now located on the driver-side B-pillar. Open the driver-side door and look at the area below the body striker.

There are apps available for free that work well to read QR codes, including Data Matrix, I-Nigma, QR Scanner, QR Droid, Barcode, and NeoReader. To read the new design label, open the application and position the sight box over the QR label area. The application will read the label and display the RPO codes as well as the VIN and other pertinent information. Most smartphone cameras will also read the QR code. Just open the camera app, point at the QR code, and click on the link that appears.

The RPO tag location and design started to change beginning in the 2018 model year. The new design tag requires a smartphone and a quick-response (QR) reader application (app) to access the vehicle's RPO information. With the app open, scan the QR label. The app will then display the RPO content on your phone.

Why You Need to Know the RPO

Why is it important to know the RPO code for the component/ system that you are attempting to repair? It's because many components are similar, but there can be some differences. This means that the part being replaced could be different—even though it may appear to be identical. In many instances, the parts person will ask for the option content or the vehicle VIN so that he or she can ensure a buyer gets the correct parts for the specific application. In addition, component repair processes and system wiring vary, so RPO information may be needed to select the correct wiring schematics or repair information.

Transmissions also have their own unique RPOs. The LCT 1000 uses the RPO M74 for the 5-speed and RPO MW7 for the 6-speed RWD applications. The following table lists all the RPO codes for the various GM Hydra-Matic/Allison 5-, 6-, 8-, 9-, and 10-speed applications for light- and medium-duty GM vehicles.

Other Allison applications and their RPO codes used in GM medium-duty truck/bus applications include A1700PTS (MA6), A1700HS (MJ0), A1700EVS (MH1), A1700RDS (MIU), A1700MH (MIX), A1750RDS (MI0), A1750EVS (MHV), A2700PTS (MB6), A2700HS (MWB), A2700EVS (MG0), A2700RDS (MIA), A2700MH (MF0), A2750RDS (MBV), A2750MH (MBW), A2750EVS (MBY), and A2750HS (MBX).

Transmission Tag Information

All Allison transmissions include a tag that helps to identify the transmission. The Allison family of transmissions uses a metal tag that is mounted to a flat surface on the transmission case. The tag is typically located on the passenger's side of the transmission case. The LCT 1000- and 2000-series tag includes the model year, model code, and serial number.

GM Hydra-Matic/Allison RPO Codes			
6T30	MH9	VT40	MRG
6T35	MNU	5ET50	MKE
6T40	MH8, MHB, MHH, MNH, MNK	AF50-8	MRC
6T45	MH7, MHC, MNP, MHG	1ET35	MMF
6T50	MHJ, MHK, M2D, MNM	CVT-7	MR8
6T70	MH2, MH7, M7W, MH4	6L45	MYA
6T75	M7V, M7X, MY9, MH6	6L50	MYB
6T80	MNM	6L80	MYC
8L45	M5T, M5N	6L90	MYD
8L90	M5U, M5X, MQE	Allison, 5/6	–
LCT 1000	MW7, M74	–	–
9T45	M3U	10L60	MI1
9T50	M3D, M3E	10L80	MF6, MQB, MI2
9T60	M3T	10L90	MGL, MI4
9T65	M3V	10L1000	–
Allison	MGM, MGU	–	–

> **TECH TIP**
>
> **Cleaning**
>
> Take care when cleaning the tag because it can be damaged. Before beginning, take a picture of the tag so that you will have the information available for the parts person if needed. ■

Some information on the tag is important when it comes to ordering parts and determining if your transmission was equipped with certain updates. A parts person may require the model year, model code, and serial number.

Model Year

The model year may not be the same as the year of the vehicle being worked on, depending on the vehicle production date.

Model Code

The model code varies, depending on the vehicle platform and the type of vehicle that the transmission is going into. Later-model Allison applications do not include the model as part of the tag information.

Serial Number

The serial number is the most important number on the tag. Allison identifies the unit series as 1000, 2000, 3000, or 4000 as well as the break points for product updates using the serial number. This means the parts person may need the serial number to order the correct parts.

On GM applications, the parts person may also need the VIN. The first two numbers of the serial number represent the transmission model: 63 or 96 = 1000 or 2000, 65 or 93 = 3000, and 66 or 94 = 4000.

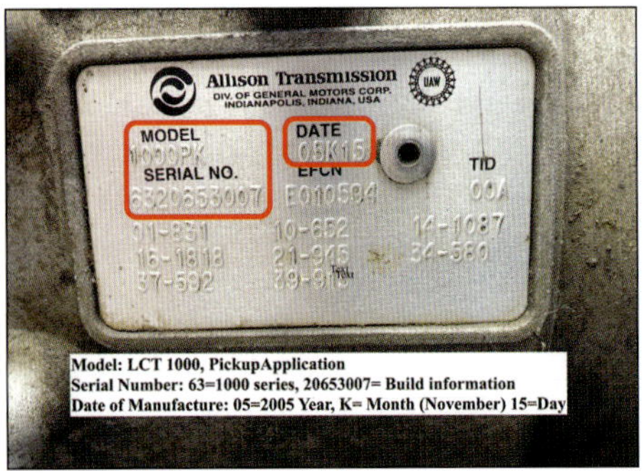

As with the RPO tag, the transmission tag contains a tremendous amount of information about the transmission, including the model code, the serial number, and the build date. Many transmission updates are attached to a specific Allison serial number. So, when ordering parts, the parts person may require the tag information to get the correct parts for the application.

LCT 1000 Unit Specifications

The Allison 1000 and 2000 are used in both GM and non-GM applications. The transmissions are available as 5- and 6-speed models. A stand-alone TCM is used with all applications. The 5- and 6-speeds use the same clutch layouts, with the difference being the hydraulic

LCT 1000 Unit Specifications	
Speeds	5-speed (2001–2005 GM, 1999–2005 non-GM); 6-speed (2006–2019 GM, 2006–present non-GM)
RPO codes	5-speed (M74); 6-speed (MW7)
TCM	Externally mounted, Bosch or Delphi product
TCM adaptive capable software	Adaptive strategies with fast-learn capabilities, both upshift and downshift controlled. Grade braking capable on most applications.
Clutches	Five clutches used: C1 (1-2-3-4), C2 (4-5-6), C3 (3-5-R), C4 (2-6), C5 (L-R); C1 and C2 are driving clutches; C3, C4, and C5 are holding clutches
Oil pump	Gear and crescent design. Pressure regulator housed in the pump assembly.
Planetary	Three used: P1, P2, and P3
Speed sensors	Up to three used: Turbine, Input (ISS), Output (OSS)
Range sensor, NSBU, IMS	2001–2005 externally mounted (1999–2005 other applications); 2006–2019 internally mounted (IMS) GM applications; 2006–current model year other applications
Input torque capacity	LCT 1000 520 ft-lbs (01–05 MY) 565 ft-lbs (05 MY) 650 ft-lbs (06–07 MY) 660 ft-lbs (08–10 MY) 765 ft-lbs (11–16 MY) 910 ft-lbs (17–19 MY)
Gear ratio	5-speed, 6-speed 1000 and 2000: 1st 3.10, 2nd 1.81, 3rd 1.41, 4th 1.00, 5th 0.71, 6th 0.61, Reverse 4.49; 5-speed, 6-speed, Allison 2500/2550: 1st 3.51, 2nd 1.90, 3rd 1.44, 4th 1.00, 5th 0.74, 6th 0.64, Reverse 5.09

LCT 1000 Unit Specifications *CONTINUED*	
Transmission weight (dry)	330 pounds (150 kg)
Fluid type	Dexron VI or Allison Transynd TES 295, TES 668, or TES 389
Fluid capacity	Dry (12.7 quarts, 12 liters) shallow pan; Filter change (7.4 quarts, 7 liters) shallow pan; Dry (14.8 quarts, 14 liters) deep pan
Pressure taps	Line pressure
Pressure specifications	2001–2003, fixed line pressure, 115–200 psi; 2004-and-later applications, at idle 70–110 psi (485–760 kPa), 1,500 rpm 125–171 psi (860–1180 kPa); Stepped line pressure starting in 2004 due to the addition of solenoid G; variable line pressure starting in 2010–2011
Grade braking feature	The TCM will downshift the transmission, providing engine braking when the correct parameters are met.
TAP shifts	The driver has the ability to manually up/down shift the unit for better control (via a button on the shifter).
Tow haul mode	The driver (via a button on the shifter) has the ability to engage tow mode, which changes the shift points and pressure controls when towing.

If equipped, the PTO drive gear is mounted to the C1 and C2 clutch drum.

and electronic systems. There are some part differences between those used in a GM application and those used in a non-GM application.

PTO and Non-PTO Applications

Both Allison and GM applications are available in two different configurations: power takeoff (PTO) and non-power takeoff (non-PTO). PTO is used on many applications to drive components, such as hydraulic pumps to operate plows and lifts. The PTO can be mounted to either side of the transmission case.

For the unit to drive a PTO, the transmission C1/C2 clutch drum must be equipped with a PTO drive gear. The PTO gear teeth also act as a speed-sensor tone ring in the PTO application. On applications not equipped with a drive gear, the drum has a speed-sensor tone wheel attached to it.

The cover mounted to each side of the transmission must be removed to provide a place for the PTO to mount to the case. If you are unsure whether a unit can/cannot be used with a PTO, remove the cover and inspect for the PTO drive gear.

Fluids and Inspection

Fluid and filter service is critical to the longevity of Allison applications. Using the correct fluid and filter can make or break the rebuild of these units.

General Motors recommends the use of Dexron VI transmission fluid. Dexron VI is far superior to Dexron III, which it replaced. Major improvements in wear control, film strength, friction durability, and oxidation

PTO covers are located on both sides of the transmission.

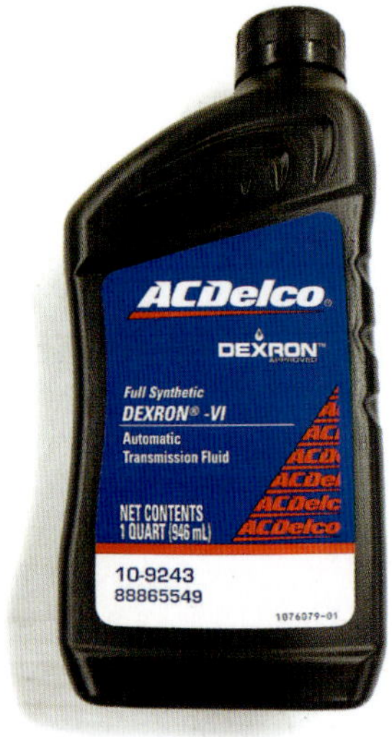

Dexron VI and Allison TranSynd are the only approved fluids for the 1000 and 2000 applications. Do not use Dexron III or other fluids in this application. Dexron VI made major improvements in oxidation resistance, lubrication capabilities, and temperature ranges compared to Dexron III. Dexron VI is licensed by several manufacturers, including Valvoline.

stability were achieved. Clutch-to-clutch-shift transmissions, such as the LCT 1000 and 2000 series as well as 6L, 6T, and 9T series require a much more robust fluid compared to previous automatic-transmission designs. Companies currently licensed to produce Dexron VI include Mobil, Chevron, Shell, SK Lubricants, and Valvoline.

Allison recommends the use of Allison TranSynd. TranSynd is available as TES 668, TES 295, or TES 389, which are acceptable in the GM and Allison 1000- and 2000-series units. Companies currently licensed to produce TranSynd fluid include Volvo, John Deere, Castrol, BP, International, Exxon Mobile, Case/New Holland, and Shell.

1000 Series Fluid Capacity

- Dry (12.7 quarts, 12 liters) shallow pan
- Filter change (7.4 quarts, 7 liters) shallow pan
- Dry (14.8 quarts, 14 liters) deep pan
- Filter change (10.6 quarts, 10 liters) deep pan

Allison TranSynd fluid TES 668, TES 295, and TES 389 are approved for the A1000- and A2000-series units.

Fluid Level

All 1000- and 2000-series units are equipped with a dipstick. The dipstick can be located on either side of the transmission, depending on application. Before checking the fluid level, perform the following:

1. Start the engine, park the vehicle on a level surface, and block the wheels.
2. Apply the parking brake and vehicle brake, place the shift lever in Park. Move the shifter to each forward gear range as well as Reverse, pausing for 3 seconds in each range. Place the vehicle in Park.
3. Allow the engine to idle for a few minutes.
4. Observe the transmission fluid temperature (TFT) using the driver information center (DIC) scan tool or by using a temperature gun to measure the oil-pan temperature.

Cold Fluid Checking Procedure

Use the cold-check procedure to check fluid level when the transmission fluid temperature is between 80°F and 90°F (27°C and 32°C). This method is not as accurate as the hot-checking procedure.

1. Locate the dipstick, flip the handle, pull out the dipstick, and wipe it with a clean rag.
2. Install the dipstick, pushing it back in all the way, wait a few seconds, and then pull it back out again.
3. Check both sides of the dipstick and use the lower level.
4. Inspect the color of the fluid and its condition.
5. If the fluid level is below the cold mark (lower), add only enough fluid through the dipstick tube as needed to bring the level to the mark.
6. If the fluid level is correct, push the dipstick back in all the way and then flip down the handle to lock the dipstick in place.
7. Perform a hot check once the transmission has reached operating temperature.

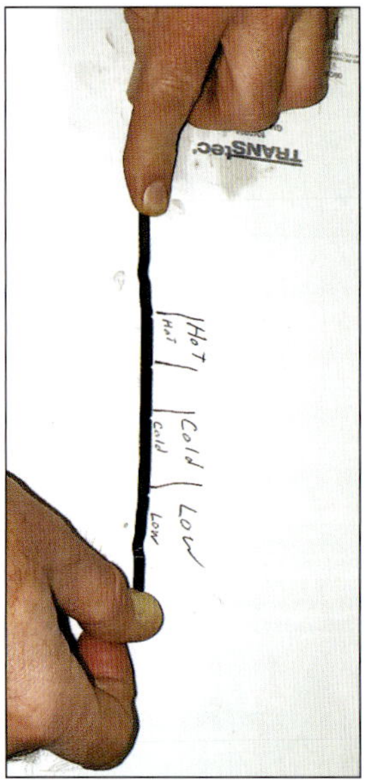

Allison applications use a dipstick to check the transmission fluid level. The dipstick includes hot and cold levels.

Hot Fluid Checking Procedure

Use this procedure to check the transmission fluid level when the transmission fluid temperature is between 165°F and 185°F (74°C and 85°C).

1. Locate the dipstick, flip the handle, pull out the dipstick, and wipe it with a clean rag.
2. Install the dipstick by pushing it back in all the way, wait a few seconds, and then pull it back out again.
3. Check both sides of the dipstick and use the lower level.
4. Inspect the color of the fluid and its condition.
5. If the fluid level is below the hot mark (upper), add only enough fluid through the dipstick tube as needed to bring the level to the mark.
6. If the fluid level is correct, push the dipstick back in all the way, then flip down the handle to lock the dipstick in place.

Filter and Fluid Service

The Allison 1000 and 2000 applications use two filters: a spin-on filter that is mounted externally on the case and the main filter that is inside the oil-pan area. In addition, two different main filters and pans are used: shallow filter/pan and deep filter/pan.

Spin-On Filter

The 1000 and 2000 applications are equipped with a spin-on filter that is mounted to the front of the case on the driver's side. Remove and replace the old filter. Clean the filter mounting surface, lubricate the filter seal, install the magnet and filter, and hand-tighten it.

Four issues have arisen regarding this filter:

1. Many of the aftermarket replacement spin-on filters are wrapped in plastic. When replacing this filter, people stick their finger through the plastic wrap and into the filter-mounting hole in an attempt to remove the plastic from the filter. This can cause a piece of the plastic to dislodge and end up in the filter. When the engine is started, the plastic can become lodged in the valve body and its spacer plate, leading to diagnostic trouble codes (DTCs) and operational issues. Never poke a finger through the plastic on any filter. Instead, remove the plastic carefully with a knife and discard it. Turn the filter upside down to make sure nothing got into the filter.
2. Make sure the filter magnet is properly installed because it regularly sticks to the old filter.
3. Many cheaper spin-on filters have holes in the filter positioned in a different location than the OEM filter. If not using an OEM filter, make sure to install a magnet on the filter to ensure the holes are not being excessively restricted, as transmission failure can occur if the flow is restricted too much.

Allison 1000 and 2000 applications use two oil filters: a spin-on type and the main filter located inside the oil pan. The spin-on filter houses a magnet between the filter and the case. The magnet must be in place and properly positioned when replacing the filter. The magnet cannot cover the holes in the filter, which is an issue with some aftermarket filters.

4. When working with the spin-on filter, make sure the sealing gasket is properly installed and lubricated with clean transmission fluid prior to installation.

Pan Filter

Changing the fluid and filter on this application is a simple process. The factory pan gasket is reusable on the LCT 1000 and 2000 applications. Always install a high-quality filter specifically designed for the application.

Some aftermarket spin-on oil filters are covered in plastic that must be removed before installing the filter. Do not poke a finger through the plastic. Instead, cut the plastic off with a knife. If a piece of the plastic gets lodged in the filter, it will travel to the valve body during operation, leading to several issues, such as no movement, slippage, and hydraulic-related DTCs.

The main filter is located inside the oil pan.

1. Remove the pan bolts and drain the fluid from the pan. The 1000 and 2000 pans are often equipped with drain plugs to make the task a little less messy.
2. Remove the filter and seal. Snap-ring pliers or a screwdriver work well.
3. Clean the pan, gasket, and case mating surface. Inspect the surfaces.
4. Install the filter seal onto the filter neck.
5. Lubricate the filter seal and filter neck with transmission fluid.
6. Install the filter.
7. Install the gasket/pan and tighten the 10 bolts to 20 ft-lbs (27 Nm) using a crisscross pattern.
8. Fill with Dexron VI or Allison TranSynd fluid.
9. Follow the fluid-level checking procedures.
10. Check for leaks.
11. Test drive the vehicle to make sure no issues are present.

Bolt and Fastener Torque Specifications

Component torque is critical to a properly functioning transmission. Be sure to follow all of the recommended torque specifications.

Tools

The tools needed to rebuild a LCT 1000 and 2000 include hand tools as well as some special tools. Hand tools (sockets, snap-ring pliers, hammers, pliers, and end wrenches) are needed to disassemble and reassemble the

Torque Specifications	
Valve Body Assembly to Main Housing Bolts	12 Nm (106 in-lbs)
Converter Housing/Oil Pump Cover Assembly to Transmission Case Bolts	56 Nm (41 ft-lbs)
Converter Housing to Oil Pump Cover Assembly Bolts	56 Nm (41 ft-lbs)
Detent Lever/IMS Assembly to Manual Shift-Shaft Bolt	10 Nm (89 in-lbs)
Detent Lever Retaining Nut	29 Nm (21 ft-lbs)
Detent Spring Assembly to Main Valve Body Bolts	12 Nm (106 in-lbs)
Engine Cooling Fan Shroud	8 Nm (71 in-lbs)
Filler Tube Bracket to Transmission Nuts	18 Nm (13 ft-lbs)
Fuel Line Bracket to Transmission Nut	18 Nm (13 ft-lbs)
Fuel Line Retainer to Transmission Bolts	2.5 Nm (22 in-lbs)
Heat Shield to Transmission Bolts	17 Nm (13 ft-lbs)
Heat Shield to Transmission Nut	25 Nm (18 ft-lbs)
Hydraulic Connector Assembly	25 Nm (18 ft-lbs)
Input Speed Sensor to Main Housing Bolt	12 Nm (106 in-lbs)
Input Speed Sensor to Torque Converter Housing Bolt	12 Nm (106 in-lbs)
Line Pressure Test Hole Plug	12 Nm (106 in-lbs)
Low and Reverse Clutch Housing to Transmission Case	56 Nm (41 ft-lbs)
Main Pressure Tap Plug	12 Nm (106 in-lbs)
Main Valve Body to Shift Valve Body Bolts	12 Nm (106 in-lbs)
Oil Cooler Line Clip to Oil Pan Nut	9 Nm (80 in-lbs)
Oil Cooler to Radiator Brace Bolts	12 Nm (106 in-lbs)
Oil Filter Adapter	30 Nm (22 ft-lbs)
Oil Pan Drain Plug	35 Nm (27 ft-lbs)
Oil Pan to Main Housing Bolts	27 Nm (20 ft-lbs)
Oil Pump Cover to Oil Pump Bolts	27 Nm (20 ft-lbs)
Output Shaft Retaining Nut	90 Nm (66 ft-lbs)
Output Speed Sensor to Rear Cover Bolt	12 Nm (106 in-lbs)
Power Takeoff (PTO) Cover to Main Housing Bolts	43 Nm (32 ft-lbs)
Pressure Control Solenoid (PCS) Retaining Bracket Bolts	12 Nm (106 in-lbs)
Shift Cable Bracket to Transmission Bolts	25 Nm (18 ft-lbs)

Torque Specifications *CONTINUED*	
Shift Cable Support to Steering Column Brace Bolt	10 Nm (89 in-lbs)
Shift Lever to Shift Selector Shaft Nut	24 Nm (18 ft-lbs)
Torque Converter Housing Inspection Cover to Transmission Bolts	10 Nm (89 in-lbs)
Torque Converter to Flywheel Bolts	60 Nm (44 ft-lbs)
Transmission Fluid Pressure Switch to Main Valve Body Bolts	12 Nm (106 in-lbs)
Transmission Mount to Transmission Support Nuts	18 Nm (13 ft-lbs)
Transmission Support to Frame Nuts and Bolts	70 Nm (52 ft-lbs)
Transmission to Engine Studs and Bolts	50 Nm (37 ft-lbs)
Transmission Mount to 4x4 Adapter	100 Nm (74 ft-lbs) first pass, +45 degrees final torque
Transmission Mount to Transmission	45 Nm (33 ft-lbs) first pass, +50 degrees final torque
Transmission Range Selector Cable Bracket Bolt	22 Nm (17 ft-lbs)
Transmission Range Selector Cable Lever Nut	25 Nm (18 ft-lbs)
Wire Harness/Vent Tube Bracket to Transmission Nut	18 Nm (13 ft-lbs)
Vehicle Speed Sensor (VSS) Bolt	12 Nm (106 in-lbs)
Yoke Assembly to Output Shaft Bolt	123 Nm (91 ft-lbs)

transmission. Some of the special tools may be improvised by using something else that is available and will accomplish the same function.

Specialty tools include a torque wrench, dial indicator, dial caliper, pump puller, and clutch compressor. These can be rented or borrowed, as they are critical for proper service.

A way to compress the clutches is also needed. A clutch compressor fixture/foot press, arbor press, or even

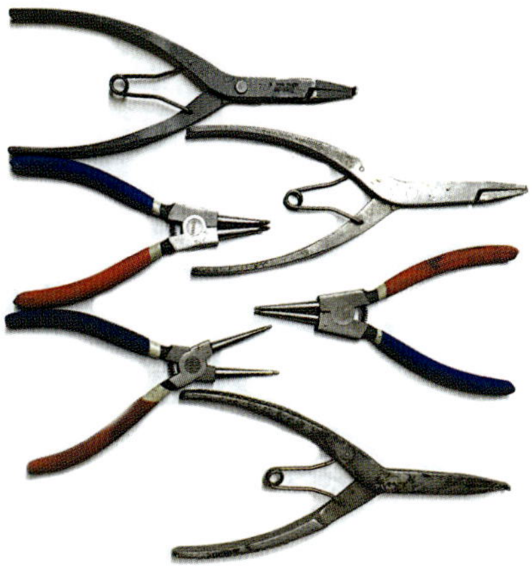

Snap-ring pliers are a necessity, as the 1000 and 2000 uses multiple different snap rings.

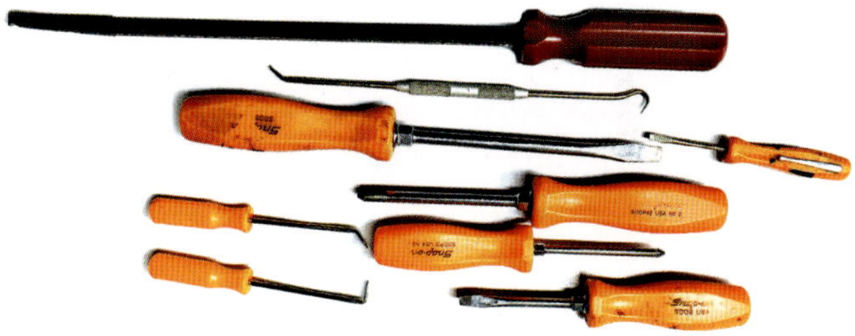

Screwdrivers and picks are used primarily to aid snap-ring and valve-body removal and installation.

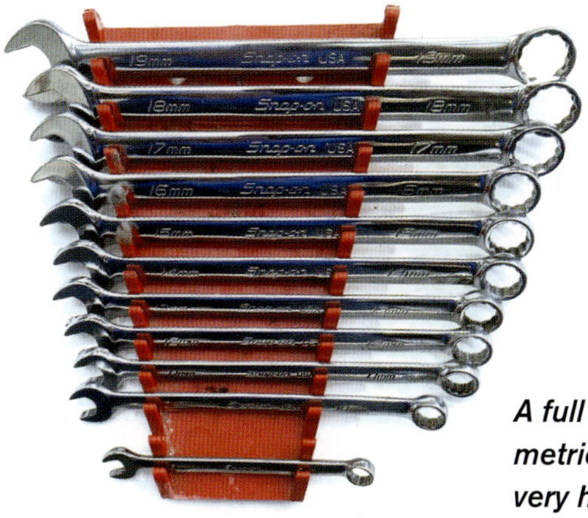

A full set of open-end metric wrenches is very helpful for 1000 and 2000 repair.

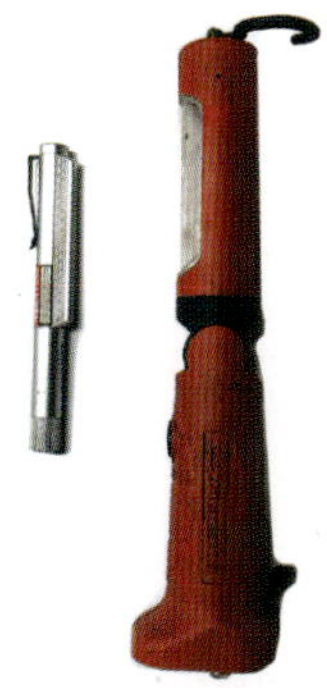

Even in well-lit work areas, handheld lights are very helpful.

As with screwdrivers, pry bars may be helpful.

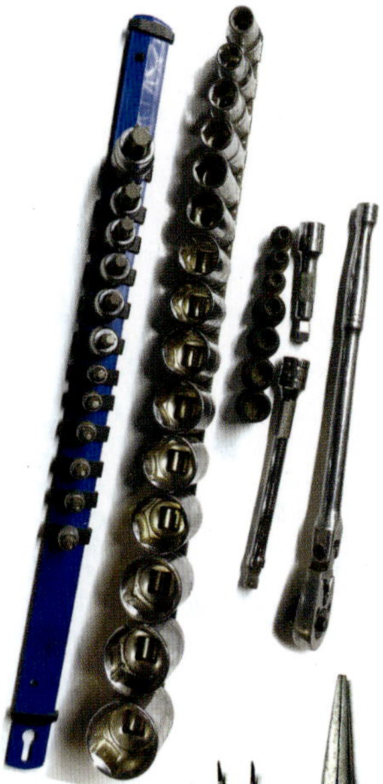

Metric and Torx socket sets are required for disassembly and reassembly.

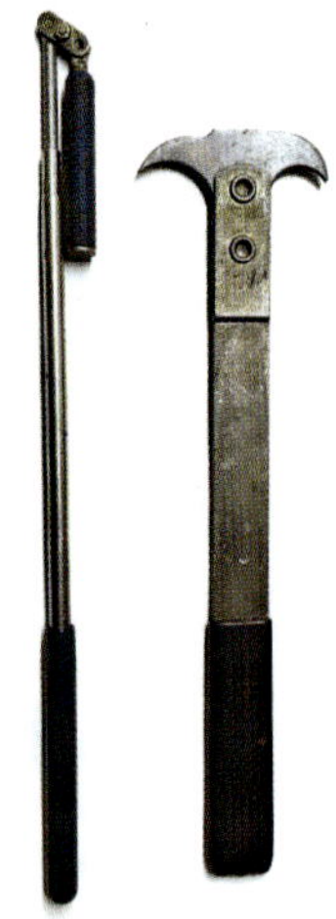

A seal remover works well for the input and output seals. A magnet is often needed to remove small parts or parts that may have fallen into spaces that are difficult to access.

Hammers and pin punches are needed to remove many of the roll pins used in the Allison.

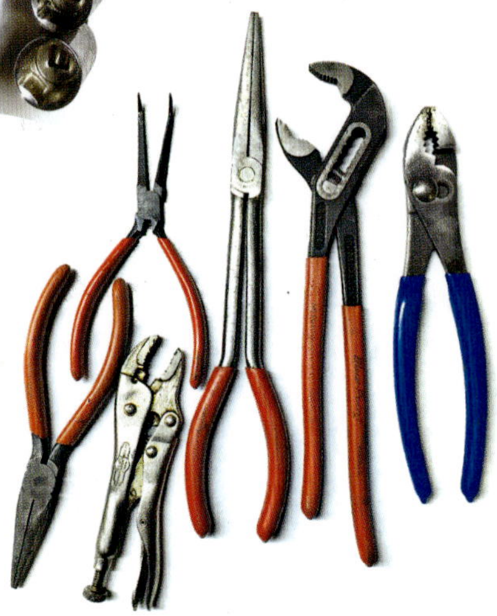

Needle nose pliers, diagonal cutters, and locking pliers are needed to easily remove and install numerous components.

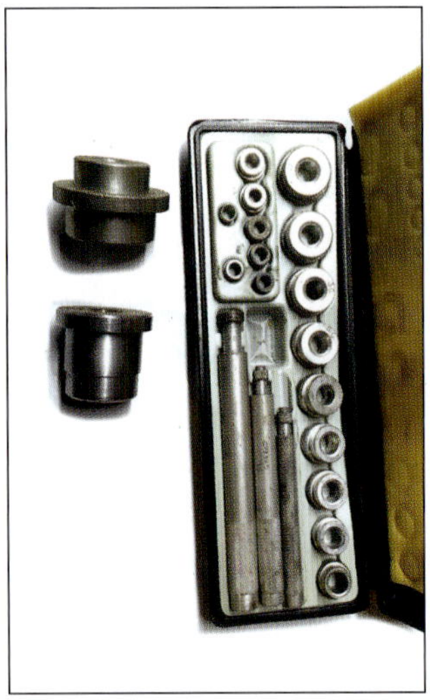

Various bushing drivers are required if you want to replace any of the transmission bushings.

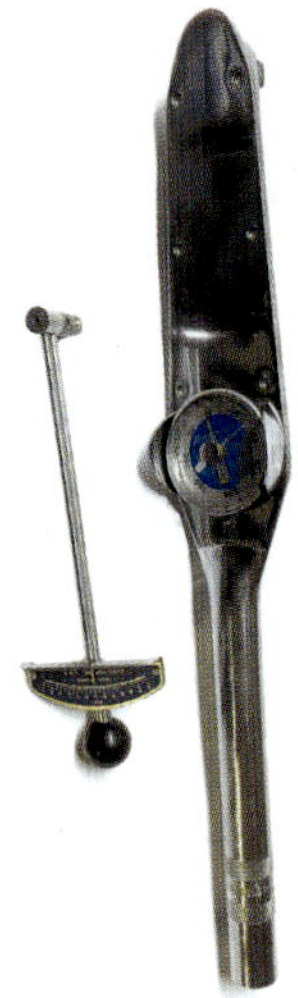

Torque wrenches are used to provide even torque at the correct value to the bolts. This is essential on components such as the pump, the valve body, and the bellhousing-to-case attaching bolts.

Air or electric impact wrenches make the job much easier, especially for disassembly. Take great care if using one for assembly purposes, as threads and bolts can easily be damaged.

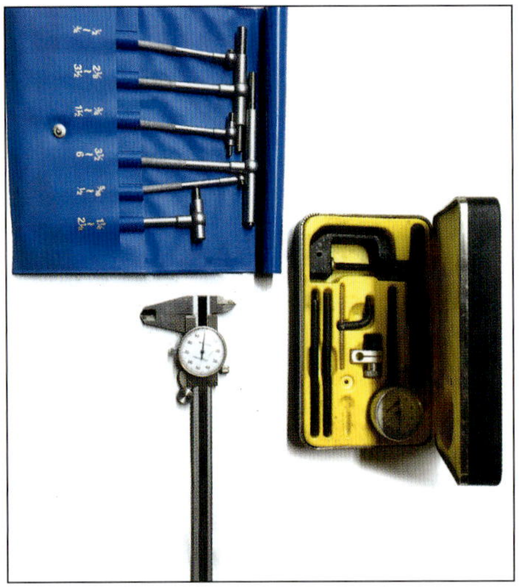

Measuring tools, such as a dial indicator, feeler gauges, and a vernier caliper, are used during transmission assembly.

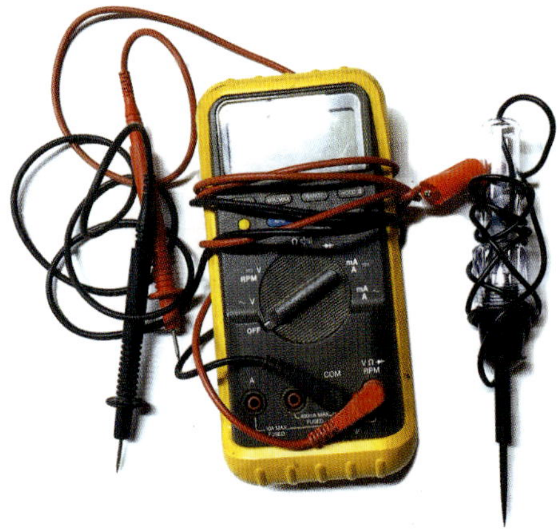

A digital volt ohmmeter is critical when testing the vehicle's electrical system as well as some transmission electronic components.

Clutch compressor tools are required for disassembly as well as reassembly of the transmission clutch packs. If a clutch compressor is not available, it is possible to improvise by using pipe or other things around the shop.

Three types of test lights are available: self-powered, low-current flow, and high-current flow. Generally, high-current-flow test lights are used to check transmission powers and grounds.

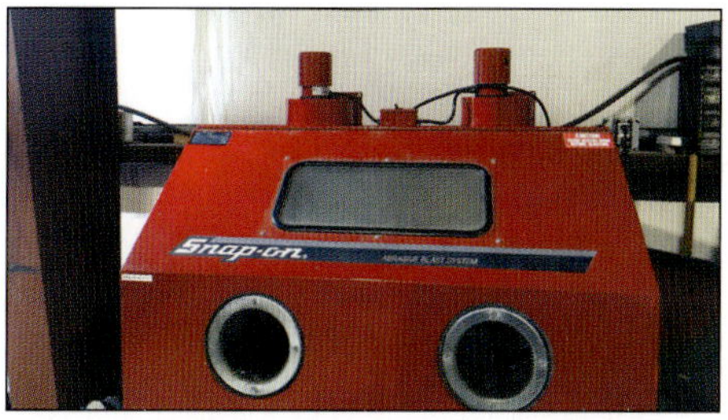

Glass bead machines work well for external components and surfaces, but do not use them on any internal transmission surface or component.

An arbor press is a great addition to any shop and can be used for many functions, such as installing bushings and bearings. In addition, an arbor press works well for compressing the clutch return springs in a transmission.

Adjustable clutch compressors are very handy, as they will fit more than one return spring assembly diameter.

Professional transmission shops use an industrial washing machine to clean transmission parts.

Some form of clutch compressor is required to compress the clutch piston return springs so that the piston snap ring can be removed. A compressor, a hand press, an arbor press, or even a drill press can be used to perform this function.

A solvent tank is a good cleaning solution for a small shop or a hobby shop. While it is more labor intensive compared to the industrial washers, it can still do a good job using Stoddard solvent.

If checking the valves in the pump, either purchase the GM/Allison tool or build a pressure-regulator valve removal tool. To make one, use either a socket or a piece of pipe. Cut notches directly across from each other that will go over the valve retaining pin.

If a tool is needed to compress a clutch return spring, consider using a drill press. With a little ingenuity, it will do the job.

a drill press (with a little ingenuity) can be used to compress the springs.

Access to a commercial parts washer saves a lot of time and effort. If you do not have access to one, a solvent tank and a pressure washer may be used. A glass-bead machine works well for cleaning parts after they have been cleaned with solvent or other cleaning processes. Do not glass bead any internal components or internal areas.

Some specialty tools are specific to the LCT 1000 and 2000 transmissions. GM has all of the tools available through Kent-Moore tools. The largest and most diverse aftermarket specialty tools are available through Adapt-a-Case tools.

Power and Ground Testing

GM applications have issues with the harness rubbing through in various locations. Harness issues can cause everything from DTCs to the transmission being stuck in limp mode.

TECH TIP

Ignition Switch

Power-related issues are not restricted to connection or battery-related problems. Ignition-switch issues are very common on GM pickup and truck applications. This condition may be intermittent in nature and can cause no movement, shift issues, and DTCs. Updated ignition switches are available to address the issue. The ignition switch is located at the base of the steering column on most applications. ■

Common areas to inspect are the frame-rail area (typically, it gets trapped by the lines), bellhousing area, chassis upper control arm, alternator and power-steering pump, transfer case, and TCM bracket.

Battery

The battery is central to proper TCM and transmission operation. It cannot be overemphasized regarding power- and ground-related issues with 1000- and 2000-series applications. Shift issues, no movement, the transmission operating in default limp mode, or DTCs are caused by either a bad battery or a connection issue on the Allison applications.

Everything starts and ends at the battery. The battery should be tested preferably with a conductance-type battery tester. Most parts stores and all dealerships have conductance battery testing equipment available for purchase.

In addition, the battery posts and cables should be cleaned and inspected. Corrosion travels up the battery cables, creating a condition known as voltage drop, which can lead to operational issues.

Poor connections are the biggest enemy of a properly operating 1000 or 2000. Always check the battery, its connections, and the transmission power and ground circuits for proper operation prior to condemning the transmission.

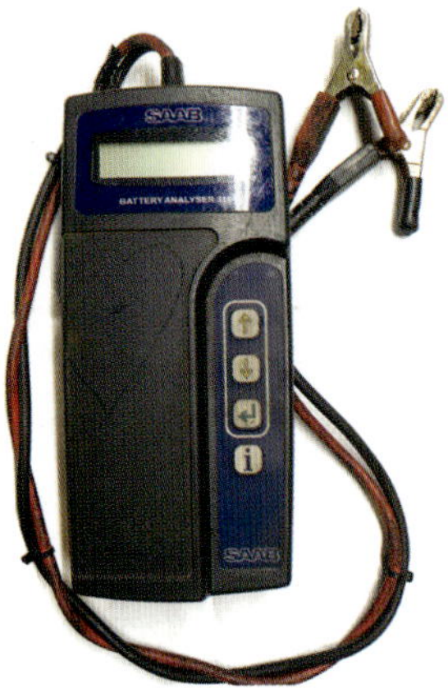

A conductance battery tester is the fastest and most reliable tool for testing a battery. On applications with two batteries, always disconnect one battery prior to testing.

The Allison 1000- 2000-series applications typically use two 12-volt vehicle batteries. When testing the batteries, always disconnect one of the batteries and test each battery independently, otherwise false readings may occur. False DTCs, shift concerns, no-movement concerns, as well as the transmission defaulting to limp mode commonly occur if any electrical issues are present.

What Is a Circuit?

When an electrical system is discussed, the term *circuit* will be used.

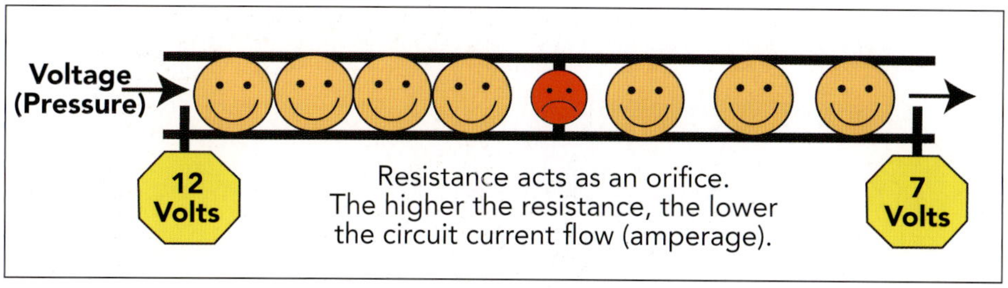

A circuit is used to describe a system that starts and ends at the battery for a particular component. A circuit consists of the following:

- A power source: B+ (typically the battery)
- A ground: typically the main ground is the negative terminal of the battery. To connect the battery ground to the rest of the circuits, manufacturers use the frame, engine block, and transmission case to transmit the current flow to the ground wiring connections at the battery.
- Conductors: typically the wiring, the connectors, and the terminals
- A load: the lights, the electrical motors, the relays, or the solenoids are typical components in a vehicle electrical circuit
- Circuit control: a switch or a computer typically used to control the load
- Circuit protection: typically a fuse, a fusible link, or a circuit breaker is used for protection from excessive current flow

Electrical Current Flow

Three terms are used when describing electrical operation in a circuit: amperage, voltage, and resistance. Amperage (current) is a measure of electron volume through a circuit. Amperage is the workhorse for the components. In other words, amperage is what illuminates the lights and operates the solenoids, relays, and electrical motors. Voltage is the electrical pressure or force that pushes the amperage through the circuit and its components. Resistance is the opposition to current flow (amperage) in the circuit. The higher a circuit's resistance, the lower the amperage is through the circuit, so the dimmer the light or the slower an electric motor will turn.

The key to understanding electrical circuits is knowing the relationship among amperage, voltage, and resistance.

Amperage

Amperage is not consumed by the electrical circuit or its components. Amperage is used to make the components operate, but it is not consumed by the component or the circuit. This means that if the amperage was measured when flowing into a light and out of the light, the amperage measurements would be the same. The aspects that change the current flow through a circuit or component are the circuit voltage and resistance. The higher the voltage and/or the lower the resistance, the higher the current flow, thus the brighter the light. The lower the circuit voltage and/or the higher the resistance in the circuit, the lower the current flow, thus the dimmer the light would be.

Voltage

Voltage is the consumable in an electrical circuit. The key is that the component (not the wiring or the connections) should be consuming the voltage. For example, if you measure the voltage being delivered to the component, and it measures 12.5 volts, the voltage on the ground side of the component should measure near 0 volts (typically it will be less than 0.5 volts) when the circuit is in operation. The component should use almost all of the circuit voltage.

For example, if a positive voltmeter lead is placed on the power-side terminal leading to a light and a negative voltmeter lead is placed on the ground-side terminal of the light and then the light is energized, the voltage that is being consumed across the light should be visible. This process is known as measuring voltage drop. In other words, close to 12.5 volts should appear on the meter display, which indicates that the light is consuming almost all of the circuit voltage.

The key is to understand that the component is the only item in the circuit that should be consuming circuit voltage. Let's say we had a bad connection in the circuit and that connection was consuming 5

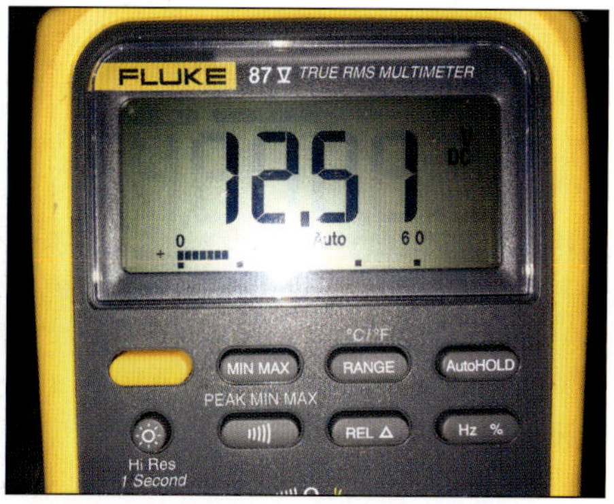

A properly charged battery should display at least 12.6 volts. Voltage supply is critical to proper transmission operation.

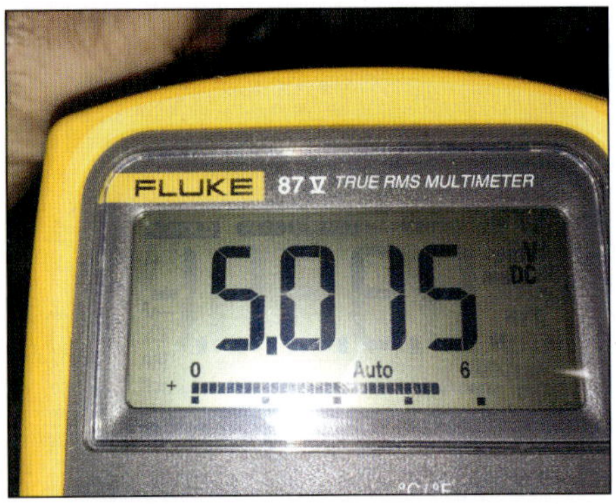

The voltage in a circuit must be consumed by the component and not the wiring or connections. Excessive voltage drop will create current flow issues in the circuit and can result in DTCs and components that operate improperly or not at all. The rule of thumb for voltage drop is 0.1 to 0.2 volts per connection with the circuit in operation. Measuring voltage drop is one of the fastest and most accurate ways of testing dynamic resistance in a circuit. A 5-volt drop is very excessive and indicates a major resistance issue.

Ohmmeter-Related Concerns

The circuit must be deenergized, otherwise the meter reading will not be accurate. Since the circuit is deenergized, it may test as "good," but it may fail to operate correctly when it is energized.

The ohmmeter only applies a tiny amount of voltage and amperage to the circuit, so it is not simulating the circuit in operation. Let's say we were measuring the resistance of a wire and that wire had all of the strands broken except for one. When the ohmmeter leads are connected to each end of the wire, the meter will measure 0 ohms, indicating a perfect connection and no issues with the wire. If that same wire was connected into a lighting circuit, the light may dim, or it may not light at all. Why? The ohmmeter does not "load" the circuit, as it is only applying a small amount of voltage and amperage to the wire being tested. Since so little voltage and amperage is being applied, the excessive circuit resistance due to the severed wires will not show up.

So, what does this mean? Ohmmeters are great for static checks of components, such as relay and solenoid windings, if the circuit is shorted or open all the time, but they will not find issues where the solenoid or relay only develops resistance or a shorted winding condition when it is energized. Ohmmeters should not be used to test battery cable and/or connections simply because of the low-current-flow characteristic of the meter, as it can easily fool you. Ohmmeters do work well for sensor grounds, as they are very low-current-flow circuits and the wires are typically very small with few strands.

The other issue is that manufacturers do not provide a lot of ohm-related resistance specifications, so a tester may be wondering if the reading is good or bad.

volts. We would have 12 volts being applied to the connection but only 7 volts available to feed the component downstream of the bad connection. Lower voltage at the component means we are now lacking the proper electrical pressure to push the amperage through the component, and it may not operate correctly or at all.

Resistance

As described previously, there is a major relationship between resistance in a circuit and the current flow through that circuit. Resistance is typically caused by bad connections. Connection issues are typically due to the following:

- Corrosion from road salt, dirt, moisture, or damaged or missing terminal seals
- Terminal fretting, microscopic corrosion, and metal transfer due to terminal vibration (fretting is a very common cause of intermittent electrical issues)
- Loose female terminals, poor pin tension (male to female)
- Loose cable attaching bolts
- Loose connections
- Damaged wiring and broken wire strands

Resistance can be measured two ways: ohmmeter and voltmeter.

Ohmmeter

An ohmmeter provides a "direct static" measurement of resistance, but it has many limitations. When a meter is placed in the "Ohm" position, it sends a tiny amount of voltage and amperage out of the positive lead and then measures how much voltage is present on the negative terminal. It then calculates the voltage drop and displays the reading as ohms on your meter. The higher the reading, the higher the resistance of the component/wiring.

Voltmeter

A voltmeter can provide an "indirect measurement" of circuit resistance. The advantage is that the circuit is active when using a voltmeter. As discussed earlier, the circuit voltage must be consumed across the component and not across the wiring or its connections. The voltage consumed across the connections can be measured with a meter by measuring the voltage drop. Excessive voltage drop across a connection or wiring indicates excessive resistance in the circuit. A general rule of thumb when measuring voltage drop is that it should not exceed 0.1 to 0.2 volts per

A 0.006 voltage drop across a circuit indicates a very good circuit connection. The voltage drop being measured in this picture is across the B+ cable between the meter-lead connections.

> **TECH TIP — Connection Issues**
>
> Before testing the LCT 1000- and 2000-series vehicle harness for power, make sure that none of the terminals have backed out of the harness side connectors. Often on Generation 1 through Generation 3 harnesses, the terminal lock releases and a terminal starts to back out, which creates a connection issue that can cause DTCs and communication- and transmission-related issues. ■

connection. Voltage-drop techniques can be used to diagnose power- and ground-side resistance related issues.

TCM Power-Side Testing the LCT 1000 and 2000

Testing the power and the ground for the TCM and the transmission varies based on the vehicle year. The Generation 1 through 3 TCM uses multiple connectors, so the pins that supply power and ground vary when compared to a Generation 4 and 5 TCM with one single TCM connector. Always refer to the proper wiring schematic for your application when testing circuits for proper operation.

Testing the power supplied to the TCM and the transmission is important. Either a voltmeter or a test light can be used to test the power feed. An old-fashioned bulb-style test light is preferable. To build one, use a bulb socket and an 1157 or other light, such as a 9004 headlight. Simply attach some wire ends to the socket for a high-quality test light that will provide sufficient load on the circuit for testing purposes.

Test lights are available as high-current-flow or low-current-flow versions. For testing powers and grounds, the higher-current-flow design should be used. A headlamp works as well as a test light. A 9004 will flow 4 or 5 amps of current, depending on which filament is used. A 1157 lamp flows about 2.5 amps of current, so it makes a great test lamp for checking power and ground circuits.

Using a digital voltmeter or an LED-type test light can lead one to believe that the transmission has power even when it does not. The digital volt ohmmeter (DVOM) and LED-type test lights require very little current to operate. Just like the issue with an ohmmeter we discussed previously, if the wire is physically damaged or there is a bad connection, the meter or LED test lamp may show there is battery voltage available to the transmission, but the circuit may not be capable of carrying enough current for the TCM or transmission to operate correctly.

2001–2005 GM Generations 1–3: Application TCM Power Test

The following steps are for connector C1 (Clear, 32 pins) and connector C2 (Red, 32 pins).

- Connect one end of the test light to a good ground.
- Disconnect the TCM connector (C1) with the ignition in the off position.
- Touch the other lead or the test-light probe to the power-supply pins in the vehicle harness connector (vehicle side) and place the ignition switch in the run position. The power feeds that need to be tested are Connector C1 (the vehicle harness connector that connects to the TCM), Pin 2 (pink wire), Pin 3 (orange), and Pin 4 (pink).
- If the light brightly illuminates, the power supplies are good.

2006–2015 GM Generation 4: TCM Power Test

- Connect one end of the high-current-flow test light to a good ground.
- Disconnect the TCM connector with the ignition in the off position.
- Touch the test-light probe to the power-supply pins in the TCM vehicle harness connector (vehicle side) and place the ignition switch in the run position. The power feeds that need to be tested are Pin 2 (some applications) (pink), Pin 63 (pink/white), Pin 70 (red/white), and Pin 10 (red/white).
- If the light brightly illuminates, the power supplies are good.

2016–2019 GM Generation 5: Application Power Test

- Connect one end of the test light to a good ground.

Generally, high-current-flow test lights are used to check transmission powers and grounds. A typical automotive test light will flow between 0.2 and 0.4 amps.

- Disconnect the TCM connector with the ignition in the off position.
- Touch the test-light probe to the power-supply pins in the TCM vehicle harness connector (vehicle side) and place the ignition switch in the run position. The power feeds that need to be tested are Pin 35 (violet/black) and Pin 66 (red/white).
- If the light brightly illuminates, the power supplies are good.

TCM Ground-Side Testing the LCT 1000 and 2000

The ground can be tested using a few different methods: voltage drop with a voltmeter or with a low-impendence, high-current-flow, bulb-type test light.

The principle of measuring voltage drop is quite simple and can be used to indirectly measure resistance in a power-side or a ground-side circuit. Let's look at making a simple ground voltage drop measurement on a battery ground to highlight the principle. To check a battery ground, do the following:

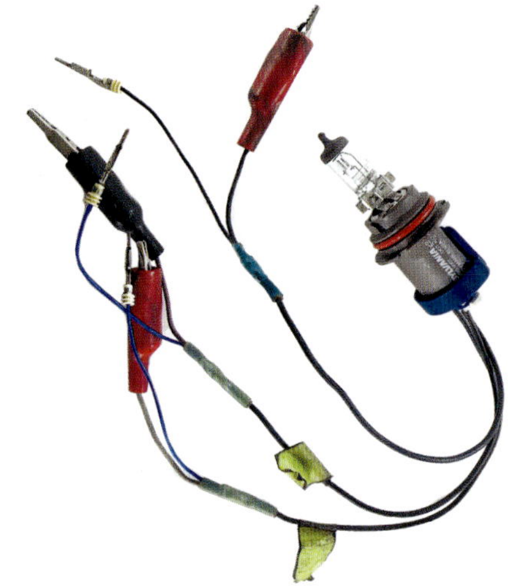

A 9004 headlight works well as a high-current-flow test light. One filament will flow approximately 2.2 amps, while the other filament will flow around 4.5 amps.

- Place the voltmeter in the DC volts position.
- Connect one of the meter leads to the negative battery cable.
- Connect the other meter lead to a point on the vehicle where the ground is connected (typically the body, frame, or engine).
- Turn the ignition into the on position.
- Turn on all electrical loads: the heater fan, headlights, radio, and all other components that can be turned on.
- Read the value displayed on the meter. Typically, it should read less than 0.1 to 0.2 volts per connection. A high reading indicates circuit resistance, which must be addressed.

Another approach is to use a test light. To do so, proceed as follows:

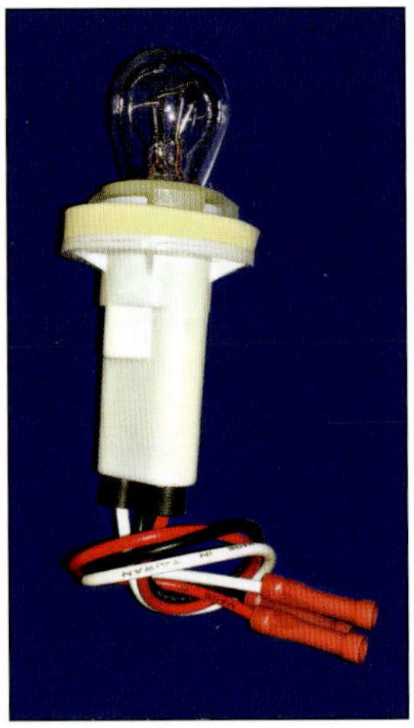

An 1157 light bulb works well, as it flows in the 2.5-amp range.

2001–2005 GM Gen 1–3: Application TCM Ground Test

The following steps are for connector C1 (Clear, 32 pins) and connector C2 (Red, 32 pins).

- Turn the key off, disconnect the TCM connector C1, and locate terminals 1 and 5 (black/white wire) in the harness-side TCM connector C1.
- Connect the test-light alligator clip to the battery positive (B+) terminal.
- Touch the test light (probe) to terminal 1 and then terminal 5.
- The light will be fully illuminated if the ground is good.
- If the light is dim or not lit at all, the ground is faulty.
- If the ground is faulty, use the

This is what a good circuit voltage drop measurement looks like.

TECH TIP: Check the Grounds

A defective Allison TCM may not be the fault of the TCM, so replacing the TCM without locating the cause can result in a repeat TCM failure. On many Allison applications, if the engine controller loses ground, the electronic control unit (ECM) will seek ground through other circuits. This may lead the ECM to seek ground through the TCM, leading to TCM circuit board failure. If a faulty TCM is diagnosed, always check the grounds, especially the ECM/TCM grounds that are typically located on the engine block. ■

voltage drop to isolate the issue (as was previously described). The problem can also be isolated using a test light.

2006–2015 GM Gen 4: TCM Ground Test

- Turn the key off and disconnect the TCM connector.
- Touch one of the test-light leads (probe) to terminal 9 and then terminal 69. Connect the test-light alligator clip to the B+ terminal.

After the transmission pass-through connector is disconnected, inspect for evidence of excessive transmission fluid in the connector. Excessive fluid in the connector can cause DTCs and transmission operational issues. If excessive fluid is found, the internal transmission harness or the transmission side harness connector seal must be replaced. Be aware, multiple different internal transmission harness configurations are available, depending on the year of the transmission.

- The light will be fully illuminated if the ground is good.
- If the light is dim or not lit at all, the ground is faulty.
- If the ground is faulty, use voltage drop to isolate the issue (as was previously described). The problem can also be isolated using a test light.

ECM and TCM grounds are located on the engine block on Duramax applications. Clean grounds are a must on these applications.

Cab grounds on older applications can cause many vehicle issues.

2016–2019 GM Gen 5: Application Ground Test

- Turn the key off and disconnect the TCM connector.
- Touch the test-light leads (probe) to terminal 65. Connect the test-light alligator clip to the B+ terminal.

For the Gen 1–3 TCM C1 clear/gray 32-pin connector, Pins 2, 3, and 4 should be tested for power. Pins 1 and 5 are the grounds that need to be tested.

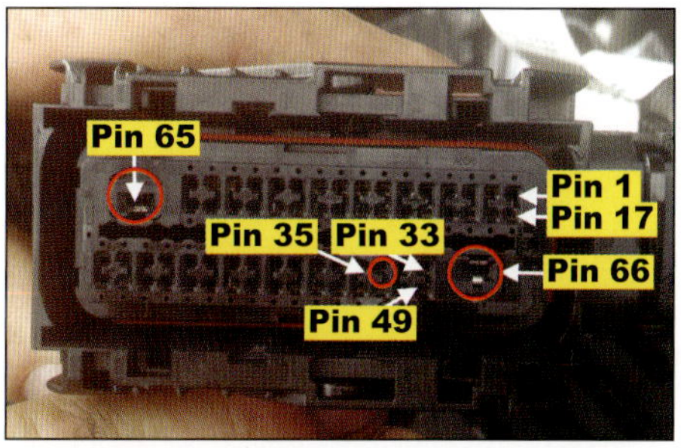

This is a GM Gen 5 2016-and-later TCM connector. Power pins to test include Pins 35 and 66, while the ground is Pin 65. A good ground and power feeds are critical to a properly functioning 1000 or 2000.

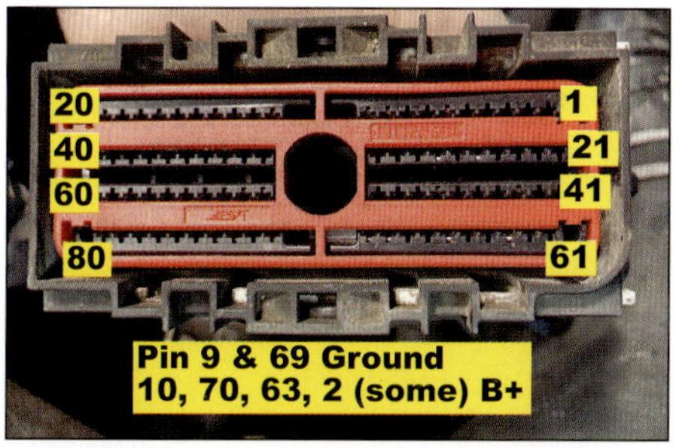

Pin 2 (some applications) (pink), Pin 63 (pink/white), Pin 70 (red/white), and Pin 10 (red/white) are the power feeds that need to be tested on the GM Gen 4 80-pin connector. Pins 9 and 69 are the grounds that need to be tested.

- The light will be fully illuminated if the ground is good.
- If the light is dim or not lit at all, the ground is faulty.
- If the ground is faulty, use voltage drop to isolate the issue (as was previously described). The problem can also be isolated using a test light.

  To isolate the faulty ground with a test light, attach the test-light lead to the B+ terminal. Trace the wiring to locate the circuit and its connectors. Backprobe each terminal/connection with a probing tool and a test light. When the light fully illuminates, the issue is found. The problem is located somewhere between the point where the light fully illuminated and the last point where the light was dim. The TCM grounds G103/G110 are located on the passenger's side of the Duramax engine block.

When disconnecting the transmission pass-through connector or the range sensor connector, examine the connectors for evidence of transmission fluid or contamination that was trapped in the connector. The connectors should not be filled with fluid. If fluid is present, any of the following symptoms may occur:

- False DTCs
- No engine crank when key is in the start position
- Transmission defaults may be present (Neutral only, 3rd gear, or 5th-gear default)
- The driver information PRNDL indicator may be blank and not show the gear position

Adhesives, Sealers, and Lubricants

None of the gaskets or seals used in the LCT 1000 require any type of sealer. Some technicians use a light coating of liquid Teflon sealer on the bellhousing bolts. In addition, they lubricate the other bolts with transmission fluid prior to installation to prevent corrosion. Rubber seals should be lubricated with Dexron VI or an approved transmission assembly lube, such as Transjel, Door Ease, or Transmission Assembly Treatment.

When installing the torque converter bolts, use Blue Loctite 242 thread locker on the threads.

Seal and Gasket Service Kits

Seals and gaskets need to be replaced any time a transmission is rebuilt. A quality kit is a necessity. Some kits include gaskets and seals only, while others include clutch plates. Some also include the filter and the molded clutch pistons. Most companies have the kits available in multiple configurations. There are several companies that sell kits for the LCT 1000 and 2000 transmissions. Precision International, TransTec, and Seal Aftermarket are some of the larger suppliers. Precision International is the OEM supplier for General Motors.

Assembly Lubricants

Transmission components, seals, bearings, and bushings need to be lubricated prior to assembling the transmission. The type of lubricant used depends on the component that is being assembled.

Several different types of lubricants are used, including automatic transmission fluid and transmission-assembly specialized lubricants, such as Transjel, Trans Assembly Goo, synthetic transmission assembly lube, Transmission Assembly Treatment, or Vaseline.

Under no circumstances should any automotive-type greases, such as chassis or wheel-bearing greases be used in an automatic transmission. Automotive greases do not break down completely and can lead to plugged filters and ultimately pump and transmission failure.

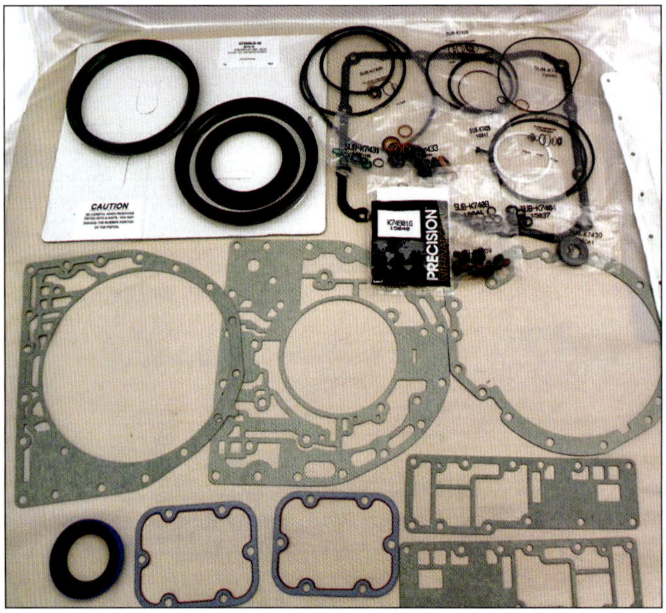

Transmission kits are available in several configurations: seals and gaskets; seals, gaskets, and clutches; seals, gaskets, clutches, and filters; and seals, gaskets, clutches, filters, bearings, bushings, and bearings. Some kits are available prepackaged with all the seals labeled. Others are delivered in bulk bags.

Assembly lubes, such as Transjel, Trans Assembly Goo, and synthetic assembly lube, are available to help with component assembly and lubrication. Do not use automotive greases, such as chassis or wheel-bearing greases because they can lead to filter restrictions and transmission failure.

Door-Ease is used by some technicians to aid in piston installation. Coat the seal with Door-Ease and then over coat the seal with clean transmission fluid.

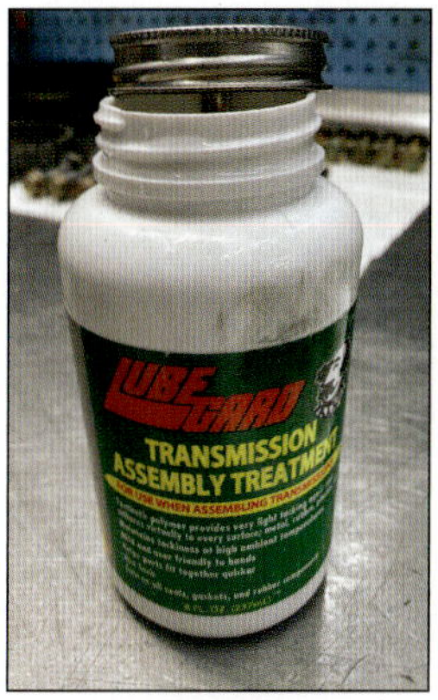

Transmission Assembly Treatment is new to the market and works very well when installing pistons on Allison applications. Coat the seal area and the bore and install the piston.

The type of lubricant used for seals, clutch piston seals, and sealing rings varies based on the preference of the assembly technician. Most rebuilders use a specialized lubricant, such as Transjel. Some old-timers use a home hardware product known as Door-Ease, which is then coated with automatic transmission fluid. Others simply coat the seals with automatic transmission fluid. A product known as Transmission Assembly Treatment works very well for some of the piston seals in Allison applications, as assembly of some clutch pistons can be a challenge.

Most of the gears and all the bearings should be lubricated with automatic transmission fluid. Bushings and thrust washers are typically coated with a specialized lubricant, such as Transjel or automatic transmission fluid. All transmission valves and valve bores should be coated with automatic transmission fluid. Most rebuilders coat the oil pump gears with a specialized lubricant, such as Transjel, or automatic transmission fluid.

Cooler Flushing

Any time the transmission is rebuilt or a new transmission has been installed, the transmission cooler must be cleaned or replaced. Contamination and metal particulates tend to pack into the cooler, restricting the cooler flow. The oil returning from the transmission is used for transmission lubrication, so a restriction in the cooler flow can result in total transmission failure. A few methods are used: a professional cooler-flushing machine, an aerosol cooler-flushing solvent, or a replacement of the

Cooler-flushing solvent is available in cans from parts stores.

Cooler flushing or replacement is critical to transmission life. Cooler return flow is fed to the transmission-lubrication circuit, so a restricted cooler can lead to a lack of transmission lubrication and transmission failure. A professional flushing machine or cooler replacement is the preferred method to address cooler contamination.

cooler or the radiator that typically houses the cooler.

Cooler lines are an issue with the GM truck applications. Be sure to inspect the lines closely for leakage and replace them as needed.

Transmission Inspection

Once the transmission has been removed from the vehicle, clean the unit with a pressure washer to remove some of the grime so that it can be inspected. Make sure to block off any openings that could allow water intrusion into the unit, including the vents, dipstick openings, the pump and turbine shaft area, electrical connectors, and the input/output shaft.

The LCT 1000 and 2000 applications tend to develop cracks in the bellhousing and the 4x4 adapter. Cracks in the bellhousing tend to be in the corner where the large rectangular opening is located. It is also imperative to inspect the engine flexplate and the 4x4 adapter for cracks.

Allison bellhousings tend to crack first in the inside area next to the large rectangular opening.

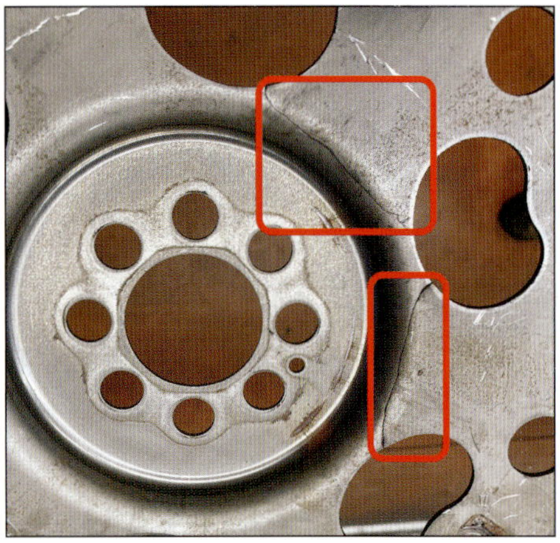

Inspect the flexplate for cracks.

Cracks

Cracks in any of these areas are not the fault of the transmission but are rather the fault of the operator, which must be addressed. Otherwise, the new part will also fail. Cracks are caused by vibration issues, including the following:

- Worn U-joints
- Excessive U-joint working angle (lift kit)
- Worn or damaged engine or transmission mounts
- Driveshaft or wheel tire balance
- Broken springs or spring hangers
- A worn carrier bearing or differential bearing

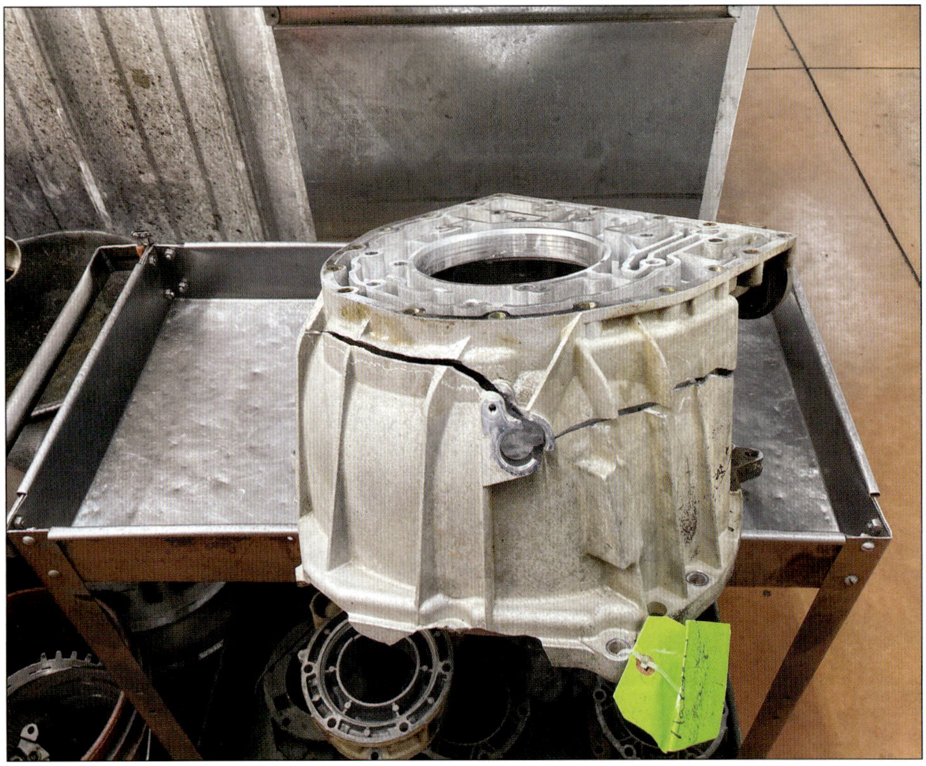

Bellhousing cracks are common on Allison application, so inspect for them.

Inspect the 4x4 adapter for cracks. Cracks are not due to a transmission issue but rather an operator issue and must be addressed. Otherwise, a repeat failure will occur.

Mechanical Components

The Allison 1000- and 2000-series transmissions use five multiple-disc clutch packs to provide either five or six speeds forward and one reverse range. Two clutches are used to drive planetary components, while three clutches are used to lock/hold planetary components to the case. The clutch packs, when hydraulically applied, drive or hold different planetary gearset members to provide the various gear ratios as well as vehicle direction. Some of the clutches are combined in one housing.

Allison refers to the clutches based on the position of the clutch in the case with C1 being closest to the front of the case and C5 located at the rear of the case. General Motors typically refers to the clutches based on the gears that the clutches will be used in: 1-2-3-4, 4-5-6, 3-5-R, 2-6, and Low/Reverse.

Starting in the front of the unit is the oil pump assembly. Behind the oil pump, the C1 and C2 clutches are located within the same drum. The C3, C4, and C5 clutches are next in line. Three planetary sets are used (P1, P2, and P3) to provide the different gear ratios as well as reverse operation. Like the clutches, the planetaries are numbered based on their position in the case: P1 is closest to the front of the case, and P3 is at the rear of the case.

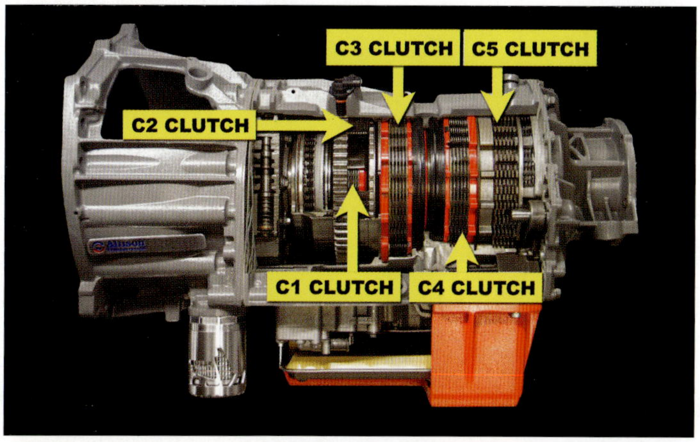

Clutch positions in the 1000 and 2000 applications are numbered from the front to the rear of this Allison Suncoast cutaway transmission. C1 1-2-3-4 and C2 4-5-6 clutches are located directly behind the pump. The C3 3-5-R clutch is located in the center of the transmission, while the C4 2-6 and C5 Low-Reverse clutches are located in the rear of the transmission. There are differences between GM LCT 1000 and 2000 applications and the Allison A1000 and 2000 applications. This means that some of the parts are interchangeable, but others are not. Components, such as the planetaries and the TCM, are different between the GM versus non-GM applications. (Photo Courtesy Suncoast Transmissions and Torque Converters)

The C1 clutch drives the P2 and P3 sun gears, while the C2 clutch drives the P2 carrier and P3 ring gear. The C3 clutch is used to lock the P1 ring gear to the case. The C4 clutch is used to lock the P1 carrier and P2 ring gear to the case. The C5 clutch is used to lock the P2 carrier and the P3 ring gear to the case.

The components are fed hydraulic pressure (clutch apply and lube pressure) via passages in the pump, the case, and the transmission shafts.

There are physical differences between GM LCT 1000 and 2000 applications and the Allison A1000 and 2000 applications. This means that some parts are interchangeable, but others are not. Components, such as the planetaries and the TCM, are different between the General Motors versus non-GM applications.

Allison versus General Motors	
Allison Name	**GM Name**
C1	1-2-3-4
C2	4-5-6
C3	3-5-R
C4	2-6
C5	Low/Reverse

Allison 1000 and 2000 Range Reference/Clutch Apply					
Gear/Clutch	**C1/1-2-3-4**	**C2/4-5-6**	**C3/3-5-R**	**C4/2-6**	**C5/L-R**
Neutral	–	–	–	–	X
1st	X	–	–	–	X
2nd	X	–	–	X	–
3rd	X	–	X	–	–
4th	X	X	–	–	–
5th	–	X	X	–	–
6th	–	X	–	X	–
Reverse	–	–	X	–	X

Range and Power Flow

The 1000 and 2000 require a combination of two clutches to provide a forward or reverse gear ratio. If only one clutch applies, the transmission will be missing the two gears that the clutch activates. If the clutch in question is starting to fail, the slip will become apparent in the highest gear that the clutch is used in prior to it slipping in both gears. This is due to the load on the clutch. The higher the gear (lower the gear-ratio number), the higher the torque load is on the clutch.

If more than two clutches are applied at one time, the vehicle will tend to tie up on that shift. Tie-up issues are typically related to internal seal cross leakage, cracks, or warpage in the pump or the valve body.

Monitoring the gear ratio with a scan tool is a great way to determine if a clutch is slipping. Each gear

The planetaries are oriented like the clutches with P1 (top) planetary located closest to the front of the transmission, P2 (middle) is the center gearset, and P3 (bottom) is the set located closest to the rear of the transmission. Keep in mind that the General Motors versus non-GM applications use different planetary tooth angles, so they are not interchangeable.

The C1 clutch drives the P2 and P3 sun gears, while the C2 clutch drives the P2 carrier and P3 ring gear. The C3 clutch is used to lock the P1 ring gear to the case. The C4 clutch is used to lock the P1 carrier and P2 ring gear to the case. The C5 clutch is used to lock the P2 carrier and P3 ring gear to the case. The General Motors and non-GM applications use different planetary tooth angles, which means they are not interchangeable.

The planetary system consists of three complete gearsets, the mainshaft, and the output shaft. Gearset and bearing updates have been implemented to address bearing-failure and gear-noise concerns.

provides a specific ratio, and the TCM calculates the ratio based on input and output speed sensor signal frequency. The TCM then provides the information to the other vehicle modules via a controller area network (CAN) data bus.

Planetary noise diagnosis is based on when the planetary is in use. Typically, the planetary will make a whining/growling noise, which may include a vibration that can vary in intensity based on the speed and torque being applied to the planetary. Use the Planetary Power Flow table (below) to identify which planetary may be causing concern.

Planetary Power Flow	
Gear	**Planetary**
1st	P3
2nd	P2, P3
3rd	P1, P2, P3
4th	Locked 1-1
5th	P1, P2, P3
6th	P1, P2, P3
Reverse	P1, P2, P3

GM planetary designs have changed along the way, so if you replace any planetary, make sure it is the correct part. If used parts are being used, visually inspect them for the proper tooth count and the correct spline angle. The spline angle for the 1999–2005 is 72 degrees, while 2006-and-later applications have an 80-degree spine angle.

LCT 1000 and 2000 Electronic Components

The Allison applications have been on the market for many years, so many updates and changes have occurred with the product line. This includes the electronics systems and its components. Changes include the TCM, solenoids, valve body, and many of the sensors.

TCM

The transmission control module (TCM) is used to control the operation of the transmission. The TCM operates a series of transmission solenoids to control the transmission shifts and, on later applications, the unit's hydraulic pressure. The TCM receives input information from various internally and externally mounted switches and sensors. Input information is used to determine solenoid operation. The TCM shares information via a CAN bus communication system with other controllers, such as the ECM, body control module (BCM), instrument panel cluster (IPC), antilock braking system (ABS), and chassis control module (CCM). TCMs are available in both 12v and 24v configurations.

A1000 and A2000 Tooth Count		
Component	**A1000 Tooth Count**	**A2000 Tooth Count**
P1 planetary pinions	25	25
P2 planetary pinions	27	27
P3 planetary pinions	27 or 29	31
P1 sun gear	61	61
P2 sun gear	57	57
P3 sun gear	49 or 53	41
P1 ring gear	111	111
P2 ring gear	111	111
P3 ring gear	111 or 103	103

The Allison TCM is located external of the transmission. The location is based on the manufacturer's needs, which means that the TCM location on a Ford may be different from the location on a Freightliner. All GM applications locate the LCT 1000 TCM near the radiator core support on the driver's side of the vehicle.

Multiple versions of TCMs have been used throughout the years, these include WTEC I, WTEC II, WTEC III, Generation 4, and Generation 5. The module generational roll out varied between General Motors and non-GM applications. General Motors did not release the Delphi Gen 5 TCM until 2015, while non-GM applications received a different updated Delphi Gen 5 control module starting in 2013. On non-GM applications, the TCM was updated to a Gen 6 version starting with the 2022 model year.

It should be kept in mind that there can be differences between the TCM used on a GM application and those used on a non-GM application, so they should not be interchanged. Motorola and Delphi are the most common manufacturers of the 1000- and 2000-application TCM. Gen 4 Motorola-built units had issues that can lead to anything from false DTCs to the transmission defaulting to Neutral. Most shops that work on a lot of Allison applications keep a Gen 4 module in the shop as a test module so that they can easily isolate module-related issues.

As was covered in Chapter 1, if a TCM fails, all of the TCM and ECM

TCM Model Years

TCM Model	Years
AL5, 466	2001–2005 (General Motors)
A40, A41, A42	2006–2008
A50, A46, T14A A52, A53, A59	2009–2015
T87, T87A	2015–2019 (General Motors)
A61, A62, A63	2013–2021 (Allison non-GM)
A6A, A6B, A6C	–
C71M, C72M, C73M	2022 Allison non-GM

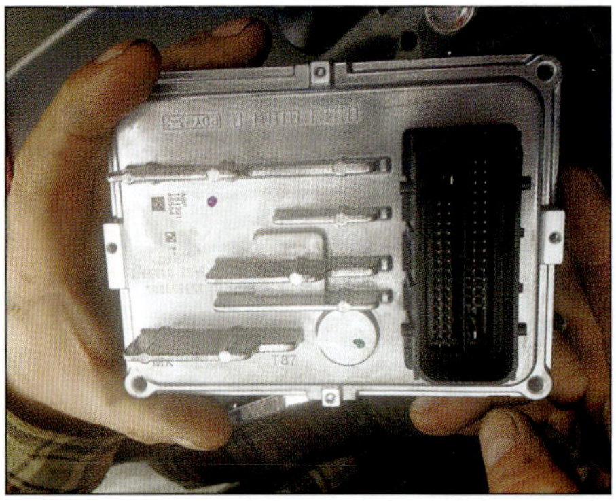

The Gen 5 module replaced the Gen 4 on 2015-and-later applications with RPO code AVF. The Delphi-built module is used on various GM applications, such as the 8L45 and 8L90, the 9T50/60/65, and the 10L1000 Allison.

grounds must be thoroughly cleaned and checked. Otherwise, a repeat module failure can occur. In addition, the battery, charging system, and its connections must be inspected.

Typically, the TCM model code is included on the tag attached to the TCM. Each of the different model modules has various part numbers available that are application dependent. As with other Allison parts, replace the TCM with the correct part-number module. Otherwise, issues with operation may occur.

Make sure to get the correct TCM part number for your application because there are differences between some part numbers.

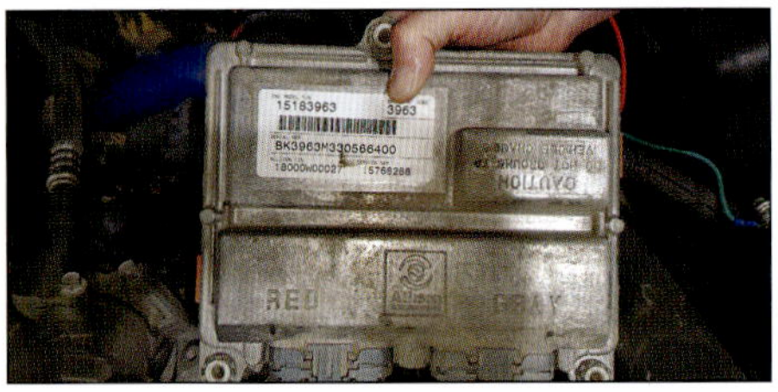

The GM Gen 1–3 applications use two 32-pin connectors and a red and a clear/gray connector. Some of the non-GM applications use three connectors.

In 2006, when the transmission transitioned to a 6-speed application, the Gen 4 module was produced by Motorola. It uses an 80-pin connector to attach the harness to the TCM. Gen 4 modules have issues with durability. If a transmission is experiencing intermittent or odd symptoms, it very well could be caused by an issue with the Gen 4 TCM. GM Gen 4 and Gen 5 TCMs are not interchangeable because the connectors are different. Non-GM A1000 and 2000 Gen 4 TCMs were replaced by the Gen 5 Delphi module. If you are ordering a Gen 4 TCM, a Gen 5 may be received as its replacement because they will interchange on the non-GM applications.

Most Allison 1000 and 2000 TCMs are programable. This means that as updates become available, the updated software can be loaded into the TCM. Some companies sell the TCM preprogramed with the

The TCM on GM applications is located near the radiator core support. It is either mounted in a bracket or directly to the fan shroud. The non-GM application TCM location varies, depending on the vehicle and the brand.

Generation 1–3 2003 Model						
Gear	Trim Solenoids		Shift Solenoids			TCC Solenoids
	A	B	C	D	E	F
R	Deenergized; C5/L-R applied	Energized; C3/3-5-R applied	ON	ON	ON	OFF
R–N	Deenergizing; C5/L-R applied	Energizing; C3/3-5-R releasing	ON	ON	ON	OFF
N–R	Deenergizing; C5/L-R applying	Energizing; C3/3-5-R applying	ON	ON	ON	OFF
N or P	Deenergized; C5/L-R applied	Deenergized; exhausted	ON	ON	ON	OFF
N–1	Deenergized; C5/L-R applied	Energized; C1/1-2-3-4 applying	ON	ON	ON	OFF
1–N	Deenergized; C5/L-R applied	Energized; C1/1-2-3-4 releasing	ON	ON	ON	OFF
1	Deenergized; C5/L-R applied	Deenergized; C4/1-2-3-4 OFF	OFF	ON	OFF	OFF
1–2	Energized; C5/L-R releasing	Energized; C4/2-6 applying	OFF	ON	OFF	OFF
2–1	Energized; C5 L-R applying	Energized; C4/2-6 releasing	OFF	ON	OFF	OFF
2	Energized; C3/3-5-R OFF	Energized; C4/2-6 ON	OFF	OFF	OFF	RPM dependent ON or OFF
2–3	Deenergized; C3/3-5-R applying	Deenergized; C4/2-6 releasing	OFF	OFF	OFF	ON
3–2	Deenergized; C3/3-5-R releasing	Deenergized; C4/2-6 applying	OFF	OFF	OFF	ON
3	Deenergized; C3/3-5-R ON	Deenergized; C2/4-5-6 OFF	ON	OFF	OFF	ON
3–4	Energized; C3/3-5-R releasing	Energized; C2/4-5-6 applying	ON	OFF	OFF	ON
4–3	Energized; C3/3-5-R applying	Energized; C2/4-5-6 releasing	ON	OFF	OFF	ON
4	Energized; C3/3-5-R OFF	Energized; C1/1-2-3-4 ON	ON	OFF	ON	ON
4–5	Deenergized; C3/3-5-R applying	Deenergized; C1/1-2-3-4 releasing	ON	OFF	ON	ON
5–4	Deenergized; C3/3-5-R releasing	Deenergized; C1/1-2-3-4 applying	ON	OFF	ON	ON

latest software, while others require programing before use. Performance TCM updates are also available from the aftermarket for higher torque and horsepower applications. If the module is not programed, the transmission will not function properly.

GM Gen 4 and GM Gen 5 TCMs are not interchangeable because the connectors are different. Non-GM A1000 and 2000 Gen 4 TCMs were replaced by the Gen 5 Delphi module. If you are ordering a Gen 4 module, a Gen 5 may be sent as the replacement because they interchange on the non-GM applications. Gen 6 TCMs (non-GM) are not interchangeable with the Gen 4 and 5 TCMs.

Solenoid State and Operation

Several different valve body designs and components have been used in the 1000 and 2000 applications. The 1999–2003 applications did not have a way to control line pressure electronically. To control shifts and shift feel, they used a pair of solenoids that are known as trim solenoids, or, as they are called out on later applications, pressure control solenoids. Trim A and B solenoids are pulse width modulation (PWM) operated to control the aggressiveness of the shift. Trim "A" is normally closed while Trim "B" is normally open. The trim solenoids control the pressure to the shift solenoids (1-2-3, C-D-E). Shift solenoid C controls the C shift valve, D the D shift valve, and E

Generation 5 2018 GM Application

Shift State	Pressure Control Solenoids		Shift Solenoids		
	PCS1	PCS2	SS1	SS2	SS3
N or P	Deenergized; L-R clutch applied	Deenergized; exhausted	ON	ON	ON
R	Deenergized; 3-5-R clutch applied	Energized; L-R clutch applied	ON	ON	ON
N–R	Deenergizing; 3-5-R clutch applying	Energized; L-R clutch applied	ON	ON	ON
R	Deenergized; L-R clutch applied	Energized; 3-5-R clutch applied	OFF	ON	ON
R Sump Temp Below –25°C	Deenergized; 3-5-R clutch applied	Deen-ergized; exhausted	ON	ON	ON
R	Deenergized; 3-5-R clutch applied	Energized; L-R clutch applied	ON	ON	ON
N–R	Deenergizing; 3-5-R clutch applying	Energized; L-R clutch applied	ON	ON	ON
R	Deenergized; L-R clutch applied	Energized; 3-5-R clutch applied	OFF	ON	ON
R–N	Deenergized; L-R clutch applied	Deenergiz-ing; 3-5-R clutch	OFF	ON	ON
N–R Temp > 20°C	Deenergized; L-R clutch applied	Energizing; 3-5-R clutch applying	OFF	ON	ON
N–R Sump Temp below –25°C	Deenergizing; 3-5-R clutch applying	Deen-ergized; exhausted	ON	ON	ON
N–1	Deenergized; L-R clutch applied	Energizing; 1-2-3-4 clutch applying	ON	ON	ON
1	Deenergized; L-R clutch applied	Deener-gized; 2-6 clutch off	OFF	ON	OFF
1–2	Energizing; L-R clutch releasing	Energizing; 2-6 clutch applying	OFF	ON	OFF
2–1	Deenergizing; L-R clutch applying	Deener-gizing; 2-6 clutch releasing	OFF	ON	OFF
2	Energized; 3-5-R clutch off	Energized; 2-6 clutch applied	OFF	OFF	OFF
2–3	Deenergizing; 3-5-R clutch applying	Deener-gizing; 2-6 clutch releasing	OFF	OFF	OFF
3–2	Energizing; 3-5-R clutch releasing	Energizing; 2-6 clutch applying	OFF	OFF	OFF
3	Deenergized; 3-5-R clutch applied	Deener-gized; 4-5-6 clutch off	ON	OFF	OFF
3–4	Energizing; 3-5-R clutch releasing	Energizing; 4-5-6 clutch applying	ON	OFF	OFF
4–3	Deenergizing; 3-5-R clutch applying	Deenergiz-ing; 4-5-6 clutch releasing	ON	OFF	OFF
4	Energized; 3-5-R clutch off	Energized; 1-2-3-4 clutch applied	ON	OFF	ON
4–5	Deenergizing; 3-5-R clutch applying	Deenergiz-ing; 1-2-3-4 clutch releasing	ON	OFF	ON
5–4	Energizing; 3-5-R clutch releasing	Energizing; 1-2-3-4 clutch applying	ON	OFF	ON
5	Deenergized; 3-5-R clutch applied	Deener-gized; 2-6 clutch off	OFF	OFF	ON
5–6	Energizing; 3-5-R clutch releasing	Energizing; 2-6 clutch applying	OFF	OFF	ON
6–5	Deenergizing; 3-5-R clutch applying	Deener-gizing; 2-6 clutch releasing	OFF	OFF	ON
6	Energized; 3-5-R clutch released	Energized; 2-6 clutch applied	OFF	OFF	ON

the E shift valve. Shift solenoids C, D, and E are on/off–design solenoids. A torque converter clutch (TCC) PWM–controlled solenoid is used to control the torque converter clutch operation.

The Allisons are unique when it comes to GM transmissions. Typically, a GM transmission makes a shift by cycling a solenoid that then moves the shift valve that is responsible for sending oil to the desired clutch. The 1000 and 2000 applications use the shift solenoids to preposition the shift valves in anticipation of the shift (staging), and then the trim/PCS solenoid is used to control the pressure being applied to the clutch.

Starting with the 2004 model year, a new solenoid was added: the solenoid G on/off line pressure solenoid. This solenoid was a pressure-reducing solenoid that was used to lower line pressure to reduce pump noise and increase lubrication flow. Adding solenoid G required the use of an auxiliary valve body and solenoid, which are bolted to the conventional valve body. Those equipped with solenoid G had stepped pressures. Four pressure curves were used: 230, 150, 95, and 80 psi.

From 2010 to 2011, the valve body was again redesigned. The trim solenoids changed to PCS designs, and solenoid G became a fully variable-modulated main line pressure solenoid, which is now located as part of the main valve body. Solenoids C, D, and E became shift solenoids 1, 2, and 3.

In 2013, the valve body received another update on 2000-series applications. Some 2000-series applications now use an additional solenoid, PC3, known as the reduced engine load at stop (RELS). This RELS solenoid is in charge of releasing the C1 clutch when the vehicle is stopped but the transmission is still in a forward range, providing a neutral idle feature. Releasing the C1 clutch places the transmission in Neutral, eliminating engine load when stopped, which improves fuel economy.

So, what does this mean? Be careful when replacing the valve body, front support, and their components, as several different versions have been used. In addition, the parameters that a scan tool will display also changed.

TFT Sensor

The transmission fluid temperature (TFT) sensor is mounted within the pressure switch manifold (PSM), which is mounted to the transmission valve body. The TFT is used by the TCM as one of the inputs to control shift points, the TCC, and shift feel. The temperature sensor is a negative temperature coefficient (NTC) type of sensor. NTC-design thermistors change resistance based on a change in temperature. The resistance change is inverse of the temperature change. In other words, as the temperature decreases, the sensor resistance increases. An increase in temperature results in the sensor resistance decreasing.

The TCM sends 5 volts to the sensor and then monitors the voltage drop across the sensor. The voltage drop is then used by the TCM to determine the transmission fluid temperature.

A high temperature may change the TCC PCS solenoid line pressure commands for the transmission in an attempt to lower excessive transmission fluid temperature. If the overheat

Pressure Switch Operation

Gear	Pressure Switch C (1) Shift Valve C (1) N/O		Pressure Switch D (2) Shift Valve D (2) N/O		Pressure Switch E (3) Shift Valve E (3) N/O		Pressure Switch R/4 Reverse N/C	
	Switch Status	Scan Tool Status	Switch Status	Scan Tool Status	Switch Status	Scan Tool Status	Switch Status	Scan Tool Status
R	Open	OFF/High	Closed	ON/Low	Closed	ON/Low	Closed	ON/Low
P/N	Closed	ON/Low	Closed	ON/Low	Closed	ON/Low	Open	OFF/High
1	Open	OFF/High	Closed	ON/Low	Open	OFF/High	Open	OFF/High
2	Open	OFF/High	Open	OFF/High	Open	OFF/High	Open	OFF/High
3	Closed	ON/Low	Open	OFF/High	Open	OFF/High	Open	OFF/High
4	Closed	ON/Low	Open	OFF/High	Closed	ON/Low	Open	OFF/High
5	Open	OFF/High	Open	OFF/High	Closed	ON/Low	Open	OFF/High
6	Open	OFF/High	Open	OFF/High	Closed	On/Low	Open	OFF/High

condition persists, the TCM will signal the BCM, which will signal the IPC driver information center. On some applications, the driver may receive a message regarding the transmission overheating that instructs the driver to pull over and stop until the transmission is no longer overheating.

Very cold fluid temperature, -49°F (-45°C), can cause the transmission to default to Neutral. In -31°F to -49°F, the transmission may default to Second gear. In -13°F to -31°F, the transmission may only have Second, Third, and Reverse. For -4°F to -13°F, the transmission may have First, Second, Third, Fourth, and Reverse. At -5°F to 71°F, the transmission may have all the gears but may inhibit TCC operation. The default actions mentioned above may vary, depending on what software level is loaded in the TCM. TFT can be monitored with a scan tool.

PSA

The pressure switch assembly (PSA) contains four pressure switches and is attached to the valve body. Unlike other GM transmission applications, the switches are used to indicate shift valve, shift solenoid operation, and clutch hydraulic application for diagnostic purposes.

Three of the switches C (1), D (2), and E (3) are normally open (N/O), while one F (4) is normally closed (N/C). The TCM provides voltage to the 4 PSM switch circuits (signal circuits). Each switch produces either an open or a ground for the TCM signal circuits. With hydraulic pressure available to the switch from the appropriate shift valve, the switch will close. This will provide a path to ground for the TCM signal circuit voltage, pulling the signal voltage low.

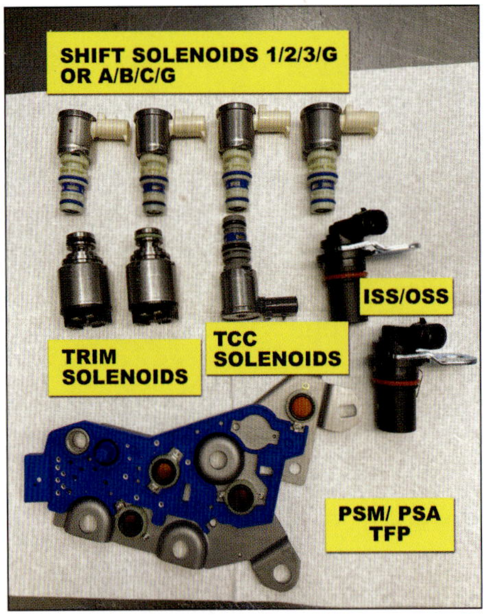

The number of solenoids and electrical components will vary, depending on the year and the generation of the unit. The shift solenoids control the shift valves to control when the clutch applies, while the trim solenoids control the shift feel. One to three speed sensors are mounted to the transmission, depending on the model and year. Keep in mind that two different design sensors have been used: AC generators and Hall effect. The pressure switch manifold is used for two functions: to provide a fluid temperature input to the TCM and to tell the TCM which clutch is receiving hydraulic pressure.

When hydraulic pressure is removed, the switch will be open, eliminating the TCM PSM signal circuit ground, which will result in the signal circuit voltage being high. The TCM then compares the PSM switch signal circuit values to the shift solenoid commanded position to determine if the appropriate clutch is receiving hydraulic pressure for diagnostic purposes.

Pressure switches 1, 2, and 3 monitor the operation of shift valves C (1), D (2), and E (3). Pressure switch 4 monitors reverse operation.

Gen 1–3 Range Sensor (1999–2005)

Early model 1000 and 2000 applications (1999–2004) have a switch mounted on the driver's side of the transmission case. Known as the transmission range (TR) switch, the assembly contains a series of mechanically operated switches. In addition, the neutral safety switch is contained within the range switch assembly. The TR switch contains five switches that are used to signal the TCM and ECM regarding the physical position of the shift lever.

The four TCM circuits are known as A, B, C, and P. The TCM feeds 12 volts to each of the four circuits. Depending on which range the shift lever is placed in, a specific switch sequence is attained. The TCM monitors the high/low voltage sequence to determine which range has been selected. The range switch is used as an input by the TCM and the ECM, and the ECM receives a signal from one switch. That information is used as a neutral safety switch input for engine starting when the transmission is in Park or Neutral.

Depending on the scan-tool software, it will display each circuit as a "Hi," "Low," or "ON/OFF." A Low or OFF indicates the switch is closed to ground and that the pin/circuit voltage is 0, while a Hi or ON indicates that the switch is open and the pin voltage is equal to battery voltage. The ON/OFF scan tool values are contrary to what one would expect. The electrical circuit works as one would expect, but depending on the scan tool software, it may not appear that the ON/OFF is properly representing the circuit voltage.

The key to the range switch diagnosis is that the values change as the

Range Sensor Operation				
Range	**A**	**B**	**C**	**P**
P	OFF/Low	ON/Hi	ON/Hi	OFF/Low
P to R Transition	OFF/Low	OFF/Low	ON/Hi	OFF/Low
R	OFF/Low	OFF/Low	ON/Hi	ON/Hi
R to N Transition	ON/Hi	OFF/Low	ON/Hi	ON/Hi
N	ON/Hi	OFF/Low	ON/Hi	OFF/Low
N to D	ON/Hi	OFF/Low	OFF/Low	OFF/Low
D	ON/Hi	OFF/Low	OFF/Low	ON/Hi
D to 3 Transition	OFF/Low	OFF/Low	OFF/Low	ON/Open
3	OFF/Low	OFF/Low	OFF/Low	OFF/Low
3–2 Transition	OFF/Low	ON/Hi	OFF/Low	OFF/Low
2	OFF/Low	ON/Hi	OFF/Low	ON/Hi
2–1 Transition	ON/Hi	ON/Hi	OFF/Low	ON/Hi
1	ON/Hi	ON/Hi	OFF/Low	OFF/Low
Fault	ON/Open	ON/Open	ON/Open	ON/Open
Fault	ON/Open	ON/Open	ON/Open	OFF/Grounded
Fault	ON/Open	OFF/Grounded	OFF/Grounded	OFF/Grounded

shift lever moves. Any value that remains locked, displaying only one value through all the shifter positions, indicates a circuit, switch, or TCM issue.

The range sensor design changed for 2004. The 1999–2003 applications used two electrical connectors, while 2004–2005 applications only used one large connector. Issues with the range sensor are very common due to moisture intrusion into the switch contacts. Default actions for range-sensor issues can vary, but be aware that one of the common defaults is the transmission defaulting to Neutral. Another common issue is the instrument panel PRNDL display blinking or going blank during operation.

On early applications, the scan tool may display: PARK=8, REV=7, NEU=0, OD=5, 3=3, M2=2, M1=1 rather than ON/OFF from each switch for each range.

Early applications used a two-connector design range sensor. Moisture intrusion with this design was common, which can lead to issues from the transmission defaulting to Neutral to a flashing or blank PRNDL display in the instrument panel.

Later applications used a signal wire connector. Like the two-connector design, it is recommended that the sensor be replaced anytime the transmission is replaced or overhauled.

Gen 4 and Gen 5 IMS (2006 and Later)

The internal mode switch (IMS) replaces the range sensor that was previously mounted externally on the transmission case. The internal mode switch is bolted to the transmission shift shaft and is mounted internally of the transmission. The IMS is connected electrically to the TCM and ECM. The TCM sends 5 volts to the sensor for operation.

As the driver moves the shift lever, the switch's internal contacts move corresponding to the movement in range position. The IMS

Internal Mode Switch Operation				
Range	**Circuit A**	**Circuit B**	**Circuit C**	**Circuit P**
P	Low/Grounded	Hi/Open	Hi/Open	Low/Grounded
P to R	Low/Grounded	Low/Grounded	Hi/Open	Low/Grounded
R	Low/Grounded	Low/Grounded	Hi/Open	Hi/Open
N	Hi/Open	Low/Grounded	Hi/Open	Low/Grounded
N to D	Hi/Open	Low/Grounded	Low/Grounded	Low/Grounded
D	Hi/Open	Low/Grounded	Low/Grounded	Hi/Open
M	Low/Grounded	Low/Grounded	Low/Grounded	Low/Grounded
D to Low	Low/Grounded	Hi/Open	Low/Grounded	Low/Grounded
1	Low/Grounded	Hi/Open	Low/Grounded	Hi/Open
Fault	Hi/Open	Hi/Open	Hi/Open	Hi/Open
Fault	Hi/Open	Hi/Open	Hi/Open	Low/Grounded
Fault	Low/Grounded	Hi/Open	Hi/Open	Hi/Open
Fault	Hi/Open	Low/Grounded	Hi/Open	Hi/Open
Fault	Low/Grounded	Low/Grounded	Low/Grounded	Hi/Open
Fault	Hi/Open	Hi/Open	Low/Grounded	Hi/Open

changes position based on the transmission shift linkage that is controlled by the driver and the shift lever. The IMS acts as the shifter lever/range position sensor or manual valve position sensor so that the TCM knows the shifter position. This information is used by the TCM to determine the number of shifts and to command manual downshifts (or manual range) when the driver manually moves the shifter.

The internal mode switch (IMS) replaced the externally mounted range sensors. Mounting the sensor internal to the transmission eliminated the moisture intrusion issues that were common on the externally mounted range sensors.

In addition, a dedicated circuit connects the P-N input from the switch directly to the engine control module (ECM) for engine start. IMS values can be monitored with a scan tool.

Speed Sensors: ISS, OSS/VSS, and TSS

GM Gen 1–4 and non-GM Gen 1–5 applications use permanent magnet-type sensors that generate an AC sine wave as their output. Sensor output voltage will vary from around 150 millivolts at low speeds to 15 volts or more at high rotational speed. The TCM converts the AC signal internally to a square wave. The TCM then monitors the frequency of the signal to determine the component rotational speed.

Three transmission-mounted speed sensors were used from 1999 to 2007: turbine speed (TSS), input speed (ISS), and output speed (OSS/VSS). The TSS was mounted in the transmission bellhousing and used the impeller fin dimples on the torque converter to make the sensor function. Starting in 2007, the TSS was eliminated, and a crankshaft sensor is now used as the calculation for turbine speed.

The ISS monitors the speed of the 1-2-3-4/3-5-R (C1/C2) clutch drum. The VSS/OSS monitors the speed of the output speed sensor tone wheel mounted on the output planetary. On 4x4 late-model applications, the VSS/OSS was removed from the transmission case and now uses the signal from the transfer case output shaft.

Turbine speed is used to calculate TCC slip. The ISS is primarily used for gear ratio and TCC slip calculations.

The 1–3 speed sensors are mounted to the transmission depending on the model and year. Two different design sensors have been used: AC generators and Hall effect, which are not interchangeable. Do not reposition the sensor mounting bracket or sensor operation issues can occur.

The OSS is used to calculate gear ratio and control up/down shifts, line pressure, and TCC.

Gen 5 GM applications use a pair of two-wire "Hall Effect, MR"–type speed sensors to feed component rotational speed information to the TCM. The sensors are fed an 8.3- to 9.3-volt supply voltage from the TCM. The sensors produce a square wave output that is fed directly to the TCM via the sensor wiring. The frequency of the square wave varies based on the component rotational speed.

Non-GM Gen 6 applications use a Hall Effect sensor as the output sensor. The other sensors are standard magnetic-type sensors, as used in previous applications.

All Allison applications use input information from various systems and inputs. ABS wheel-speed-sensor issues can cause transmission-shifting issues on many applications, even though the TSS is operating properly.

The speed sensors have a mounting bracket attached to the sensor. Do not rotate the bracket in relation to the sensor. Changing the bracket position may affect the sensor's operation.

The speed sensor wiring is made of twisted pairs for EMI protection. If a wiring repair is performed, the wiring must be twisted at a rate of nine revolutions per foot. If a connector or terminal issue is present, General Motors sells harness terminals as well as harness pigtails.

On applications that generate a turbine speed signal from the torque converter fins, damage to the fins will cause sensor and transmission operational issues.

TCM Shared Data and Additional Inputs

While the TCM receives information from sensors/switches mounted internal of the transmission, most of the information the TCM requires is supplied by other modules, such as the ECM, BCM, CCM, and electronic brake control module (EBCM).

The throttle position sensor (TPS), accelerator pedal position sensor (APP), brake pedal position sensor (BPP), engine speed, engine coolant temperature sensor (ECT), manifold absolute pressure sensor (MAP), mass airflow sensor (MAF), intake air temperature sensor (IAT), TAP switches, and pitch/yaw sensor are examples of externally mounted sensors that are used by the TCM to control transmission operation. Sensor information is transmitted to the TCM from the other modules via a CAN communication bus.

TECH TIP — Scanning

When scanning data and DTCs on all applications, it is imperative to monitor the data and the DTCs on all the vehicle's systems. Issues with other systems will cause transmission operational issues and false DTCs. ■

Proper transmission operation is dependent on accurate information from the sensors that act as inputs to the TCM. With that in mind, any time there is a transmission concern, make certain that the issue is not related to something other than an internal transmission–related issue prior to condemning the transmission.

Scan Tool Diagnosis, Data Parameters, DTCs, and Programing

A quality scan tool is critical to assist with the diagnosis of related issues. The scan tool should allow checking for DTCs that are stored, freeze-frame and failure record information related to the DTCs set, and sensor data. The tool should also provide output override capabilities that allow control of the transmission via the scan tool.

Data Parameters

Dozens of parameters are available on 1000 and 2000 applications. Parameters are related to sensor input values, TCM calculations (such as ratio and torque), and output commands (such as the solenoids and pressure control). Data parameters are provided by the different control modules to aid in diagnosis.

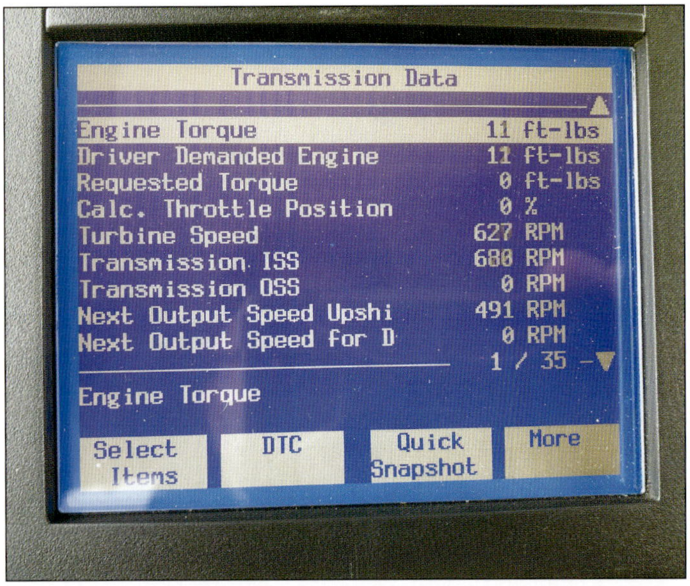

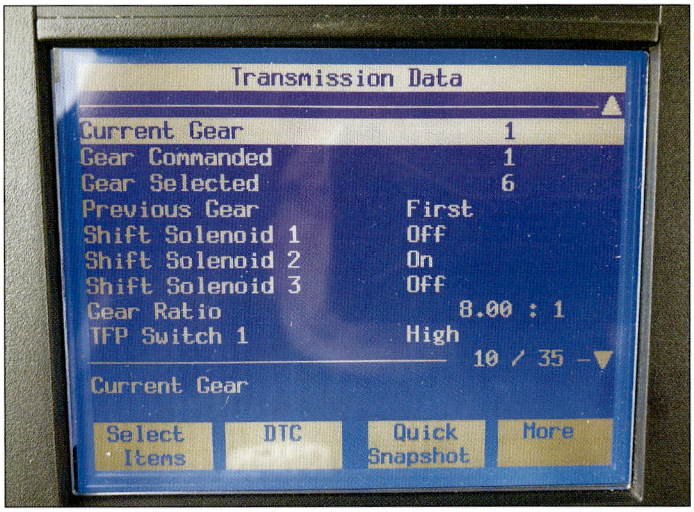

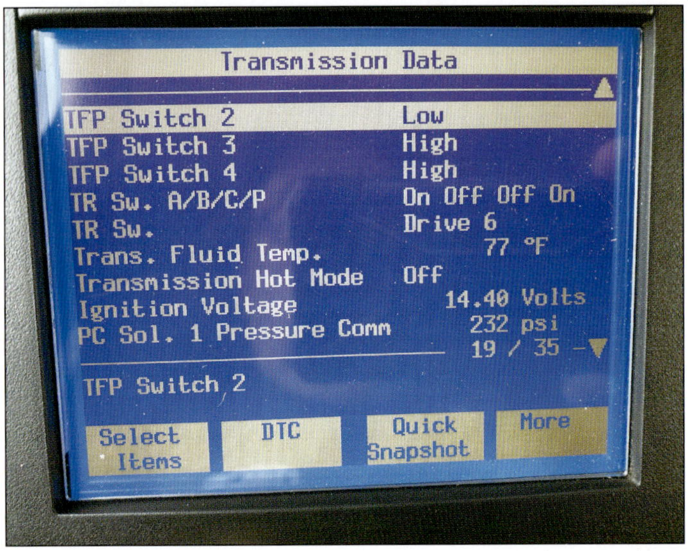

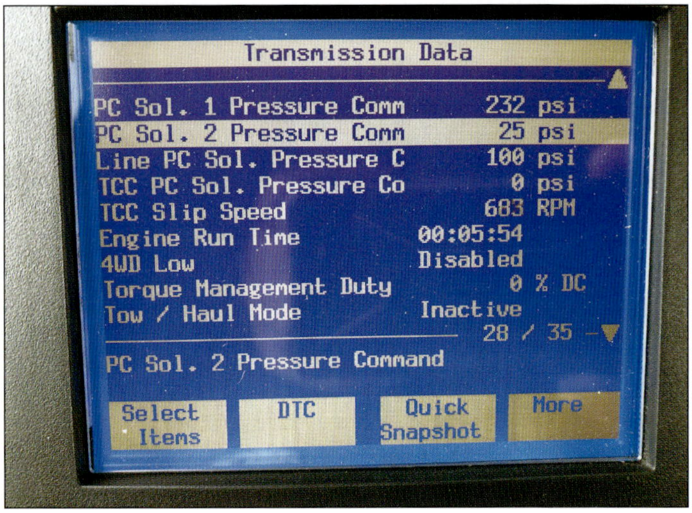

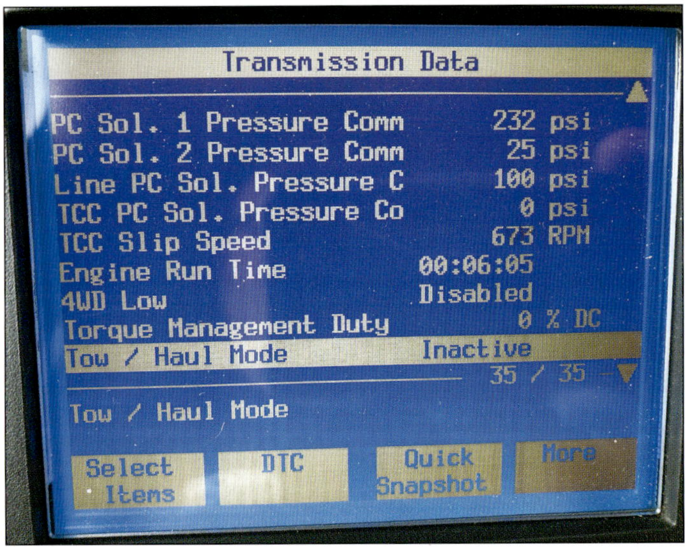

The normal key on, transmission in Neutral, and engine running at idle values are shown for a 2009 GM K2500 application.

DTCs

DTCs are a form of "contact tracing" for a vehicle. A DTC indicates the area of the vehicle system that has an issue. It does not necessarily mean the component is faulty, but it does indicate that something is likely wrong that relates to that component, circuit, or system. For example, let's say there is a DTC related to the IMS. Several possibilities exist: an issue with the wiring, a problem with the IMS connection to the manual valve, a faulty TCM, or a faulty IMS.

It is imperative to scan all vehicle modules, because in simple terms "today's transmission is no longer a transmission." It is part of a complete powertrain system. This means that issues in other systems can and will cause issues with transmission operation.

A common example is clutch damage on late-model applications with variable line pressure. This may be caused by an owner using an oil coated–type aftermarket air filter. The oil from the filter coats the factory MAF sensor element, skewing the MAF sensor airflow value being sent to the ECM. The ECM communicates the incorrect engine load value to the TCM. The TCM then calculates the wrong line pressure solenoid command value, which leads to low clutch pressure and ultimately transmission clutch failure. General Motors has issued several bulletins regarding this issue.

All LCT 1000 and 2000 DTCs are OBD-II-compliant five- or seven-digit (enhanced) codes. Five-digit codes are the standard OBD-II-compliant DTCs, while the sixth and seventh digits on a seven-digit-enhanced DTC are symptom indicators. This enhanced DTC design helps to separate things such as a short-to-ground condition from a short-to-voltage condition. The additional sixth and seventh digits of an enhanced DTC cannot be read with some brands of scan tools.

Character	Meaning
P	Powertrain
0 or 1	"0" is a generic DTC, so the meaning is the same for any manufacturer. "1" is a manufacturer-specific DTC.
7	Transmission-related concern
11	Component or concern causing the DTC. In this instance, the concern indicates an issue that is related to the fluid temperature sensor or circuit.

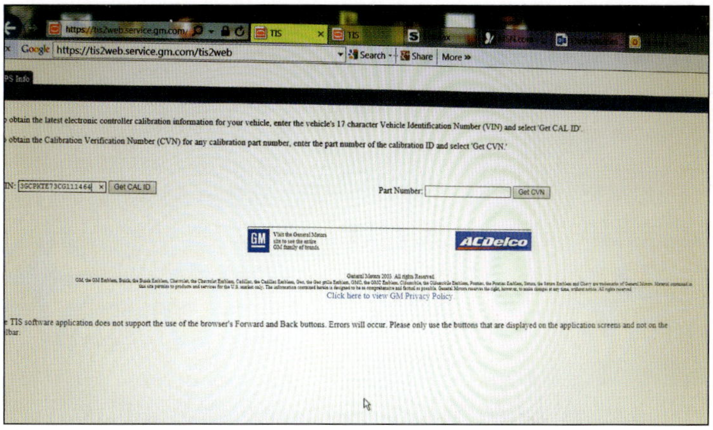

The software level can be checked for free by accessing the GM TIS2 website. Simply enter the vehicle identification number (VIN) and click on the "Get Cal ID" button.

The nearby table shows an example of an OBD-II-compliant five-digit DTC for P0711.

Late-model vehicles may not be able to clear the DTC and/or its default actions—even though the scanner indicates the DTC is cleared. For example, if a "Service Engine Soon" or "Check Trans" lamp is illuminated, the DTC is cleared, but the lamp may not go off. So, how does one get the SES lamp off after the DTC is cleared with a scan tool? Review the parameters the controller used to set the DTC. Operate the vehicle, making sure to match the DTC parameters used for setting the code. Typically, this takes more than one drive cycle. The controller will test for the fault, and if all is well, it will turn out the lamp and fully clear the DTC. This whole process was implemented because people were trying to cheat to get their vehicles through their local emission certification for vehicle licensing.

If a DTC is set, make sure to access the appropriate shop manual information.

Programing

The TCM requires programing to function correctly if it was replaced. Programing the TCM requires the use of a J2534 programing interface, a quality scan tool, and a subscription to the GM Special Programing Service (SPS) via AC Delco for GM applications. If you do not have access to the programing equipment, a dealer or qualified independent shop needs to do the programing. If you are reusing the TCM, check its software level to see if it is equipped with the latest software load. The GM software level can be checked for free by accessing the GM TIS2 website (tis2web.service.gm.com/tis2web/).

Once the site is accessed, load the VIN into the VIN box on the screen and press the "Get Cal Id" icon. The next screen to load displays the calibration tables for the VIN. Various controllers can be accessed to get the calibration numbers available.

If the TCM/transmission icon is chosen, the next screen displays the calibration numbers available for that VIN's TCM application. The display shows the various calibrations that are available for that application and typically the reason for the update. Compare the numbers displayed on the GM TIS2WEB SPS system to the value listed as "CAL ID" in the scan tool data parameters. If the value displayed on the scan tool is the same as the latest one displayed on the GM website, the calibration is up to date. Keep in mind that this website format

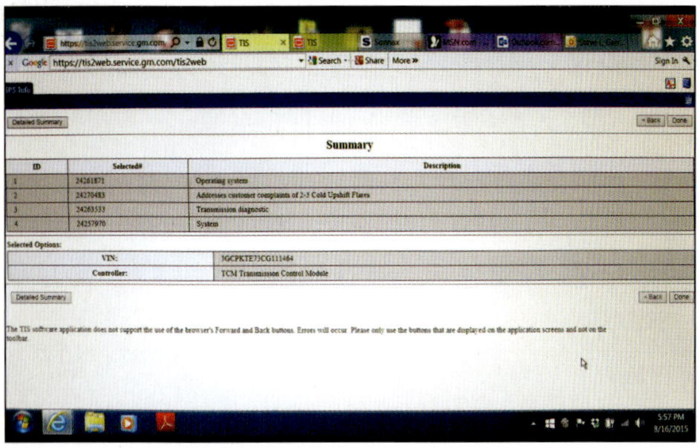

The website shows the software levels available for the application based on the VIN. Using a scan tool, compare the Cal ID number stored in the TCM to the values displayed on the screen to see if a software update is available for the application.

changes often, so the screens may not look exactly as the picture portrays.

Adaptive Learning, Clearing Adapts, and Relearning Adapts

Adaptive learning is the most misunderstood feature used with today's transmissions. The Allison family of units are equipped with various adaptive functions that are designed to protect the transmission from damage while providing good performance for the customer. Shift adapts, garage shift adapts, and study state adapts are common terms used to describe today's transmission adaptive features. These features are comprised of a software algorithm that is transparent to the customer but is essential to proper transmission operation.

Adaptive Learning

The 1000 and 2000 software is equipped with a feature known as adaptive learning. Adaptive learning is designed to ensure that the transmission shifts and operates the same at 100,000 miles as it did at 100 miles. Multiple types of adaptive learning are used, but the most common type is the upshift/downshift adapts.

The TCM has the ability to learn the shift times of all the transmission upshifts and downshifts. This is known as shift adapts. The TCM measures the clutch apply/release rates to determine the shift time. This is accomplished by the TCM monitoring the shift command, the ISS, and the OSS frequency during the shift. The TCM commands a shift and then monitors for a change in the ISS frequency. The TCM can determine shift time by measuring the time between when the solenoid was commanded to make a shift and when it sees an input speed sensor change showing that the shift is complete.

The measured shift time is then compared to the desired shift time for that vehicle load and shift by the TCM. If the shift time was too short, the TCM will command less pressure the next time that particular shift is commanded again. If the shift time was too long, the TCM will increase the pressure when that particular shift happens again. The corrected shift pressure offset positive and negative values are stored in the TCM memory to be used on the next shifts. While the system is very sophisticated, the TCM monitors the shift times for all the upshifts and downshifts at various throttle openings and fluid temperatures and stores that information in the TCM memory for use on the next shift that meets that criterion.

Clearing Adapts and Relearning Adapts

The shift adapts should be cleared and relearned if any of the following occur:

- The transmission was replaced
- The transmission was rebuilt
- The valve body was replaced or repaired
- Any repair that could impact shift times was performed, including replacing or reprograming the TCM

TECH TIP: Clearing Adapts

Clearing the adapts on all 1000- and 2000-series applications will not result in all the values resetting to 0. The values will reset to predetermined software values that may or may not be 0. ■

The shift adapt pressure offset values are learned and stored in the TCM memory for each shift at specific loads and temperatures. If repairs are performed on the transmission, that can affect shift times. It is important that the shift adapt stored values be reset and relearned.

Clearing Adapts

Clearing the adaptive memory is accomplished with a quality scan tool. The reason the adapts must be cleared is because the transmission was likely repaired because of an issue with the transmission. The TCM will have learned and attempted to correct for the issues present within the transmission. For example, if the seal for the 2-6 clutch was worn, the 1-2 and/or 5-6 shifts may flare or slip. The TCM will learn the shift time

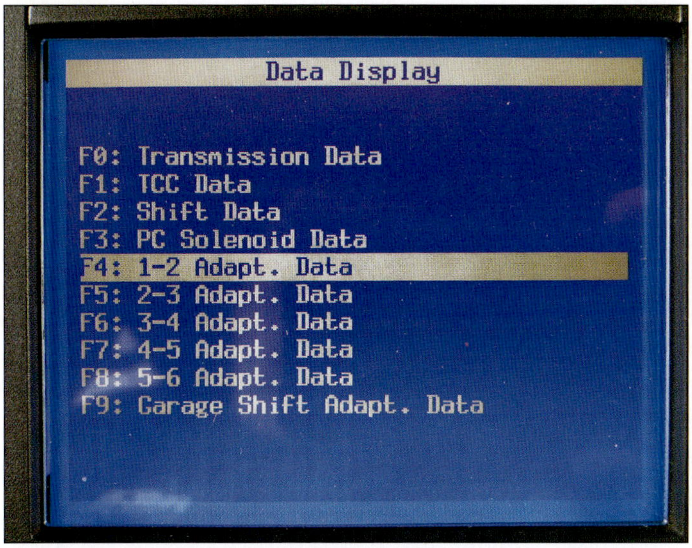

Shift adapt values are available for each shift. Choose the shift to view to retrieve the adapt values.

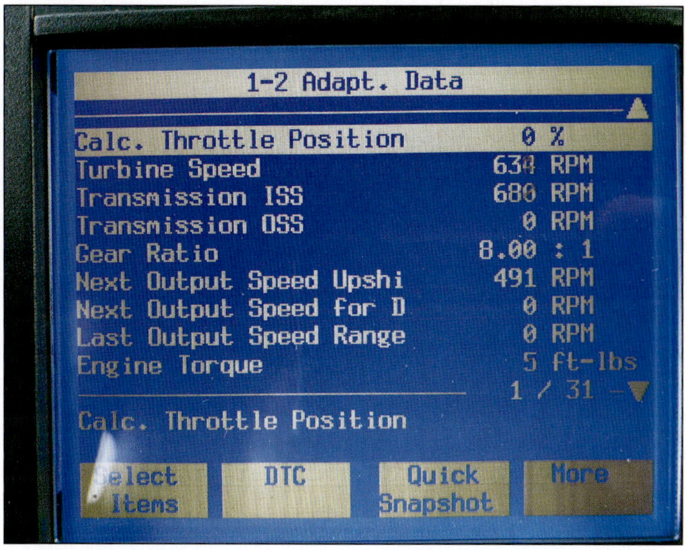

The normal key on, transmission in neutral, and engine running at idle values are shown for a 2009 GM K2500 application.

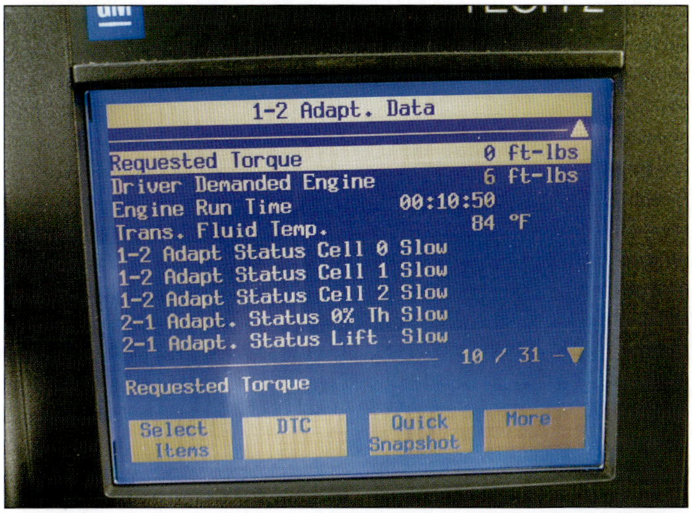

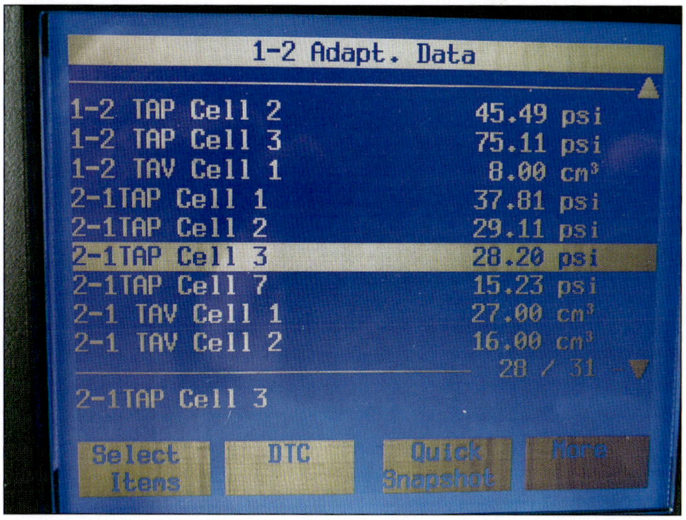

The normal key on, transmission in Neutral, and engine running at idle values are shown for a 2009 GM K2500 application. Shift adapt information represents the last adaptable shift values stored.

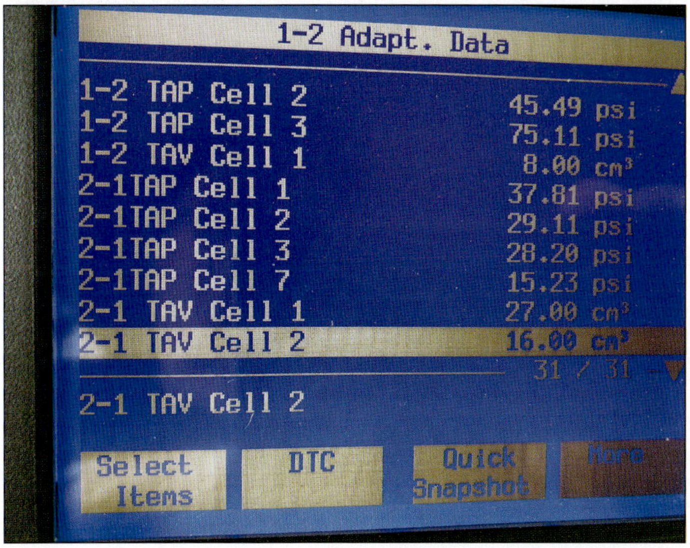

and provide a positive pressure offset in an attempt to correct for the worn seal on the next shift.

Now, the transmission is repaired, and new seals were installed. The leakage is no longer present, but of course, the TCM does not know the transmission was repaired. The TCM then shifts the transmission using the pressure offsets that were stored for the worn transmission. This can cause transmission damage as well as an upset customer, as it takes many shifts at various throttle openings and temperatures to get the values relearned for the new transmission.

Relearning Adapts

Clearing the adapts clears all the adaptive memories. Clear all DTCs prior to clearing the adapts. Follow the instructions on the scan tool to clear the adapts. Once the adapts are cleared, new transmission adapts need to be relearned. Some scan tools have the ability to perform a "fast learn," which shortens the length of time it takes to relearn the adapts. This typically occurs when the adaptive values are cleared on an Allison. The TCM starts the relearn process in "fast learn mode." After the adaptive shift values have been "roughed in," the TCM will switch to "slow learn mode." This process is repeated for each shift and gear. Typically, this process is referred to as shift convergence. Once all the shifts have converged, the relearn process is complete.

Once the adaptive relearn process has been performed, a complete road test should be performed, upshifting and downshifting the transmission through all gears at various different throttle openings. If the scan tool does not have the ability to perform a fast learn, then a very extensive road test will need to be performed, operating the vehicle through all the up/downshifts at various throttle openings and temperatures.

On-Vehicle Repairs and Adjustments

As with all other transmissions, the Allison applications may require some on-vehicle adjustments to make it operate correctly. In addition, proper operation is not just the function of the transmission but also many other vehicle components.

Shifter Cable Adjustments and New Cable Installation

Use the following steps to adjust the shifter cable or install a new cable.

1. The steering-column shift lever should be placed in the Park position with the wheels blocked.
2. The transmission manual shaft lever should be placed in the Park position.
3. Open the cable white cover by using a screwdriver to unlock the cable-locking teeth. Grasp the shift-cable shifter end in your left hand and the shift cable transmission end (new cable) in your right hand. Align the two ends and slide them together. Once the two-piece cable is slid together, it will no longer come apart, as it locks permanently into position.
4. Release the transmission end, allowing the spring to apply tension to the cable.
5. Open the white cover on the shifter end of the cable. Push the natural-colored lock button down. This engages the locking teeth on the transmission end of the cable.

The white cover on the cable is used to lock and unlock the cable position. The cable needs to be adjusted with the transmission shifter and the transmission positioned in the Neutral position.

Transmission Mounts, U-Joints, Driveshaft Bearings, and Vehicle Springs

Vibration issues can cause case, bellhousing, flexplate, and 4x4 adapter cracks and failure, so any type of vibration must be addressed when working with a 1000 or 2000 transmission application. Always closely inspect the bellhousing, flexplate, and 4x4 adapter for cracks and damage.

The transmission mounts should be inspected for wear and damage. A collapsed mount can cause vibrations to be transmitted into the vehicle body, leading to owner complaints as well as transmission damage. Inspect the mount for cracks and the rubber for being separated from the metal.

Always inspect the U-joints and any driveshaft carrier bearings for wear and damage. If the vehicle has a lift kit installed, always check the driveshaft U-joint working angle. Always inspect the vehicle springs, spring hangers, and bushings for wear and damage.

2006-and-Later Applications

Diagnosis of the IMS can be accomplished with the scan tool prior to transmission disassembly by monitoring the IMS values outlined earlier in this chapter. If the values do not match the table, the IMS, the wiring, or the TCM is likely defective.

The IMS can be bench tested using an ohmmeter, but that takes a lot more effort. It is easiest if the IMS is tested prior to removing the IMS from the transmission. Disconnect the sensor connector from the harness. Using a terminal probing tool or a paper clip, touch the ohmmeter to the appropriate IMS pins. Move the shift lever located on the driver's side of the transmission through the ranges. As the shifter is moved, the meter should display a resistance reading of fewer than 10 ohms or open circuit (OL), depending on which range is selected.

As it moves through the ranges, the reading will show some ranges with continuity, while other ranges will indicate OL. All we are looking for is that the switch is capable of closing and opening. If the meter stays locked on OL or it stays locked in one position, the IMS is faulty. If the first circuit tests "good," move to the other circuits and repeat the process.

- Connect one meter lead to Pin C and the other to Pin F on the IMS.
- Connect one meter lead to Pin D and the other to Pin F on the IMS.
- Connect one meter lead to Pin E and the other to Pin F on the IMS.
- Connect one meter lead to Pin B and the other to Pin A on the IMS.

To replace the IMS, remove the electrical connector and then remove the valve body. Remove the IMS Torx 27 bolt. Remove the spherical pin from the case using a pair of pliers, being careful not to damage the case. Remove the shift shaft and IMS. For installation, reverse the removal process. The Torx bolt is coated with Loctite, so either recoat the bolt or replace it with a new bolt that is included in some gasket kits.

This shows the location of IMS Pins A–F for IMS testing purposes. The IMS can be bench tested using an ohmmeter if it was not tested prior to removing the transmission from the vehicle.

The IMS must be properly positioned with the shift shaft, rooster comb, and parking-pawl linkage. The retaining bolt and dowel pin are then installed. If removing the IMS for any reason, it is always a good practice to replace the shift-shaft seal.

Testing and Replacement: PSM, PSA, TFP Switch, and TFT

The pressure switch manifold (PSM), which is also known as a PSA or TFP, and transmission fluid temperature (TFT) sensor are one assembly. An ohmmeter can be used to test the PSM and the TFT. Remove the PSM/TFT assembly from the transmission valve body. Disconnect the wiring connector. Connect the ohmmeter to the following pins:

- Connect one meter lead to PSM Pin A and the other to the metal body of the PSM.
- Connect one meter lead to PSM Pin B and the other to the metal body of the PSM.
- Connect one meter lead to PSM Pin C and the other to the metal body of the PSM.
- Connect one meter lead to PSM Pin D and the other to the metal body of the PSM.

TECH TIP

PSM Details

Early-design PSM assemblies contained six hydraulic switches, but only four were used. Replacement PSM assemblies contain four switches that interchange with the earlier-design application. ■

Using a pencil eraser, press on the switch membrane. The meter should measure less than 10 ohms or OL as the membrane is pressed if the switch is good. Repeat for each switch. If a switch is found to be faulty, the PSM will require replacement.

Connect one meter lead to PSM Pin E and the other to Pin F of the PSM to test the TFT.

The reading will depend on the ambient temperature. At 70°F, the sensor will register between 3,360 and 3,600 ohms. If the sensor has an issue, the PSM will need to be replaced.

To replace the PSM/TFT assembly, remove the oil pan, filter, and wiring connector. Remove the six bolts attaching the PSM/TFT to the transmission. Install the new PSM/TFT

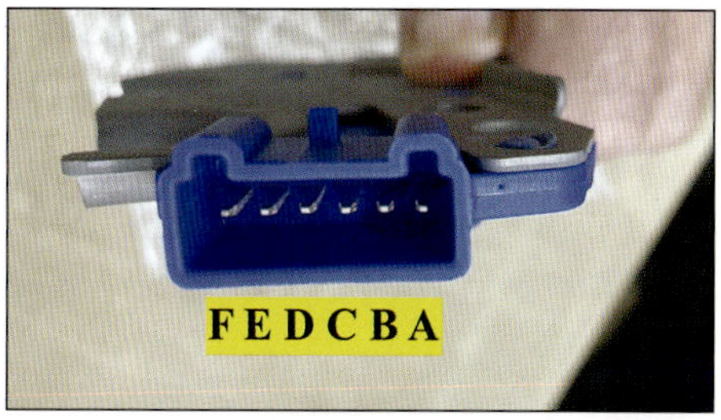

The PSM can be bench tested using an ohmmeter. Connect an ohmmeter to the appropriate pins outlined in the text. Use a pencil with an eraser to depress each PSM switch. The switches should change position, which will be indicated by the meter reading of OL or continuity.

assembly and O-ring seals. Torque the six attaching bolts to 106 in-lbs (12 Nm). Install the wiring connector, filter, and pan/gasket and fill the unit with fluid.

Speed Sensor Replacement and Testing

Magnetic speed sensors (GM Gen 1–4 and non-GM Gen 1–5) can be tested with an ohmmeter. Disconnect the wiring connector. Touch the ohmmeter leads to the speed-sensor terminals. Resistance should measure between 1,930 and 4,260 ohms, depending on temperature.

The speed sensors have a mounting bracket attached to the sensor. Do not rotate the bracket in relation to the sensor. Changing the bracket position may affect the sensor operation.

The speed sensor wiring is twisted pairs for EMI protection. If a wiring repair is performed, the wiring must be twisted at a rate of 9 revolutions per foot. If a connector or terminal issue is present, General Motors sells harness terminals as well as twisted pair harness pigtails.

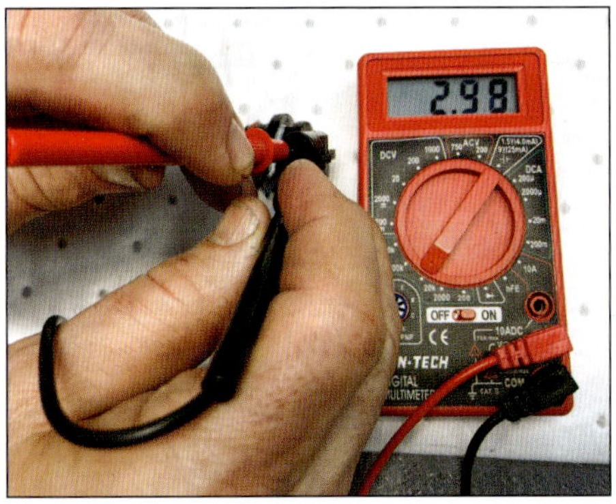

LCT 1000 and 2000 and the A1000 and 2000 applications with permanent magnet speed-sensor designs will allow the use of an ohmmeter to bench test the speed sensors. Connect the ohmmeter leads to each sensor pin and measure the resistance. The specification is 1,930 to 4,260 ohms. GM Gen 5 and Gen 6 non-GM applications use Hall sensors and cannot be tested as described.

The GM Gen 1–4 and non-GM Gen 1–5 permanent magnet-type sensors are not interchangeable with the GM Gen 5 or non-GM Gen 6 MR Hall–type sensors.

To replace, remove the bolt attaching the sensor to the transmission. Remove the sensor. Install the new sensor with the O-ring. Tighten the attaching bolt to 108 in-lbs (12 Nm). Attach the wiring connector to the sensor.

Range Sensor Replacement

Removal of the switch wiring connectors may be difficult due to the sealer that is used in some of the connectors in an attempt to prevent moisture intrusion into the switch. Do not pull too hard on the wires. Otherwise, damage can be done to the terminals. Lightly heating the connector with a heat gun or a propane torch to loosen the sealer works well if it is an issue.

Shift the transmission to Neutral. With the connector(s) disconnected, remove the shift-shaft nut. Remove the two bolts holding the sensor to the case and remove the sensor from the shift shaft. Inspect and address any burrs on the shift shaft.

Leave the foam in place (as shown) when installing the range sensor.

TECH TIP

Range Sensor

Issues with the range sensor are very common. It is always recommended that the switch be replaced rather than bench tested and reinstalled. Issues created by the switch can be anything from the truck dropping into Neutral and no longer moving forward or in Reverse to multiple DTCs and default actions. Updated designs were released to address the issues. ■

Make sure the Neutral assurance clip is installed on the new sensor. With the transmission still in Neutral, install the new sensor. Tighten the two sensor-case-attaching bolts to 20 ft-lbs (27 Nm). Remove and discard the Neutral assurance clip. Install the shift-shaft lever and tighten the nut while holding the lever to 18 ft-lbs (24 Nm). Do not use an impact on the shaft nut. Attach the wiring connector(s).

The range-sensor design changed for 2004. The 1999–2003 applications used two electrical connectors, while 2004–2005 applications only use one large connector. In 2006,

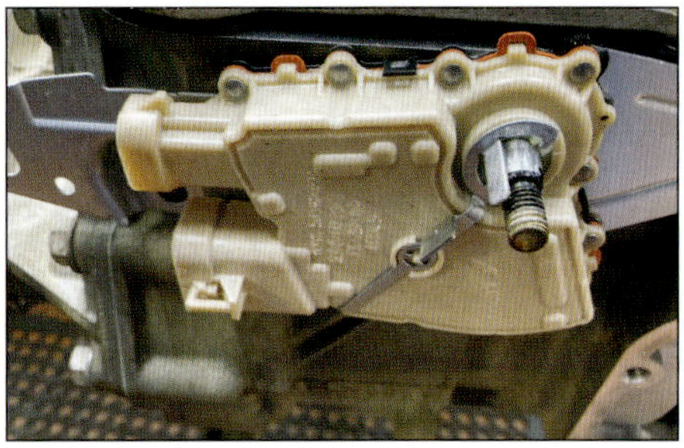

With the transmission and the shifter in Neutral, lubricate the shift shaft and install the sensor. Install and properly torque the bolts. With the sensor installed, remove the Neutral position assurance clip and install the wiring connectors.

the sensor was eliminated with the advent of the IMS.

Pressure Testing, Clutch Testing, and Road Testing Components

When issues arise that may indicate problems with the transmission, in-depth testing processes help isolate the cause of the concern. Some of the processes require the use of a pressure gauge, while others require the use of a scan tool. In addition, some diagnostics require the inspection of components to isolate the problem.

Pressure Testing

Pressure tests are used to isolate hydraulic issues with the transmission. This process typically requires the use of a pressure gauge and a scan tool. Pressure testing the Allison consists of measuring the line pressure, which is a product of the pump and regulator valve circuits. This process provides insight into the health of the transmission hydraulic system.

1. Block the wheels, start the engine, set the parking brake, and place the transmission in Park. Use a scan tool to inspect for any current or past DTCs. If current DTCs are set, address those first, as high line pressure is a default action for numerous DTCs on many applications.
2. Check the transmission fluid level and adjust as necessary.
3. Turn the engine off. Inspect the manual shift linkage at the transmission for proper function.
4. Remove the line-pressure test-port plug on the bottom of the transmission bellhousing next to the spin-on filter. Install a pressure gauge into the test port.

The line pressure tap is located at the front of the bellhousing next to the spin-on oil filter.

5. Start the engine. With the engine speed at approximately 600 rpm and TFT between 71 and 93°C (160–200°F) (74–85°C/165–185°F on 2012-and-later models), place the transmission in Drive. With the vehicle stationary, use the scan tool to command the transmission through each forward gear and repeat the reading.
6. Pressure should measure between 101 and 200 psi (1999–2010) or 75 to 111 psi (2011 and later) in each gear when at idle.
7. Readings exceeding the specifications by plus-or-minus 10 percent indicate an issue with the transmission, such as issues with the line-pressure-control solenoid (if equipped), pressure regulator valve, filter, or fluid level. If the pressure is not correct in some gears but it is correct in others, inspect the clutch that is applied in those gears for leakage. Turn the engine off and disconnect the scan tool.
8. Remove the line-pressure gauge. Install the line-pressure plug and tighten to 108 in-lbs (12 Nm).

Clutch Testing

The 1000 and 2000 applications have the ability to test the clutches with the vehicle stationary by using a scan tool.

1. Block the wheels, set the parking brake, connect the scan tool, and select the transmission output controls feature on the scanner.
2. Firmly apply the brake, place the transmission in the D range, raise the engine speed to 1,400 rpm, and shift the transmission through each gear using the scanner.
3. Monitor the input/turbine speed-sensor values. If the clutch is working correctly, the RPM will drop and stay at 0 in each gear. If the input/turbine speed does not drop to 0, note which clutches are on in those ranges. Use the clutch-apply table to diagnose which clutch is slipping.

Road Testing

Perform this procedure first to ensure the electronic transmission components are functioning properly. If these components are not checked, a simple electrical condition could be misdiagnosed.

1. Connect the scan tool.
2. Ensure the gear selector is in Park and that the parking brake is set.
3. Start the engine. Scan for DTCs and address any current DTCs set before moving to the next step.

   NOTE: Scan all modules for DTCs, as Allisons use information from multiple modules. Issues with other module components can cause transmission-related issues.
4. Verify that the following scan tool data can be obtained and is functioning properly.

Monitor the data values at key on, engine off, and engine running and compare to the service manual standards or to data from another known good vehicle.

Garage Shifts

Perform the following steps for garage shifts.

1. Set the parking brake. Start the engine and allow the transmission to warm up. With the engine running, apply the brake pedal.
2. Move the gear selector through each gear range: P/R, R/P, R/N, N/R, N/D, D/N, D/M, M/D.
3. Pause 2 to 3 seconds in each gear position. Verify that the gear engagements are not delayed (engagements should take less than 2 seconds) and are not harsh. Monitor the engagement with the scan tool by observing the ISS/turbine shift speed-sensor value. ISS should drop to 0, showing when the engagement is complete.

Harsh engagement may be caused by high engine idle speed, incorrect line pressure, or high line pressure resulting from a DTC being set.

Delayed engagement may be caused by low idle speed, low fluid level, incorrect line pressure, TFT to cold, shift-selector linkage out of adjustment, or incomplete adaptive learning.

TCC and Shift Controls

The TCM calculates the upshift/downshift points based on MAP, MAF, TFT, ECT, throttle position, and vehicle speed. The TCM compares the values to those stored in a shift point table located in the vehicle software set. When it is appropriate for the vehicle to make an upshift or downshift, the TCM commands the appropriate pressure control solenoid (or trim solenoid) on or off.

The key parameters to monitor for shift-control operation include gear ratio, TCC slip, PCS and trim solenoid commands, TCC PCS commands, and feedback values.

This design makes it difficult to feel the TCC apply, as it uses a PWM control system to control TCC apply and release slippage. After the TCC is fully applied, it will indicate an issue with the system, such as a faulty torque converter, TCC apply valve or TCC regulator valve stuck or worn, TCC circuit hydraulic leakage, or a faulty TCC PCS.

Downshifts

1. Attach the scan tool and monitor the commanded gear-shift time parameters. Accelerate the vehicle in Drive range at light throttle (5 to 15 percent) until Third gear is just achieved.
2. Quickly increase the throttle angle until the commanded gear position indicates that a downshift to Second gear was commanded. Note the shift feel and shift time. Repeat this process for each shift, 4-3, 5-4, and 6-5.
3. Note any harsh, soft, or delayed shifts as well as slipping conditions. Note any noise or vibration.
4. The same process should be conducted using manual shift control either with the shift lever or by using the driver shift controls on the steering wheel.

Cleaning Components

Proper cleaning and cleanliness are the most important things that one can do to ensure a properly operating transmission. Even trace amounts of dirt and debris can cause major operational issues. Inspection of the components for wear and damage will prevent installation of a faulty part, which can lead to additional time and costs regarding the repair.

A commercial washer is the most efficient way to wash most transmission parts. If you do not have access to a commercial washer, a pressure washer and solvent tank can be used.

Brake cleaner works well for small parts, including valve-body components.

The most critical process when rebuilding a transmission is making certain all the components are clean when they are installed. Cleaning the case and its components can be accomplished using various processes, including a commercial washer, solvent tank, or brake parts cleaner. Commercial washers are used by professional shops to clean components. A solvent tank can be used if you do not have access to commercial washing equipment. Spray cans of brake cleaner work well for smaller parts as well as the valve body.

Cooler

The transmission oil cooler requires flushing any time it is rebuilt or a remanufactured unit is installed. A clean cooler is critical for transmission operation and life. The cooler tends to trap contamination from the damaged transmission. The contaminants will travel into a newly built transmission, causing valves/ solenoids to stick as well as major lubrication issues with the new transmission. This can lead to premature transmission failure. Cooler flushing can be accomplished by using a commercial transmission-flushing machine, which is the preferred method, or by using multiple cans of spray cooler flush available from local parts stores.

Component Inspection

Planetaries, shafts, drums, clutches, bearings, snap rings, the valve body, oil pump, case, and bushings must be inspected for damage and wear.

Planetaries

Inspect the planetary gear teeth for cracks and excessive wear. The pinion washers should be inspected for damage. Most transmissions will have a measurement for pinion washer wear that can be accomplished with the use of a feeler gauge. The feeler gauge is placed between the pinion washer and the pinion. If excessive, the planetary carrier will require replacement on most applications.

Shafts

Shafts should be inspected for spline wear, cracks, and twisting.

Drums/Housings

Drums should be inspected for cracks. If cracked, the drum needs to be replaced. In addition, the drum splines and bushings should be checked for wear and replaced if needed.

Clutches

Typically, clutches are replaced during a rebuild, so inspection is not generally required. It is suggested that an OEM clutch be used, such as BorgWarner, Exidy, or Raybestos. Raybestos and Alto offer performance clutches for the applications. Both the friction and the steel plates should be replaced. If reusing the clutches, the friction discs need to be inspected for thickness, flaking, discoloration, warpage, spline wear, and for being burnt. The steel plates need to be inspected for flatness, lug wear, heat checks, and general wear. While clutch damage can occur with any of the clutch packs, the 4-5-6 is the most prone to damage on this application.

Bearings

Clean the bearings with solvent. Most transmission bearings cannot be disassembled to inspect, so if you are reusing them, apply force to the bearing while rotating it. If any roughness is felt, replace the bearing. Most transmissions have bearing kits available that provide all the bearings for the unit under one part number. Several bearing updates have been implemented on the Allison applications.

Snap/Retaining Rings

Snap rings can be damaged during disassembly. Inspect the snap ring for distortion and damage/wear to its surfaces. If in doubt, install a new snap ring.

Valve Body

Valves and valve bores in the valve body and pump need to be inspected for wear and damage. Valves/valve bores can be inspected by performing a vacuum test or by visual inspection. Several updated valve kits are available via the aftermarket.

Oil Pump

The oil-pump components require inspection for damage and wear. Metal from a failing torque converter migrates to the oil cooler and pump, which leads to damage.

Case

Inspect the case for cracks and wear in the lug areas.

Bushings

All bushings should be inspected for wear and damage. General Motors does not service most of the bushings and requires the dealer to replace the component if a bushing is worn or damaged. Bushings are available through aftermarket suppliers. Be aware of some cheap bushings, as they may not maintain the correct tolerances and may perform worse than the bushing that was taken out. A quality US company producing bushings is Durabond, as it is an OEM supplier for many engine and transmission bushings.

Inspecting the Transmission

1 *Inspect the planetary gears and thrust washers for damage and wear. If the washers or planetary show wear, make sure to fully inspect for lubrication circuit restrictions and leakage as well as the transmission fluid cooler for restrictions. Tooth damage is generally due to bearing failure somewhere in the unit and pieces of the bearing migrating back into the gears, which result in damage.*

2 *Inspect the planetary gears for broken and cracked teeth.*

3 *Inspect the planetary pinions and sun gears for wear and damage to the teeth.*

4 *Inspect the shaft splines for twisting and cracking. If performance software is installed in the ECM, consider making various performance updates to the transmission, as excessive torque will damage the transmission. Inspect the shaft bushings for wear.*

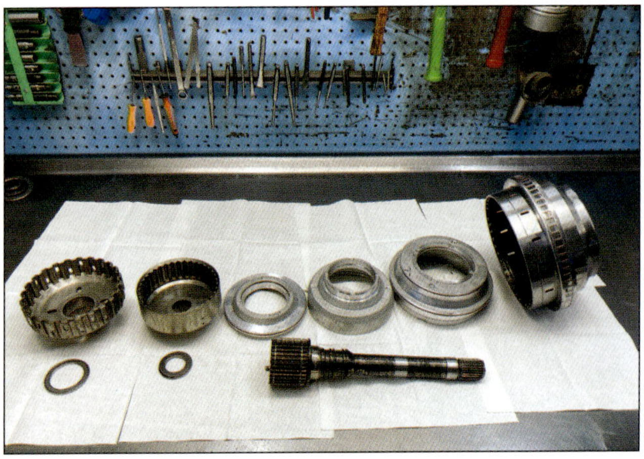

5 *Inspect the clutch drums for spline wear. Inspect the drum bushings for wear. Inspect the pistons for cracks and wear. Inspect the splines where the clutch discs ride for wear. Grooves in the drum splines can lead to the discs sticking in those splines and clutch failure.*

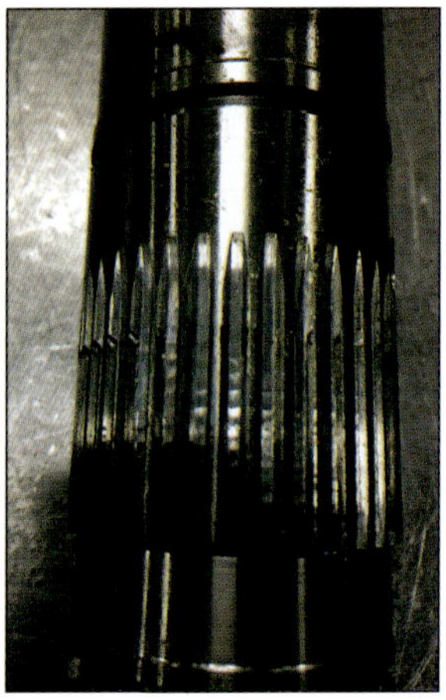

6 *The stator support, also known as a ground sleeve, should be checked for spline wear. Wear in this area is common, so always inspect for excessive wear.*

7 On high-torque applications, the stator support tube (ground sleeve) may shift position in the pump, leading to fluid flow issues. Always inspect the tube position. The feed hole in the tube should line up with the flange in the pump body (as shown) if the tube is in the correct position. If shifted, components need to be replaced.

8 The stator support tube (ground sleeve) will shift position vertically. Always inspect for this issue. If the tube has moved up (shown here), it can lead to feed problems. In this instance, the pump likely requires replacement.

9 Inspect all of the valves and valve bores for damage and wear.

10 Visually inspect the pump components for wear and damage. Several measurements can be made on the pump components to determine if they are excessively worn.

11 Inspect or replace all the bearings. Some bearings in the 1000 and 2000 applications have been updated because of premature bearing failure.

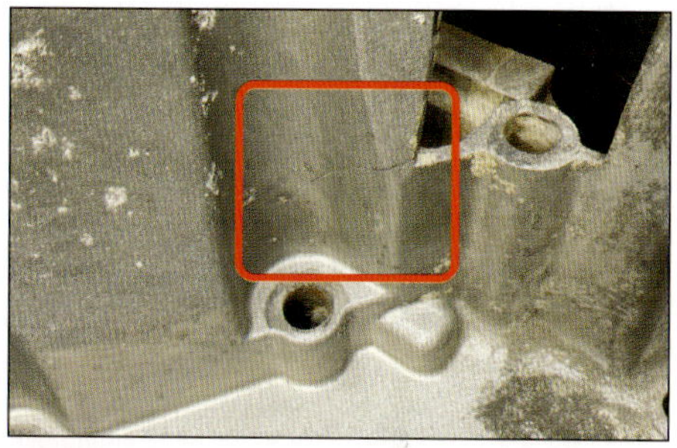

12 The 1000 and 2000 applications are very sensitive to vibration-related issues. Vibrations will cause the bellhousing and/or 4x4 adapter to develop cracks. Cracking is not caused by faulty parts, so the vibration must be addressed. Otherwise, a repeat failure will likely occur.

13 Clutches are typically replaced during an overhaul. If not replacing the clutches, inspect them for flaking, spline damage, and warpage. Inspect the steel plates for lug wear, warpage, and excessive heat indications.

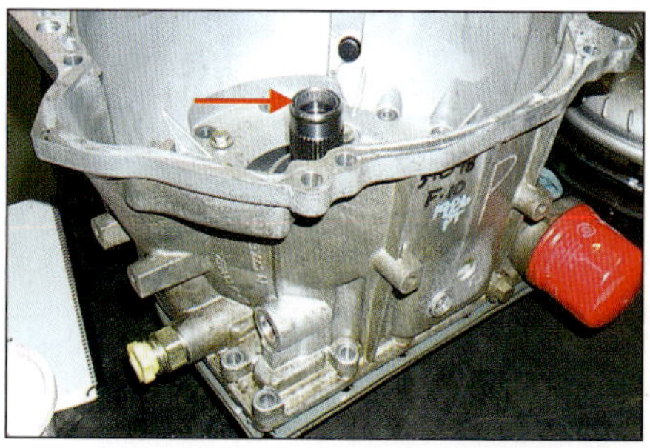

14 Transmission bushings are used to support and hold the components in proper alignment within the transmission. Think of them as a bridge to cross a river. The bridge holds all the cars crossing the bridge in proper position, allowing them across the river. If the bushings are worn, the shafts and housings will lose alignment, leading to clutch failure, as the seal rings in the unit may no longer be properly aligned. Inspect the bushings for wear and damage. If worn bushings are found, closely inspect the lubrication circuit and cooler for evidence of a flow issue.

Component Service Disassembly and Assembly

Before beginning component servicing, the first task is to clear and clean a workspace. The Allison transmissions are very heavy, so getting assistance to lift and move it is required.

Hand tools are required for disassembly, as many of the pieces are retained by bolts. Keep the workspace clean and organized. Lay the parts out in the order they were removed from the transmission to make the inspection and assembly tasks easier.

Torque Converter Removal

To remove the torque converter, rotate and pull/lift the converter from the pump assembly. GM makes lift tools for this task (J46409 T-handles). Otherwise, you can make one with some bolts and a welder. The torque converter is quite heavy (60-plus pounds). If you plan to reuse the converter, flip it upside down in a drain pan and drain as much fluid as possible. Once drained, flip the converter with the hub side facing up and cover the hub hole.

Set the converter aside in a place where it cannot be damaged.

TECH TIP — Inspect for Damage

Always examine for converter external fin damage on units that have a turbine speed sensor mounted in the bellhousing. Damaged fins, dents, and dings in the fins can skew the turbine speed reading and lead to DTCs and operational issues. ■

Holding Fixture

The GM J44723 holding fixture bolts to the PTO area of the case and can be mounted to a workbench or an engine stand. Do not use the PTO cover bolts to mount the holding fixture, as they are not long enough. Use six M10x1.5 bolts that are long enough to provide 3/4 to 1 inch of thread engagement into the case with the fixture installed.

If you do not have access to a transmission-mounting fixture, some technicians stand the transmission on its end on a pair of boards over a

After the torque converter has been removed, remove the PTO covers on both sides of the transmission. Do not use the PTO cover bolts to attach the holding fixture, as they are too short to fully hold the weight of the unit. Use six M10x1.5-mm bolts that will provide 3/4 to 1 inch of thread engagement.

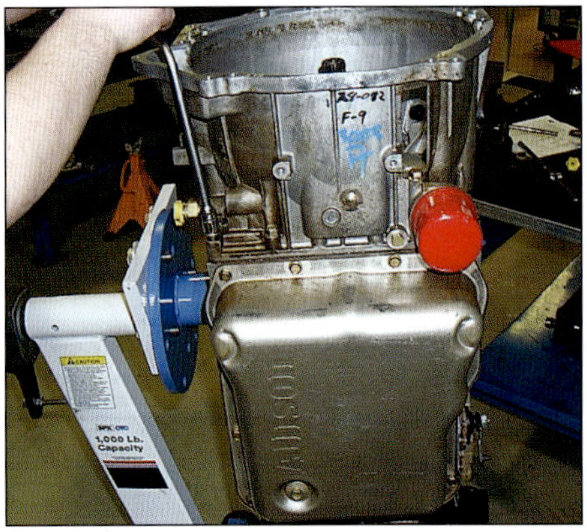

The case is mounted onto GM fixture J44723.

Purchase or build your own fixture. Please use caution, as these units weigh more than 300 pounds. Care must be taken. Otherwise, an injury may result.

small bucket or use an old transmission case as a stationary stand.

Spin-On Filter, Speed Sensors, and Transmission Range Sensor Removal

One to three speed sensors are mounted to the transmission, depending on the year and application. Remove the sensor bolt and each sensor. Do not rotate the sensor in its bracket, otherwise sensor operational issues can occur.

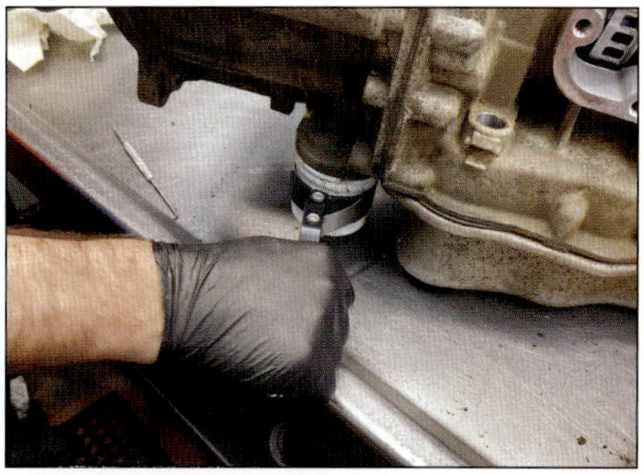

Remove the spin-on oil filter with a filter wrench.

TECH TIP

Safety

The 1000- and 2000-series transmissions are very heavy (300-plus pounds), so care must be taken to avoid personal injury and damage to the unit. Always use lifting equipment. Always properly support the transmission. ■

The filter magnet often sticks to the filter. Make sure to remove it, as it is important that it be reinstalled when a new filter is installed.

Remove the speed sensors. Do not rotate the sensor in its bracket.

Remove the bolts attaching the range sensor (if equipped) to the transmission, and remove the range sensor. Sensor replacement is always recommended on the 1000- and 2000-series applications.

Using an oil-filter wrench, remove the spin-on oil filter. The magnet often sticks to the filter. Make sure not to lose the magnet.

Oil Pan and Filter Removal

Rotate the transmission with the input shaft facing up and allow any fluid to drain. Once it is drained, rotate the transmission with the oil pan facing up and remove the 12 bolts. Remove the pan and gasket (an OEM gasket is reusable). Rotate and pull the filter to remove it.

It is always as good idea to break the filter apart to inspect the

Remove the 12 bolts that attach the pan and drain the fluid. Typically, the pan bolts will require a 13-mm socket.

The 2005-and-earlier applications use a range sensor mounted eternally on the case. Remove the attaching bolts and remove the sensor.

contamination. This provides a good idea of what is needed to inspect for when the transmission is fully disassembled. Use a screwdriver or snap-ring pliers to remove the filter seal.

Remove the pan, gasket, and filter. The OEM gasket is reusable if it is not damaged.

Twist and lift the filter to remove it.

Remove the seal with your fingers, a flat-blade screwdriver, or a pair of snap-ring pliers.

TECH TIP

Updates

Several updates have been made to numerous thrust bearings in 1000- and 2000-series applications. It is recommended to replace all the thrust bearings with the updated designs. ■

End Play Measurement

It is critical that end play be checked prior to disassembly. Rotate the transmission so the input/turbine shaft is facing up. Mount a dial indicator so it can measure the turbine/input shaft vertical movement. Using a large screwdriver, pry up the C1/C2 drum and read the shaft movement. Do not pry against the speed-sensor tone ring.

The specification should read between 0.011 and 0.061 inch (0.279 and 1.549 mm). If not within specifications, it is likely that worn or damaged components will need to be addressed during repairs. Write down the value that was measured so it can be referred to during reassembly.

Extension Housing and 4WD Adapter Removal

Two methods can be used to disassemble/assemble the 1000 and 2000 applications. Some technicians work from the front to the rear of the unit, while others work from the rear to the front. The method you choose will determine when the adapter/extension housing removal/installation steps will be followed. If working from the front to the rear of the unit, do not remove the extension housing at this point. If working from the rear toward the front, the extension housing needs to be removed as outlined before proceeding.

This book is laid out based on how General Motors and Allison approach the rebuild process, disassembling front to back and assembling back to front. So, leave the housing in place for now.

For either approach, the 4x4 output-shaft nut should be removed now. Do not attempt to replace a damaged adapter/extension housing with the transmission in the vehicle, as components can fall out of place, leading to issues.

Housing Removal

The housing removal procedures for 4x4 and 2WD are outlined below.

4x4

- With the rear of the transmission horizontal, place the transmission in Park.
- Remove the output shaft nut by using a hub socket (DT 50869 for 2010-and-later applications or J43769 for earlier applications) or an equivalent.
- Remove the housing bolts and remove the housing.

2WD

- Remove the yoke and output-shaft seal.
- Remove the large snap ring.
- Using three J43910 puller legs and the J24420-B puller (or an equivalent), remove the bearing from the housing. The legs lock into the bearing races. Tighten the puller and remove the bearing.
- Remove the housing bolts and the housing.

On 4x4 applications, a nut is used to retain the 4x4 adapter along with the 16 bolts that attach it to the case. The nut requires a spanner socket to remove it.

Two different nut designs have been used. GM tools DT50869 for late models, J43769 for early models, as well as sockets from companies such as Adapt-a-Case are available.

Lock the shifter into the Park position and remove the nut by rotating the socket counterclockwise on the 4x4 unit.

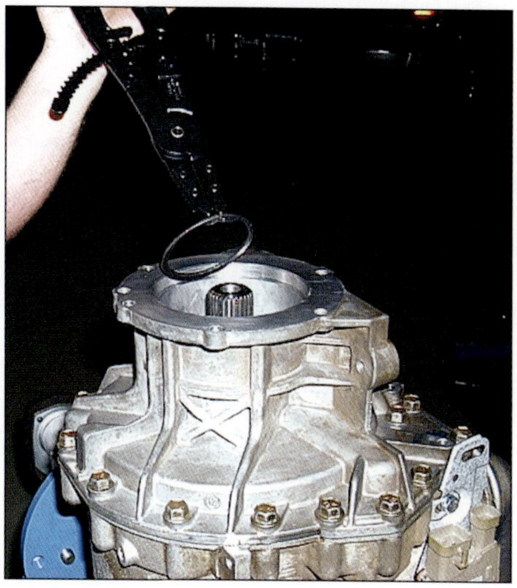

At this point, you will need to decide how you want to disassemble the unit. If you choose to work from the front to the back of the case as outlined in the text, skip to the valve-body removal steps and come back to these steps when the C1, C2, and C3 clutches and planetary components are removed. If you choose to work from the rear of the case forward, complete the steps listed now. The rear seal will need to be removed to access the snap ring. Remove the snap ring with a large pair of snap-ring pliers. On 2WD applications, the output speed-sensor tone wheel and end-play shim are located under the output bearing.

On 2WD applications, use a bearing puller (J24420-B with J43910 legs) or an aftermarket equivalent.

Care must be taken not to damage the bearing, so it is critical that the puller legs fit properly into the bearing race.

The 2WD applications use an extension housing while the 4x4 uses a transfer-case-adapter housing. The housings on both applications are held in place by 16 bolts.

The selective end-play shim is located on the output shaft under the bearing on both applications. Do not lose the shim. In addition, the parking-pawl pivot pin often sticks in the housing.

Valve Body Removal

As with the extension/4x4 adapter housing removal, valve body

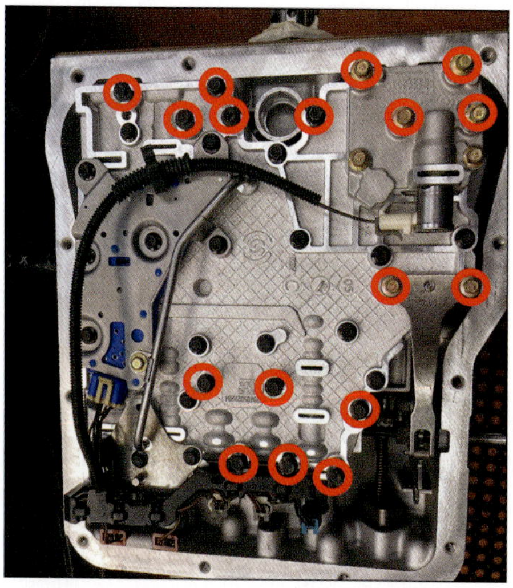

Remove the detent spring and the 15 highlighted bolts, wiring harness, and any pipes that may interfere with removal of the valve body.

Removing the Valve Body

- Remove the detent spring.
- Remove the 15 bolts holding the valve body to the case. Do not remove all the bolts, as some are used to hold the valve-body halves together.
- Remove the piping if needed.
- Place a clean rag in the case below the manual-valve case opening. Move the manual valve pin to allow the valve body to be separated from the case. Lift and slide the valve body from the case, making sure to protect the manual valve and pin from falling.
- Set the valve body aside for repair. Valve body service will be covered in Chapter 4.
- Some technicians choose to remove the harness with the valve body, and some prefer to remove it prior to removing the valve body. To remove the harness, disconnect the wiring connectors from all of the solenoids, PSM, and the IMS (if equipped). Fold the harness out of the way. Two horseshoe valve-body clips hold part of the harness in position over the trim solenoids. The harness can be removed from the case either now or after the valve body has been removed by using a 30–32 mm ($1^{3}/_{16}$ inch) deep socket to compress the plastic retainers that hold the harness pass-through connector in the case. Push the harness toward the valve body to remove the harness from the case.

removal varies with the technician. Some technicians remove the valve body prior to removing the transmission internal components, and some remove the valve body after all of the transmission components have been removed from the case.

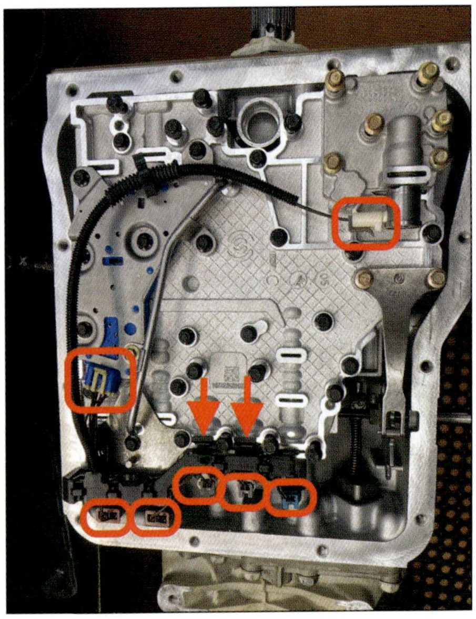

Two methods can be used. One is to remove the valve-body wiring harness and fold it out of the way. The other is to disconnect the pass-through connector, pushing the connector into the case. This allows the harness to stay connected to the valve body when removing the valve body from the case.

Shift Shaft Removal

Once the valve body has been removed, the shift shaft can be removed. Do the following to remove the shift shaft:

- Remove the shift-shaft pin.
- Loosen the shift-shaft nut.
- Remove the shift shaft and detent (rooster comb) and the IMS (if equipped).
- Remove the shift-shaft seal.

Place a rag in the case opening below the manual valve. Lift the valve body from the case.

Be careful not to lose the valve pin in the end of the manual valve.

Removing the Shift Shaft

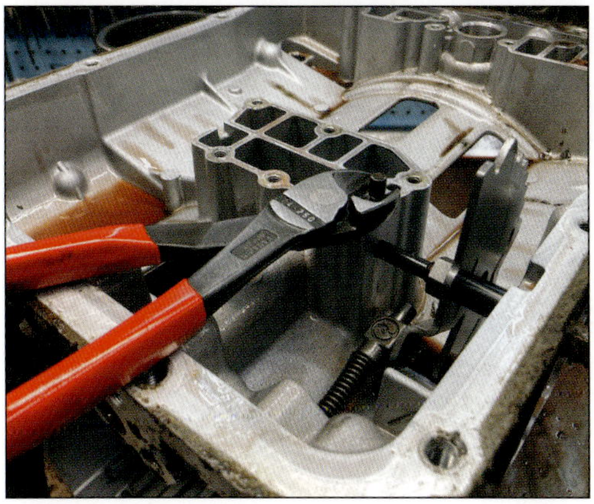

1 *With the valve body removed, use a pair of pliers or diagonal cutters to remove the shift-shaft pin.*

2 *Remove the shift-shaft nut with an open-end wrench.*

3 *Slide the shift shaft out to allow for detent/rooster comb removal. With the shaft removed, the detent/rooster comb is free to be removed.*

4 *Carefully remove the shift-shaft seal from the case. Be careful not to damage the case bore where the seal rides.*

Bellhousing and Pump Service

As with other components to be serviced, the pump is a single-service process that includes disassembly, inspection, and assembly. The completed pump assembly will then be set aside for installation at a later point.

Pump Service

The front seal should be removed before removing the pump/bellhousing from the transmission. The bellhousing can be removed individually or with the pump. Most technicians remove the pump and bellhousing separately due to the weight of the components. To remove the bellhousing/pump as one assembly, remove the 20 outer bellhousing bolts.

If removing the bellhousing and pump separately, also remove the 10 inner bellhousing bolts. The pump/bellhousing inner bolts have O-ring seals. Some of the bellhousing bottom bolts have copper washers on later applications.

With the bolts removed, lift the bellhousing from the case while pushing on the stator support to separate the two components. With the bellhousing removed, lift the pump and separator plate from the transmission.

With the pump/separator plate on the workbench, flip it over and remove the five bolts. They are generally 15-mm heads, but the problem with trying to nail this kind of thing down is that it changes depending on the generation of the part. The pump has had numerous updates as to what is holding the pump halves together.

The pump parts can now be serviced. Remove the pump gears and inspect the components. Remove the sealing rings on the stator support and the large O-ring from the pump body.

TECH TIP

Bolt Length

Keep all the bellhousing attachment bolts separated from those used to attach the extension/adapter housing. Installing the incorrect-length bolts can cause case damage. ■

Pump Removal and Disassembly

1 *Remove the 15 bellhousing pump bolts as shown. If removing the bellhousing and the pump as one assembly, remove the bolts shown here and the bolts shown in Step 2. If separating the pump from the bellhousing during disassembly to make the components lighter to lift, also remove the bolts shown in Step 3 at this time.*

2 *Remove the six external bellhousing bolts.*

3 *To separate the pump from the bellhousing, remove the 10 inner bellhousing bolts.*

5 *Some of the outer bellhousing bolts may have copper washers that will be replaced during overhaul. The inner bolts have sealing rings.*

6 *Separate the pump from the bellhousing.*

7 *Remove the cooler fittings from the bellhousing. The fittings will be reused after new seals have been installed.*

8 *The pump and channel plate need to be separated, so access to the pump and channel plate can be gained for service. The pump and channel plate are held together with five bolts.*

9 *Remove the sealing rings with your fingernails or a pick.*

10 *Remove the five bolts holding the pump halves together. Typically, the bolts will require a 12-mm socket for removal.*

11 *Separate the pump cover from the channel plate and pump body. Remove the seals on the stator support.*

12 *The channel plate can now be removed from the pump body. Remove the channel plate gaskets. Remove the wear plate and inspect it for wear and damage.*

Pump Cleaning and Assembly

The pump parts can be cleaned with solvent or brake cleaner. Some technicians fully disassemble all of the valves from the pump, while many simply use a pick to carefully check for movement, as the pump valves on these applications typically do not have many wear issues. Flat-blade screwdrivers and picks work well to help check or remove the components. However, be careful that you do not damage the valve or the bores.

If you are disassembling the pump valves, lay the valves, springs, and retainers on a clean cloth so that they can be inspected and cleaned. The valves and their bores need to be inspected for wear and damage. Any orifices need to be cleaned.

The stator support pump body and bellhousing pump surfaces need to be checked for flatness with a straightedge. Inspect all of the pump channeling for damage. Many shops flat sand the pump halves.

Pump Wear Measurements

The pump received several changes through the years. One of the major updates was during the 2004 model year. The fluid channeling, the valve spring dimensions, and the number of gear teeth changed. The gear tooth count for the inner gear changed from 31 teeth to 22 teeth, and the outer gear teeth went from 37 to 26 teeth, which affects pump noise. In addition, the wear plate changed. An updated pump that will back service the early design is available, and it includes the pump and wear plate in kit 29542796. Individual early and updated parts are not interchangeable. In 2015, the pump received another major update with the elimination of the C1/1-2-3-4 exhaust backfill valve.

Once the pump components have been separated and cleaned, the components can be inspected for wear and damage.

General Motors and Allison sell pump body kits that consist of the body with gears, bushing, and front seal. Some of the individual pump parts are not available separately.

Wear and Damage Inspection Checklist

- ❒ The pump gears should have directional marks (dots) on the inner and outer gear. The OEM gears position the marks facing the pump housing. Note the position when removing the gears so that they can be installed in the same direction they were removed.
- ❒ Remove the sealing rings from the stator support. Allison uses measurements to determine if the wear is excessive.
- ❒ Inspect the pump bushing for wear and damage. The front pump bushing maximum inside diameter dimension is 2.3015 inches (58.458 mm).
- ❒ Inspect the stator tube bushing for wear and damage. The maximum stator shaft bushing inside diameter measurement is 1.3315 inches (33.820 mm).
- ❒ Inspect the gears and the gear pocket for damage. Measure the pocket depth. The maximum pocket depth is 4.3392 inches (110.216 mm).
- ❒ Inspect the pump gear pocket bore and measure the distance across the pocket where the outer gear rides. The maximum width measurement is 2.0537 inches (52.165 mm).
- ❒ Inspect the outer gear for wear and tooth damage. Measure the outside diameter of the outer gear. The minimum outside diameter is 4.3302 inches (109.987 mm).
- ❒ Inspect the inner gear for wear and tooth damage. Measure the gear's inside diameter between the torque converter drive flats. The maximum distance is 2.0537 inches (52.165 mm).
- ❒ Inspect for excessive wear by measuring the outer gear-to-housing clearance. The maximum measurement is 0.009 inch (0.23 mm).
- ❒ Inspect for excessive wear by measuring the outer gear-to-crescent clearance. The maximum measurement is 0.010 inch (0.26 mm).
- ❒ Measure the housing-to-gear end clearance. Install the pump gears. Place a feeler gauge between a straightedge and the pump gears. The maximum measurement is 0.0029 inch (0.074 mm).
- ❒ Inspect the pump wear plate for wear and damage. The minimum thickness is 0.116 inch (2.950 mm). Keep in mind that the wear-plate design must match the pump design being used. Otherwise, pressure issues occur.
- ❒ Check the dowel pins for wear and damage. Dowel pin installed height should measure 0.420 to 0.440 inch (10.7 to 11.3 mm).
- ❒ Check the channel plate/separator plate for damage. Several orifice changes have occurred. If the plate needs to be replaced, make sure to compare the old and new plates.
- ❒ Inspect the stator tube's inside diameter for wear in the area where the input shaft seals ride. The maximum inside diameter measurement in the area that the shaft seals ride is 1.7894 inches (45.45 mm).

Inspecting and Measuring Pump Components

1 *Remove the large O-ring from the pump body. Clean and inspect the pump gears and pump body bore for damage and wear. Note the position of the gear identification dots to make reassembly easier. The OEM position has the dots facing the pump body.*

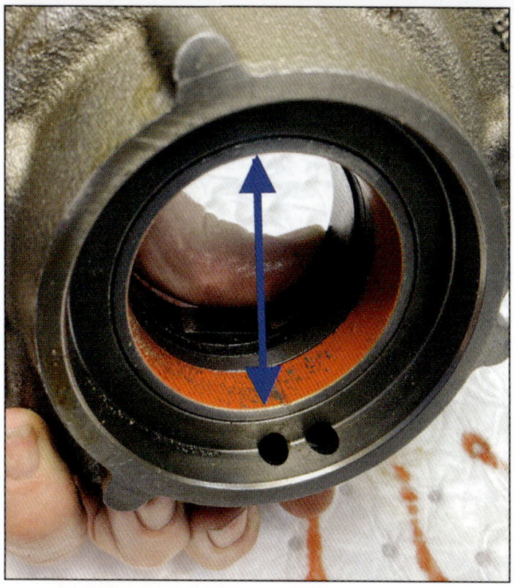

2 *Visually inspect the pump bushing for wear and pitting. Measure the bushing inside diameter, which should have a maximum dimension of 2.3015 inches (58.458 mm).*

3 *Visually inspect the stator bushing for wear and pitting. Measure the bushing inside diameter, which should have a maximum measurement of 1.3315 inches (33.820 mm).*

4 *Measure the pocket depth. Maximum pocket depth is 4.3392 inches (110.216 mm).*

5 *Some technicians perform this measurement if they are having pressure issues. Measure the gear thickness in multiple places. A variance of more than a few thousands indicates an issue with the gear.*

6 *Measure the outside diameter of the outer gear. The minimum outside diameter is 4.3302 inches (109.987 mm).*

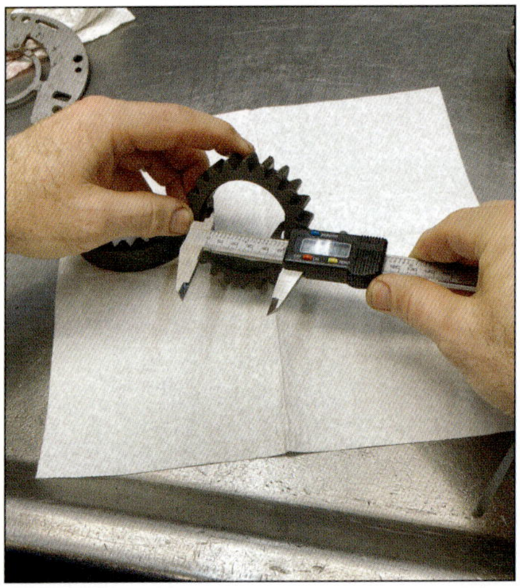

7 *Measure the gear inside diameter between the torque converter drive flats. The maximum distance is 2.0537 inches (52.165 mm).*

8 *Using a feeler gauge, measure the clearance between the outer gear and the pump body. The maximum measurement is 0.009 inch (0.23 mm).*

9 *Using a feeler gauge, measure the clearance between the outer gear and the pump body crescent. The maximum measurement is 0.010 inch (0.26 mm).*

10 *Install the pump gears. Place a feeler gauge between a straightedge and the pump gears. The maximum measurement is 0.0029 inch (0.074 mm).*

11 *Inspect the plate for warpage and wear. The minimum thickness is 0.116 inch (2.950 mm). Keep in mind that the wear plate design must match the pump design being used. Otherwise, pressure issues will occur. Inspect the dowel pins for wear. Dowel pin installed height should measure 0.420 to 0.440 inch (10.7 to 11.3 mm).*

12 *Inspect the plate for wear, warpage, and damage. Plate updates have occurred throughout the years, so if replacing it, make sure to compare the old and new plates.*

13 *Inspect the inside diameter of the stator support for wear where the turbine/input shaft seals ride. Measure the inside diameter. The maximum inside diameter where the seals ride is 2.9154 inches (74.05 mm).*

Pump Bushing Service

Service of the front pump bushing is common, as wear and pitting occurs. Bushing maximum inside diameter measurement should not exceed 2.3015 inches (58.458 mm). If the bushing requires replacement, the pump must be disassembled. The gears and front seal must be removed. To remove the bushing, some technicians use a chisel to split the bushings so that it can be removed, while others use a bushing driver (such as J43771 or an equivalent) to remove and install the bushing.

The only bushing that should be used in this application is a Teflon-coated bushing, which is typically burnt orange in color. Clean the bore and apply Loctite #620 to the bore. Lay the pump on a set of wooden blocks for support and press or drive the bushing into place using bushing driver J43771 or an equivalent. The bushing can be oriented in any position, but the preferred orientation is to have the split in the bushing aligned with the pump casting numbers. If the dowel pins were removed, install the dowel pins and set the pin height to 0.420 to 0.440 inch (10.7 to 11.3 mm). Clean the pump housing and bushing once the tasks are complete.

Front Seal Installation

With the bushing installation complete, the front seal can now be installed. Align the seal with the lip on the seal facing the pump body. Using the J43772 seal driver or an equivalent tool, press or tap the seal into position in the pump body. The seal should be installed flush to 0.010 inch (0.25 mm) below the surface of the pump body.

Pump Assembly

Lubricate the front seal, bushing, gears, and pump body bore with Transjel or an equivalent. Insert the outer gear and inner gear with the dot on the gears facing the pump body. Install the large-diameter O-ring seal on the outside diameter of the pump body. Install the wear plate, aligning it with the dowel pins in the pump body. Install the separator plate/channel plate, aligning it with the dowels.

Remove the bushing with a driver, a blind hole puller, or by carefully splitting it with a chisel. Apply Loctite #620 to the clean bore. Press the new bushing in using the J43771 driver or an equivalent tool. The bushing should be installed flush to 0.010 inch (0.25 mm) below the drum. Use only a Teflon-coated bushing. With the bushing installed, install the pump seal flush to 0.010 inch (0.25 mm) below the pump body.

Assembling the Pump

1 *The pump has a dot on each gear for directional identification. The OEM version installs the gears with the dots facing the pump body (down in the pocket).*

2 *Lubricate the front seal and the bushing with Transjel.*

3 *Lubricate the pump body with Transjel.*

4 *Install the outer gear into the pump body in the OEM position with the dot toward the pump body.*

5 *Install the inner gear into the pump body in the OEM position with the dot toward the pump body.*

6 *Double-check your work on the pump.*

7 *Install the wear plate and the large O-ring on the pump body.*

8 *Install the channel plate on the pump body. Align the plate with the body dowel pins.*

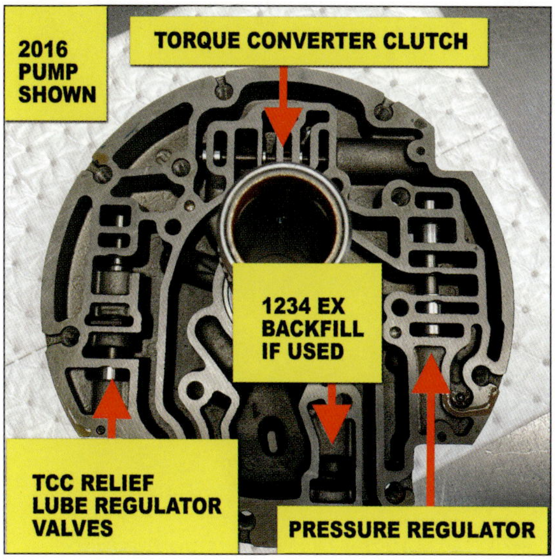

Shown here are the torque converter clutch, TCC relief and lube regulator, pressure regulator, and C1 1-2-3-4 clutch exhaust backfill.

A homemade pressure regulator compressor tool can be made from a piece of pipe or a socket with two notches cut in it 180 degrees across from each other. The homemade tool is shown in Chapters 1 and 4.

This is an example of an early application pressure regulator.

The converter relief valve (early application shown here) is designed to protect the torque converter from being over pressurized when TCC is in the off position. Relief pressure is set at 114 to 162 psi (786 to 1117 kpa).

The C1/1-2-3-4 clutch exhaust backfill valve (early application shown here) prevents air from entering in the clutch circuit by maintaining approximately 2 psi (14 kpa) in the clutch circuit when the clutch is off.

The torque converter clutch (TCC) valve (early application shown here) controls operation of the TCC. This valve controls the pressure feeding the torque converter clutch piston within the torque converter.

The Stator Support

The stator support pump cover, or the front support (as Allison refers to it), houses either three or four valves, depending on the year. As was discussed earlier, the C1/1-2-3-4 exhaust backfill valve was eliminated in later-model applications. In addition, several spring changes have also occurred with the valves in the support, including converter relief and lube regulator valves.

All of the valves are made of steel. The pressure regulator valve and the main lube/converter relief valve are difficult to remove/install unless you have access to tools J43770 and J24459-5 or equivalents. A tool can be made with a piece of small pipe with two slots cut in it (as shown in the pictures on page 15). The slots are positioned directly across from one another.

Some technicians do not remove the pump valves unless the unit has large amounts of metal contamination. Instead, they simply use a pick to check that the valve is not stuck. Other technicians remove all the valves and inspect the bores and the valves for damage. To do this, lay the valves out on a clean workbench with them correctly oriented as they would be in the pump half/support assembly. The valves and support are then cleaned, lubricated with clean transmission fluid, and reassembled.

Inspect the stator tube (ground sleeve) for proper position (both rotational and vertical) as outlined on page 47. If the tube has changed position, clutches that feed via the tube passages may be affected, leading to clutch failure.

Inspect the stator tube bushing for wear and spline damage. The maximum stator shaft bushing inside diameter measurement is 1.3315 inches (33.820 mm). If the bushing requires replacement, many technicians use a chisel to carefully split the bushing so that it can be removed. Others use a blind hole puller, such as J44529, to remove the bushing. To

The stator support tube is replaceable, or it can be purchased as part of the pump cover assembly. Inspect the splines and the tube inside diameter for wear. Inspect the tube for being shifted in the pump cover as was outlined in Chapter 2.

install a new bushing, use bushing driver J43774 or an equivalent. Pressing the bushing into place is the preferred method. The bushing should be installed flush or up to 0.010 inch (0.25 mm) below flush in the tube.

The stator support tube is replaceable if it is worn or damaged. As outlined previously, measure the tube's inside diameter and inspect the area where the input shaft seals ride for excessive wear. Inspect the stator splines for excessive wear.

Most technicians will not have the tools to replace the tube/sleeve, so they typically replace the complete pump cover assembly, including the stator support/ground sleeve. If you have access to the tools (J43765 ground sleeve installer/remover tools), press the tube/sleeve out of the pump cover/front support.

If the stator tube bushing needs to be replaced, use a blind hole puller (J44529) or carefully split the bushing with a chisel.

The holes in the new stator tube must be properly aligned with the holes in the pump cover/front support. The J43765-1 tool is then installed with the lip facing the pump half/front support. With J43765-1 in place, flip the pump half over in the press while supporting the J43865 tool. Using tool J43765-3, apply pressure using the press to push the pieces together until the parts are fully seated. Install the completed assembly in a lathe to check the stator support runout. The maximum runout allowed is 0.008 inch (0.20 mm).

The needle bearing in the stator support can also be replaced. Remove the bearing and install a new bearing if needed. A blind hole puller (J26491 or an equivalent) can be used. Install the bearing using a bushing driver, such as J43775 or an equivalent. Make sure to sit the tube on a metal press plate or piece of wood when pressing the new bearing into position, as you do not want to move the stator support tube/ ground sleeve in the pump cover/front support.

The plastic thrust washer on the back of the pump cover/front support should be inspected for wear. The minimum thickness measurement is 0.059 inch (1.49 mm). Install the washer using Transjel to retain it on the back of the pump half/front support.

Install the bushing using bushing driver J43774 or an equivalent. The bushing installed height is either flush or up to 0.010 inch (0.25 mm) below flush in the tube.

Pump Component Assembly

Place the pump on a workbench with a hole in it or on some flat blocks of wood. Place the pump over the hole with the front seal facing the hole in the bench. Make sure the bushing, front seal, outside-diameter O-ring seal, gears, dowel pins, wear plate, and separator/channel plate were previously installed.

Make sure the valves were previously installed in the pump cover/front support. Place the pump cover/front support with the stator support splines facing the pump body and separator/channel plate that was previously placed on the workbench. Align the bolt holes in the pump cover/front support with the threaded holes in the pump body and install the five pump bolts. Tighten the bolts in a crossing pattern to 18 to 21 ft-lbs (24–29 Nm).

If not previously installed, install the separator/channel plate gasket and the plastic thrust washer. Install the seal rings on the back of the pump cover/front support. Install the two seal rings onto the front side of the pump cover/front cover stator support. Retain all of the above-mentioned parts with Transjel.

Set the completed pump assembly aside on the workbench for installation later. Cover the pump to keep it clean.

Reassembling the Pump Components

1 *Align the pump cover to the pump body.*

2 *Install the five pump bolts finger tight.*

3 *Torque the pump bolts in a crossing pattern to 18 to 21 ft-lbs (24 to 29 Nm).*

4 *Inspect the pump thrust washer. Minimum thickness measurement is 0.059 inch (1.49 mm). Install the washer using Transjel to retain it on the back of the pump half/front support.*

5 *Carefully install the seal rings on the back of the pump support.*

6 *Install the stator support seal ring. Install the channel/support plate gaskets. Retain them with Transjel. Set the completed assembly aside for later installation.*

Clutch and Planetary Removal and Service

While the clutches can be removed starting at either end of the transmission, many technicians work from the rear of the unit if they have removed the extension housing/4WD adapter. Others leave the extension housing/4WD adapter in place and work from the front of the unit. In our example, we are going to work from the front of the unit, as we previously discussed.

C1 (1-2-3-4) and C2 (4-5-6) Clutch Drum Removal and Service

Lay the parts out in the order/position they were removed. Place the input/turbine shaft vertical. Lift the C1/C2 clutch drum from the case. Do not lose the thrust bearing located between the sun gear and the planetary.

Position the clutch drum with the input/turbine shaft facing down through a hole on the workbench. Remove the snap ring retaining the P1 flange and sun gear to the C1/C2 clutch drum. Remove the P1 sun gear and flange plate.

P1 sun gear-to-flange spline wear is fairly common on heavy-duty applications and must be inspected. If the P1 flange-to-P1 sun gear splines strip, the transmission will lose Third, Fifth, and Reverse operation.

Remove the thrust washer along with the C2 drive hub. Remove the C1 drive hub and the bearing sitting on top of the C1 drive hub. Remove the thrust bearing sitting on the end of the turbine/input shaft. It may be stuck inside the C1 drive hub or sitting on the end of the turbine shaft.

Remove the C2 clutches. Remove the C1 backing plate spiral snap ring. Remove the snap ring from the C1 backing plate and remove the C1 backing plate and the C1 clutch pack.

The turbine/input shaft can be removed by removing a snap ring. It is easiest if the snap ring is marked for its vertical position, as it is directional. Remove the snap ring and remove the turbine/input shaft. Remove the turbine shaft from the clutch housing. Remove the two seal rings from the turbine shaft.

Remove the C1 balance piston snap ring and then the C2 balance piston snap ring. Install a clutch compressor, such as J43777 or an equivalent, and lightly compress the return springs. Remove the retaining ring. The C1 return springs, C1 piston, and C1 balance piston can now be removed from the drum.

Mark the C2 piston snap ring for vertical position. Install a clutch compressor (such as J43776-1 or an equivalent) and lightly compress the C2 piston return springs. Remove the C2 retaining ring. The C1 piston housing and C2 return springs can now be removed from the drum.

Remove the C2 piston and C2 balance piston from the housing. Remove the O-ring from the clutch housing inner hub. The C2 piston has three seal rings on this model year that will need to be removed.

C1/C2 Clutch Disassembly

1 Remove the C1/C2 clutch drum. If the transmission is sitting vertically, lift the drum straight up and out of the transmission case. If the transmission is sitting on a bench, pull the drum from the case.

2 The sun-gear bearing will sometimes stick to the sun gear. Make sure not to lose or damage the bearing when removing the C1/C2 drum.

3 *If you are going to do transmission work, it is always best to have either a clutch-drum holding fixture or a hole in your workbench that the clutch drum shaft can be placed in to hold the drum. With the C1/C2 drum vertical, remove the P1 flange and P1 sun gear snap/retaining ring from the clutch drum.*

4 *Remove the P1 flange and P1 sun gear from the drum. Inspect the sun gear-to-flange teeth for wear, as it is common in heavy use applications.*

5 *Remove the C2 drive hub from the C1/C2 drum. The C2 drive hub will house a bronze thrust washer that must not be lost.*

6 *Remove the C1 clutch hub and thrust bearing. The thrust bearing may stick to either the top of the C1 hub or the bottom of the C2 drive hub.*

7 *Remove the thrust bearing that sits between the end of the turbine/input shaft and the C1 drive hub. The thrust bearing may stick to either component.*

8 *Remove the C2 clutch pack from the C1/C2 drum. If planning to reuse the clutches, inspect and measure the parts as outlined in the text.*

9 *The C1 clutch is a small-diameter clutch pack. The top plate is the clutch backing plate.*

10 *The C1 clutch pack uses two snap/retainer rings to hold the pack in place in the drum. Remove the top snap/retainer ring using either snap-ring pliers and a pick or a screwdriver.*

11 *Remove the spiral snap/retainer ring using a pick and a screwdriver.*

12 *Remove the C1 clutches and backing plate from the drum. The clutch stake-up varies depending on the year of the transmission, as this clutch pack was updated in later-model applications. If you plan to reuse the clutches, inspect and measure the parts as outlined in the text.*

13 *Many snap/retaining rings in the Allison applications are directional. Rather than taking the time to identify which direction the snap ring goes, it is easiest to simply take a pick and mark the snap ring for its up position. When the ring is put back in during assembly, simply place the ring with the mark facing up.*

14 *Using snap-ring pliers, remove the turbine/input shaft snap/retaining ring so that the shaft can be removed from the drum.*

15 *Remove the turbine/ input shaft.*

16 *Remove the turbine/ input shaft seal rings from the shaft. The seals are butt-cut designs, so they are easily removed.*

17 *Using a pick or a small screwdriver, remove the snap/retaining ring holding the C1 balance piston.*

18 *Using a pick or a small screwdriver, remove the snap/retaining ring from the C2 balance piston.*

19 *Compress the C1 return spring and remove the snap ring. Using J43777 or an equivalent tool, lightly compress the C1 clutch return springs and remove the snap/retainer ring.*

20 *With the snap/ retainer ring removed, remove the C1 clutch return springs.*

21 Remove the C1 balance piston. Care should be taken to not damage the seal area of the piston.

22 Remove the C1 piston housing. Care should be taken to not damage the sealing area for the C1 balance piston. Pry in the spring pocket area.

23 An alternate method is to use two pairs of needle-nose pliers to remove the C1 piston housing. Care should be taken to not damage the sealing area for the C1 balance piston.

24 Many snap/retaining rings in the Allison applications are directional. Rather than needing to take time to identify which direction the snap ring goes, it is easiest if one simply takes a pick and marks the snap ring for its up position. When the ring is put back in during assembly, one can simply place the ring in with the mark facing up.

25 Using J43776-1 or an equivalent tool, lightly compress the C2 return springs so the snap/retaining ring can be removed.

26 Remove the C2 piston snap/retaining ring.

27 *Place a pry bar into the balance piston snap-ring groove and lightly pry in alternating locations to remove the C1 piston housing.*

28 *Remove the C2 piston return springs.*

29 *Using needle-nose pliers or a pry bar, carefully remove the C2 piston.*

30 *Using a pick and a small screwdriver, remove the C1/C2 drum O-ring seal. Note the position of the groove in the housing so you can easily identify the position during assembly.*

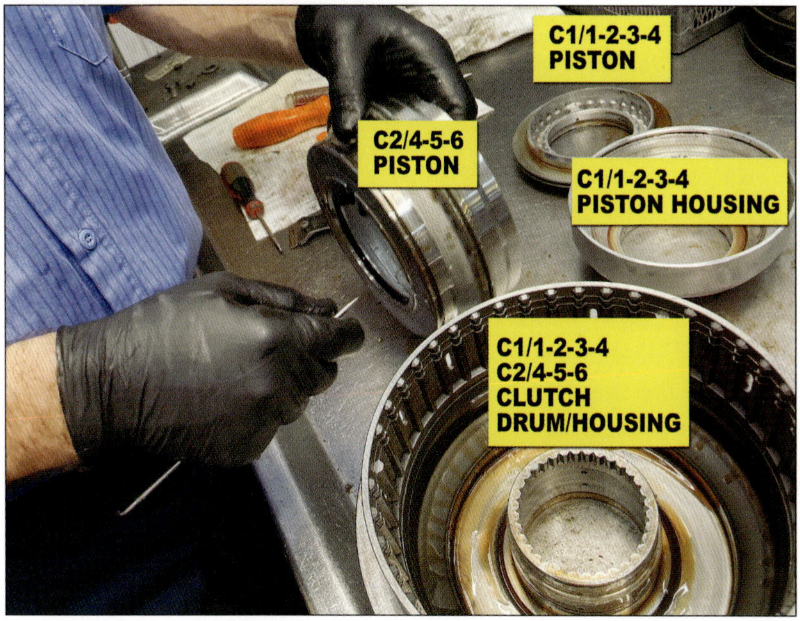

31 *C1/C2 drum components include the C1/1-2-3-4 piston, C1/1-2-3-4 piston housing, C2/4-5-6 piston, and C1/C2 clutch drum/housing. Your components may look slightly different from those shown, as later drums used different design components.*

The PTO gear is attached to the C1/C2 drum. If damaged, the drum needs to be replaced.

The turbine/input speed-sensor tone wheel is housed staked to the C1/C2 drum on non-PTO applications.

This design ring is replaceable if damaged. Using tools J43768 tone wheel driver and J43767 tone wheel staking tool, a new tone ring can be installed.

C1 (1-2-3-4) and C2 (4-5-6) Drum Service

Clean all of the parts removed and inspect the drum and pistons for wear, cracks, and damage. Inspect the inside diameter of the drum, where the pump hub seals ride for wear and damage. The maximum inside diameter where the seals ride is 2.9154 inches (74.05 mm). Inspect the C1 piston housing check ball for leakage and for being stuck. Shake the C1 housing and make sure the ball is free. Pour some solvent or ATF onto the ball to make sure it seals.

Inspect the return spring and snap rings for damage. Inspect the speed-sensor tone wheel for damage. Inspect the clutch drum bushing for wear and damage.

If the drum bushing is damaged or worn, it can be replaced. The maximum inside diameter of the bushing is 3.0776 inches (78.17 mm). Remove the bushing using a blind hole puller or by carefully splitting the bushing to remove it. Install the bushing using the J43778 bushing driver or an equivalent. Using a press to install the bushing is the preferred method. The bushing should be installed flush to 0.010 inch (0.25 mm) below the drum surface.

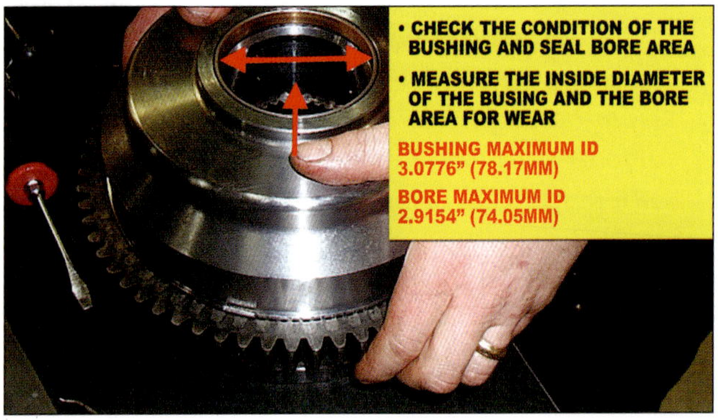

Inspect the C1/C2 drum bushing and bore for size and damage. Inspect the inside diameter of the drum bore, where the seals ride, for wear and damage. The maximum inside diameter where the seals ride is 2.9154 inches (74.05 mm). If the bushing is damaged or worn, it can be replaced. The maximum inside diameter of the bushing is 3.0776 inches (78.17 mm). Remove the bushing using a blind hole puller or by carefully splitting the bushing. Install the bushing using the J43778 bushing driver or an equivalent tool. Using a press to install the bushing is the preferred method. The bushing should be installed flush to 0.010 inch (0.25 mm) below the drum surface.

The tone wheel can be replaced, but it requires some special tools: J43768 tone wheel driver and J43767 tone wheel staking tool. If a replacement is required, grind the stakes from the drum and remove the old tone wheel. Install the new tone wheel and press it into position using J43768 to properly position it on the drum. Use the staking tool to attach the tone wheel to the drum in four positions 90 degrees apart. The tone wheel should be staked using 9 tons of force.

If the vehicle is equipped with a PTO gear and it is damaged, it is recommended that the drum be replaced. The gear can be replaced, but it requires precise measurements to position the new gear onto the drum.

C1 (1-2-3-4) and C2 (4-5-6) Drum Assembly

The C1/C2 housing and piston designs have changed through the years. This means the appearance of the components within the drum as well as the number of seals used has changed. In this book, we are using pictures from a 2005 model year, but we also explain the procedure for a later-model unit.

The C2 piston was updated, eliminating a 0.040-inch (1-mm) bleed hole while adding a seal, so a replacement piston may look different than the one being replaced. If a piston is equipped with an orifice, make sure it is not restricted.

Early-Design Drum/Housing and Pistons

Position the drum with the clutch opening facing up. Install the inner hub O-ring into the bottom groove of the clutch drum. Install three new seals onto the C2 piston and lubricate them with transmission assembly lubricant or an equivalent. Install a smaller-diameter seal with the lip of the seal facing away from the aluminum piston.

Lubricate the C2 balance piston and install it into the C2 piston with the rubber side facing the C2 piston. Push the C2 piston and the C2 balance piston down far enough to expose the snap-ring groove in the drum for the C2 piston and C2 balance piston. Make sure they are fully seated, as they are a very tight fit into the drum. Push the C2 balance piston below the snap-ring groove in the drum. Install the piston-retaining snap ring into the drum. Make sure the snap ring is fully seated.

Align the notches in the C2 piston return spring with the tangs on the C2 piston and install the return spring. Lubricate and install the C1 piston housing into the C2 clutch piston. Using J43776-2 or an equivalent clutch compressor, compress the return spring enough to expose the snap-ring groove in the inner hub of the clutch drum. Install the retaining ring. Make sure the retaining ring is fully seated. Remove the clutch compressor.

Install two new seals on the C1 piston. One seal fits on the inside diameter of the piston, while the other fits on the outside diameter. The inside-diameter lip-style seal installs with the lip facing away from the return-spring pockets in the piston. Lubricate the seals with transmission assembly lubricant or an equivalent. Install the C1 piston into the drum piston housing with the indents facing up. Make sure the piston is fully seated. Install the return springs with the springs fitting into the spring pockets in the C1 piston. Using J43777 or an equivalent spring compressor, compress the springs far enough to allow the installation of the retaining ring into the groove in the drum hub. Make sure the retaining ring is fully seated. Remove the compression tools.

Lubricate the seals on the C1 balance piston with transmission assembly lubricant or an equivalent. Install the balance piston with the rubber side toward the drum. Push the C1 balance piston in so that it is below the snap-ring groove in the C1 piston housing. Install the retaining ring. Make sure the retaining ring is fully seated.

Later-Design Drum and Pistons

Position the drum with the clutch opening facing up. Install the inner hub O-ring into the bottom groove of the clutch drum. Install two new seals onto the C2 piston and lubricate them with transmission assembly lubricant or an equivalent. The bottom inside diameter seal is a lip-style seal. Install it with the lip of the seal facing away from the aluminum piston.

Install the C2 piston into the C1/C2 drum. Make sure the piston is fully seated. Install a seal ring onto the C1 piston housing and lubricate it with transmission assembly lubricant or an equivalent. Align the return springs so that the notches in the spring retainer are aligned with the tangs of the C2 piston and install the springs. Install the C1 piston housing into the drum.

Install clutch compressor J47339-1 or an equivalent and lightly compress the return springs. Install the retaining ring in the snap-ring groove into the hub of the drum. Make sure the retaining ring is fully seated.

Install the two new seals onto the C1 piston. The bottom inside-diameter seal may be a lip-style seal. Install it with the lip of the seal facing away from the aluminum piston and lubricate it with transmission assembly lubricant or an equivalent. Install the C1 piston and make sure it is fully seated. Align the return springs with the return spring pockets in the piston and install the return springs. Lubricate the C1 balance piston with transmission assembly lubricant or an equivalent. Install the balance piston with the rubber side facing the drum and C1 piston.

Install clutch compressor J47339-1 or an equivalent and lightly compress the return springs. Install the retaining ring and remove the compressor.

Rebuilding the Drums and Pistons

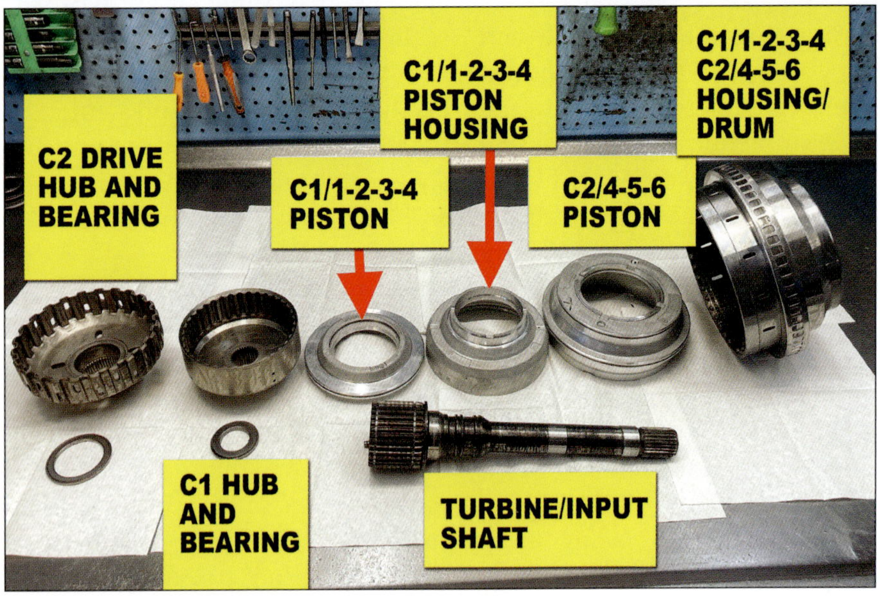

1 *Here are the C1/C2 drum components: C1/1-2-3-4 piston, C1/1-2-3-4 piston housing, C2/4-5-6 piston, C1/C2 clutch drum/housing, C2 drive hub, C1 drive hub, and the turbine shaft. Your components may look slightly different from those shown, as later drums used differently designed components. Clean and inspect the drum and all components so that they are ready for assembly.*

2 *Remove the seals and inspect the C2 piston check balls or orifices.*

3 *Install the C2 piston seals. The inside-diameter seal lip faces toward the drum and away from the piston return spring area. The number of piston seals vary with drum design.*

4 *Install the C1/C2 drum O-ring into the O-ring groove in the housing.*

5 *With the new seals installed onto the C2 piston, lubricate them with transmission assembly lubricant or an equivalent. Install the piston into the C1/C2 drum. This is typically a tight fit.*

6 *Make sure the C2 piston is fully installed.*

7 *Align the notches in the C2 piston return spring with the tangs on the C2 piston and install the return spring.*

8 *Lubricate the C2 balance piston seals and bore with transmission assembly lubricant or an equivalent and install the piston.*

9 *Make sure the C2 balance piston is fully installed.*

10 *Install the C2 balance piston snap/retainer ring with a screwdriver. Make sure it is fully seated in the C1/C2 drum.*

11 *If not previously installed, install the C2 piston return springs.*

12 *Install the C1 piston housing into the drum.*

13 *Make sure the C1 piston housing is fully installed.*

14 *Compress the C1 piston using J43776-1 or an equivalent tool and install the snap/retaining ring onto the hub groove bore in the C1/C2 drum. Install the snap ring with the marking previously made facing up, or if unmarked, the flat side of the snap ring should be facing up.*

15 *Make sure the snap/retaining ring is fully installed and seated.*

16 *Install the C1 piston seals. Lubricate the C1 piston seals and bore with transmission assembly lubricant or an equivalent and install the piston.*

17 *Push the C1 piston in evenly until it is fully seated.*

18 *Make sure the piston is fully seated.*

19 *Install the C1 return springs and orient the snap ring with the narrowest taper on the snap ring opening facing the snap-ring pliers. Look at the end of the snap-ring opening so that you can see what I am referring to. This is true on all snap rings of this design for installation so that the snap-ring pliers will not slip off if the ring needs to be removed.*

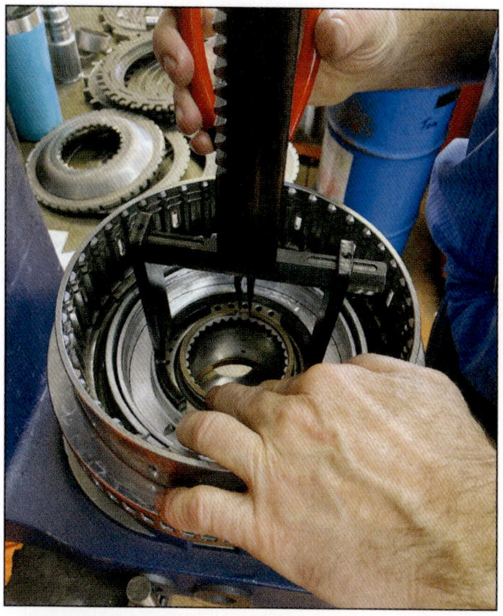

20 *Using J43777 or an equivalent spring compressor, compress the springs far enough to allow the installation of the retaining ring into the groove in the drum hub. Make sure the retaining ring is fully seated.*

21 *Inspect the C1 balance piston seal. Lubricate the C1 balance piston seal and bore with transmission assembly lubricant or an equivalent.*

22 *Lubricate the C1 balance piston seal and bore with transmission assembly lubricant or an equivalent and install the piston.*

23 *Make sure the C1 balance piston is fully seated.*

24 *Make sure the C1 balance piston snap/retaining ring is fully seated.*

25 *Using Transjel, lubricate the C1/C2 drum inside bore and bushing.*

Turbine and Input Shaft Installation

Check the turbine shaft bushing for wear and damage. The maximum inside bushing diameter should not exceed 0.7920 inch (20.117 mm). If the bushing requires replacement, use a blind hole puller, such as J44526-1 or an equivalent, or carefully split the bushing with a chisel and remove it.

Use a bushing driver, such as J43791 or an equivalent, to install the bushing. The bushing should be installed flush to 0.010 inch (0.25 mm) below the inner turbine shaft surface.

Install the two butt-cut seal rings onto the shaft on the large spline end of the shaft. Install the TCC seals on the other end of the shaft. Install the turbine shaft into the C1/C2 clutch drum splines. Install the snap ring to retain the shaft in the drum. The snap-ring direction should be installed with the marks that were previously made on it facing up. If you did not make marks, install the snap ring with the flat side facing away from the clutch drum.

Turbine Shaft Rebuild and Reinstallation

1 *Inspect the turbine/input shaft bushing for wear and damage. The maximum inside bushing diameter should not exceed 0.7920 inch (20.117 mm). If the bushing requires replacement, use a blind hole puller, such as J44526-1 or an equivalent, or carefully split the bushing with a chisel and remove it. Use a bushing driver, such as J43791 or an equivalent, to install the bushing. The bushing should be installed flush to 0.010 inch (0.25 mm) below the inner turbine shaft surface.*

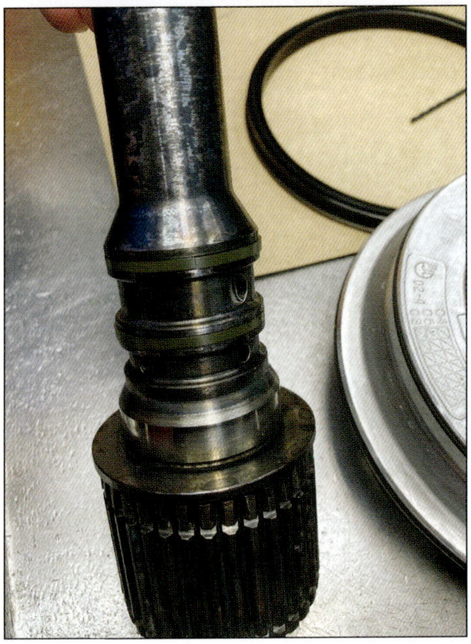

2 *Clean and inspect the turbine/input shaft journals and seal-ring grooves for wear.*

3 *Install all of the turbine shaft seal rings. Lubricate the seals with Transjel.*

4 *Install the turbine shaft into the C1/C2 drum. Align the splines.*

5 *The snap/retaining ring will fit into the groove on the shaft.*

6 *Install the snap ring with the marking that was previously made facing up. If unmarked, the flat side of the snap ring should face up.*

Inspect the Friction Discs

Check for the following:

- Burnt lining (Due to the design, it is normal for the Allison linings to slightly discolor on the inboard edge of the lining.)
- Exposure to antifreeze or water
- Flaking lining
- Damaged splines
- Excessive wear
- Warped discs

Inspect the Steel Plates

- Lug wear
- Heat spots (Slight discoloration in a few areas is normal; heavy heat spotting is not normal)
- Warpage

C1 Friction Disc Measurements

- Minimum disc thickness: 0.0935 inch (2.375 mm)
- Minimum oil groove depth: 0.0079 inch (0.200 mm)
- To determine warpage/coning, lay the disc on a flat surface. Measure between the flat surface and the friction material. The maximum cone for each plate is 0.010 inch (0.255 mm).

C1 Steel Plate Measurements

- Minimum thickness: 0.0841 inch (2.135 mm)
- To determine warpage/coning, lay the disc on a flat surface. Measure between the flat surface and the disc. The maximum cone for each plate is 0.0079 inch (0.200 mm).

C1 backing plate measurements are based on the backing plate ID number stamped into the plate.

Backing Plate ID Numbers

Plate ID #	Minimum Thickness	Friction Plate Count
8521	0.4661 inch (11.840 mm)	6
8522	0.4835 inch (12.280 mm)	6
8523	0.5012 inch (12.730 mm)	6
8524	0.5189 inch (13.180 mm)	6
8525	0.5366 inch (13.630 mm)	6
6221	0.4661 inch (11.840 mm)	7
6222	0.4835 inch (12.280 mm)	7
6223	0.5012 inch (12.730 mm)	7
6624	0.5189 inch (13.180 mm)	7
6225	0.5366 inch (13.630 mm)	7
2420	0.4488 inch (11.400 mm)	7

C2 Friction Disc Measurements

- Minimum disc thickness: 0.0935 inch (2.375 mm)
- Minimum oil groove depth: 0.0079 inch (0.200 mm)
- To determine warpage/coning, lay the disc on a flat surface. Measure between the flat surface and the friction material. The maximum cone for each plate is 0.0089 inch (0.225 mm).

C2 Steel Plate Measurements

- Minimum thickness: 0.0841 inch (2.135 mm)
- To determine warpage/coning, lay the disc on a flat surface. Measure between the flat surface and the disc. The maximum cone for each plate is 0.0094 inch (0.240 mm).

C1 and C2 (1-2-3-4/4-5-6) Clutch Measurements

Most technicians replace the clutches during a rebuild. OEM and Performance clutches are available. Allison makes the clutch plate specifications available if one would like to see if the clutches can be reused.

C1 (1-2-3-4) Clutch Installation

Starting with an internally splined steel plate, alternately install the steel internally splined plates and the externally splined friction discs. With all the plates installed, install the C1 backing plate and the two retaining rings. The spiral retaining ring is installed last. Make sure both rings are properly installed.

Depending on the design, the number of C1 clutch plates may vary. Early applications use six friction and six steels; later applications use seven friction and seven steel plates.

With the clutch fully installed, lubricate and install the T1 thrust bearing onto the end of the turbine shaft. The bearing should be installed with the blue stripes facing up, with the inside-diameter lip facing up. Install the C1/1-2-3-4 clutch drive hub over the clutch plates. Wiggle and turn the hub until it is fully seated against the T1 bearing.

Clutch Clearance (Factory Method)

The C1 clutch does have a clearance check, but it requires a special tool to accomplish the task if using the factory method. As we discussed earlier, updates to the C1 clutch have been implemented through the years. The unit serial number determines which tools and backing plates are to be used. Units starting with serial number 6310415454 (Indianapolis) and 6320442099 (Baltimore) use the updated C1 backing-plate design and tools with silver coloring to make the measurement. The early-design packs require tools that are all black in color.

Install the C1 clutch pack minus the backing plate. Using tools J44525-1 or J44525-5, place the tool onto the turbine shaft. Install the J44525-1 with the inner edge facing down. Slide the inner edge of the J44525-1 into the snap-ring groove in the turbine shaft. Align the holes in the J44525-1 with the holes in either the J44525-2 or J44525-5.

Install the tool bolts and torque them to 16 in-lbs (1.8 Nm). Place the tab of tool J44525-3 (black) or J44525-4 (silver) into the turbine shaft snap-ring groove. The tab of the tool will have four sides with numbers printed on the tab. Read the number from the tab that fits in the groove. That number should be the same as the number stamped on the backing plate. If no tab fits in the groove, select a plate with an ID of 6221 or 8521. Select the correct backing plate.

> **TECH TIP: Lubrication**
>
> Some technicians install the friction plates dry, while others presoak the discs in transmission fluid prior to installation. If installed dry, operate the transmission in Neutral for a few minutes upon initial start to provide lubrication for the linings. ■

Clutch Clearance (Alternative Method)

If you do not have access to the tools to check the clutch clearance, you can use an alternative method. Take some shims from another transmission, such as a 4T60/4T65E final drive, bend them at a 90-degree angle, and use them as a go/no go tool. Another option is to use a stack of feeler gauges. Typically, one would shoot for 0.080 inch to 0.110 inch with a target of 0.090 inch. Determine how far your pack is off from the target and add or subtract that value from the backing plate you have. Find a backing plate in the included table that is in that range and install the selected backing plate.

C2 (4-5-6) Clutch Installation

Lubricate and install the C1/1-2-3-4 drive hub thrust bearing onto the previously installed C1/1-2-3-4 drive hub with the blue strips facing up/away from the drive hub; place with the outside-diameter lip facing up. Install the C2/4-5-6 drive hub with the lugs facing the drum. Starting with a steel plate, alternately install the C2/4-5-6 seven steel and six friction plates.

Note: Some technicians install the friction plates dry, while others presoak the discs in transmission fluid prior to installation.

Lubricate and install the bronze thrust washer into the C2/4-5-6 drive hub. Inspect the P1 sun gear and flange for wear and for pitting in the area where the thrust bearing rides. Install the P1 sun gear in the P1 drive flange. Align the wide lugs on the drive flange with wide notches in the C1/C2 drum and install the drive flange and sun gear. Install the retaining ring. Make sure the ring is fully seated.

Set the C1/C2 completed drum aside on the workbench for installation later.

C1 and C2 Clutch Pack Assembly

1 *Early-design transmissions use fewer discs than the late-model applications. If reusing the discs, inspect them for wear as outlined in this chapter.*

3 *Start the assembly of the C1 clutch pack with a steel/inner splined disc.*

2 *Late-design transmissions use more discs than the early-model applications. If reusing the discs, inspect them for wear as outlined in this chapter.*

4 *Following the steel plate is a friction disc. Presoak the friction discs with transmission fluid prior to installation.*

5 *The pack installation alternates between steel/inner splined discs and friction/outer splined discs until all the plates are installed. The top plate is the backing plate, which is selective in this application.*

6 *Two methods can be used to check the C1 clutch pack clearance. The factory method involves using tools J44525-1 or J44525-5, J44525-2, J44525-2, or J44525-4, depending on the year. The tab of the tool is stamped with numbers that correspond with the numbers stamped on the backing plate. Use the chart and procedure in the text to select the correct backing plate.*

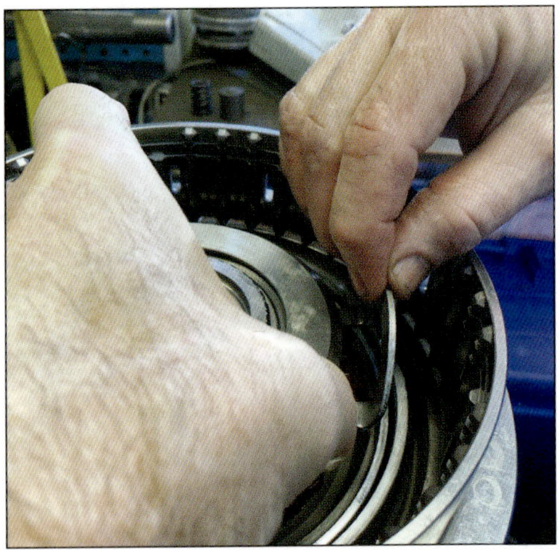

7 *For the alternate method, locate some shims that range between 0.080 and 0.110 inch that will fit into the area in the drum shown. The 4T65 final-drive shims or angled feeler gauges work well. Bend the shims to a 90-degree angle. Install the backing plate.*

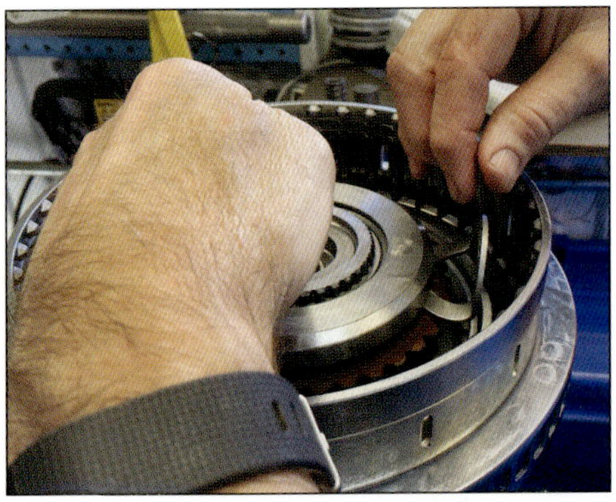

8 *The alternate method is to slide the selective measuring shims or feeler gauges between the backing plate and the top disc. The target is 0.080–0.110 inch, with 0.090 being the optimum value. Select the backing plate from the chart that will move the pack clearance into the target. Be aware that the backing plates available are based on the clutch design (pack plate count). Install the correct backing plate.*

9 *The selective size coding is stamped on the backing plate. Use the chart in the text to determine size.*

10 *Install the snap/retaining ring. Make sure it is fully engaged. Orient the snap ring with the narrowest taper on the snap-ring opening facing the snap-ring pliers. Look at the end of the snap-ring opening so that you can see what I am referring to. This is true on all snap rings of this design for installation so that the snap-ring pliers will not slip off if the ring needs to be removed.*

11 *Install the spiral second retaining ring. Rotate the ring into position.*

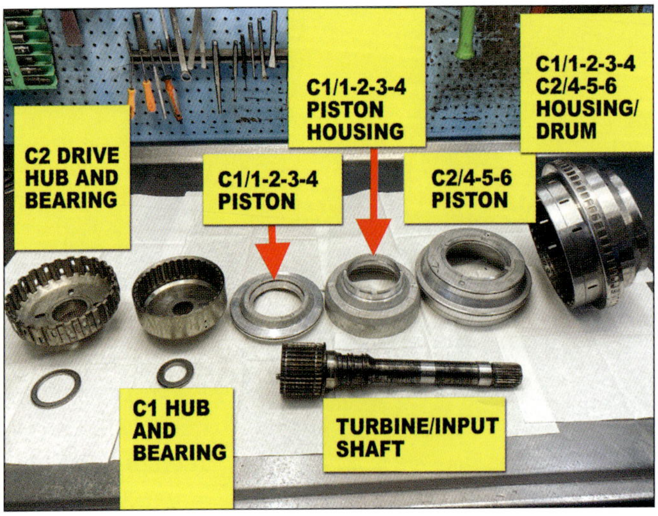

12 *Observed here are the C1/C2 drum components: the C1/1-2-3-4 piston, C1/1-2-3-4 piston housing, C2/4-5-6 piston, C1/C2 clutch drum/housing, C2 drive hub and bearing, C1 drive hub and bearing, and turbine/input shaft. Your components may look slightly different from those shown because later drums used different design components.*

13 *Install the thrust bearing with the blue markings up. If the bearing is not marked, the side attached to the inside-diameter race should face up. Lubricate the bearing with transmission fluid prior to installation. Double-check the direction the bearing was installed.*

14 *Install the C1 clutch drive hub. Wiggle and rotate the hub until it is fully installed.*

15 *Install the C2 hub thrust bearing with the blue markings up onto the C1 hub. If the bearing is not marked, the side attached to the outside diameter race should face up. Lubricate the bearing with transmission fluid prior to installation. Double-check the direction the bearing was installed.*

16 *Install the C2 hub over the C1 hub and C2 bearing previously installed.*

17 *Check the C2 hub's bronze thrust washer for thickness and damage. The minimum thickness is 0.102 inch (2.59 mm).*

18 *Install the bronze C2 hub thrust washer into the notches in the C2 hub. Lubricate and retain the washer with Transjel.*

19 *The C2 clutch includes six frictions, seven steels, and one flange plate. If reusing the discs, inspect the discs for wear as is outlined in this chapter. Presoak the pack prior to disc installation.*

20 *Install a steel (outer-splined) plate first.*

21 *Install a friction (inner-splined) plate next.*

22 *Alternate between friction and steel plates until all the plates are installed. Never have two frictions stacked on top of each other.*

23 *Install the P1 sun gear as shown into the C2 flange plate.*

24 *The lugs for the P1 sun gear fit into lugs in the C2 flange plate.*

25 *Install the flange plate with the P1 sun gear into the lugs of the C1/C2 clutch drum.*

26 *Install the snap/retaining ring into the C1/C2 drum. Make sure it is fully engaged in all of the drum lugs.*

27 *Make sure the C2 clutch is free. Use a pick or a small screwdriver through the slots in the drum to make sure the clutch pack is free.*

28 *A drill bit works well if you would like to get a specific clutch pack clearance measurement.*

29 *Install the P1 sun gear bearing with the side with the blue ink markings up. If the bearing is not marked, the side attached to the inside-diameter race should face up. Lubricate the bearing with transmission fluid prior to installation.*

30 *Double-check the direction of the bearing installation.*

C3 (3-5-R) and C4/C5 Clutch Removal, and P1, P2, and P3 Planetary Service

The C3/3-5-Reverse clutch is mounted on the bellhousing side of the case below the C1/C2 drum. Remove the C3 clutch snap/retaining ring from the case. Remove the P1 carrier/P1 ring gear and the C3 clutch components.

Discoloration on the inside diameter of the C3 friction discs is considered normal due to the design.

The P1 carrier houses a plastic spacer; set it aside with the planetary components. Remove the C3 clutch piston using two flat-blade snap-ring pliers or air pressure. Rotate the transmission to access the output shaft.

If not already done, remove the extension housing or 4x4 adapter (as outlined previously in this chapter). The 2WD applications use an extension housing while the 4x4 uses a transfer-case adapter housing. The housings on both applications are held in place by 16 bolts.

4x4

- With the rear of the transmission horizonal, place the transmission in Park.
- Remove the output shaft nut by using a hub socket (DT 50869 on late-model applications or J43769 on earlier applications) or equivalent tool.
- Remove the housing bolts and remove the housing.

2WD

- Remove the yoke and output shaft seal.
- Remove the large snap ring.
- Using three puller legs (J43910) and the puller (J24420-B) or an equivalent, remove the bearing from the housing. The legs lock into the bearing races, so tighten the puller and remove the bearing.
- Remove the housing bolts and the housing.

A selective shim is located on the output shaft under the bearing on both applications; do not lose the shim. In addition, the parking pawl pin tends to stick in the housing. This can damage the pawl spring, so make sure the pawl pin stays in the case when removing the extension housing/4x4 adapter.

C3 Clutch Disassembly

1 *Locate the snap/retaining ring for the C3 clutch.*

2 *Remove the snap/retaining ring for the C3 clutch from the case.*

3 *Grab the planetary and remove the P1 ring and P1 carrier/P2 ring gear to remove the planetary and clutches.*

4 *The C3 clutch stacks up as follows: four frictions, four steels, and one backing plate. The discoloration on the inside diameter is normal for this pack due to the design. If you plan to reuse the clutches, inspect and measure the parts as outlined in the text.*

5 *The three thrust plates need to be measured for wear, as is outlined in the text.*

6 *This is Dimension B. The difference between the two measurements is Dimension C. The minimum thrust-plate wear area thickness is 0.1150 inch (2.920 mm). Repeat this process for all three thrust plates.*

7 *Remove the P1 ring gear from the P1 carrier/ P2 ring gear.*

8 *Remove the plastic spacer ring from the P1 carrier/P2 ring gear.*

9 *Remove the C3 piston from the case by using air pressure or a pair of flat-blade snap-ring pliers to pull the piston out.*

10 *The C3 piston is a molded-design piston. Note the orifice in the piston that acts as an air bleed for the circuit.*

Extension Housing Removal

1 *If the extension/4x4 adapter has not already been removed, remove the 16 bolts holding the housing in place after removing the output shaft nut (4x4) or the output seal and bearing (2WD), as described in the text.*

2 *Removing the 4x4 adapter bolts will allow you to remove the housing once the output shaft nut has been removed.*

3 *To remove the 2WD extension housing, remove the rear seal.*

4 *To remove the 2WD extension housing, remove the bearing snap ring.*

5 *Remove the 2WD output bearing using a bearing puller.*

6 *Lift the 2WD output bearing from the rear extension housing.*

7 *Remove the 4x4 adapter or extension housing by lightly prying evenly around the housing. Take care that the park pawl pin stays with the case. Otherwise, damage to the pawl spring can occur.*

8 *Check the adapter housing for cracks (common). Cracks are due to vibration issues that must be addressed.*

9 *Do not lose the end-play shim (4x4).*

10 *The end-play shim and output speed-sensor tone wheel are housed on the output shaft and can be accessed by removing the extension housing (2WD).*

C4/2-6 Clutch and C5/Low and Reverse Clutch Removal and Disassembly

With the extension housing/4x4 adapter removed, remove the park pawl, park pawl spring (note how the spring is attached), and park pawl pin. Remove the park pawl shaft cam guide.

Grab the output shaft and lift it from the case. This will remove the output shaft and the P3 carrier. Set the carrier and output shaft aside. Remove the P3 sun gear. The thrust bearing may stick to the output carrier or the P3 sun gear. Remove the thrust bearing and keep it with the sun gear. Remove the C5 return spring assembly.

Remove the mainshaft, the P2 sun gear, and the P2/P3 sun gear spacer by grabbing the shaft and lifting the components from the case. Remove the P3 ring gear/P2 carrier assembly and the thrust bearing from the case. Remove the C5 clutch plates and the backing plate from the case. The thrust bearing may stick to the P2 carrier or the P2 sun gear.

Remove the snap rings retaining the C4 clutch discs in the case. Two snap rings are used. The outer ring is a conventional clutch snap ring while the inner ring is a thinner-cushion snap ring.

Remove the C4 clutches from the case. Use air pressure or two flat-blade snap-ring pliers to remove the C4 piston from the case.

The piston for the C5 clutch is located in the extension/4x4 adapter housing. Gently pry the C5 piston from the housing. The two seals are replaceable on the C5 piston. Closely inspect the housing for cracks and damage. The extension housing contains the output speed-sensor tone ring on 2WD applications.

C3/C4/C5 Clutch Inspection

Many technicians replace the clutches during a rebuild. Allison makes the clutch plate specifications available if one would like to see if the clutches can be reused.

Clutch Plate Inspection

- ❒ Burnt lining (Due to the design, it is normal for the Allison linings to slightly discolor on the inboard edge of the lining)
- ❒ Exposure to antifreeze or water
- ❒ Flaking lining
- ❒ Damaged splines
- ❒ Excessive wear
- ❒ Warped discs

Inspect the steel plates for:

- ❒ Lug wear
- ❒ Heat spots (Slight discoloration in a few areas is normal but heavy heat spotting is not)
- ❒ Warpage

C3 Friction Disc Measurements:

- ❒ Minimum disc thickness: 0.093 inch (2.375 mm)
- ❒ Minimum oil groove depth: 0.0079 inch (0.200 mm)
- ❒ To determine warpage/coning, lay the disc on a flat surface. Measure between the flat surface and the friction material. The maximum cone for each plate is 0.0089 inch (0.225 mm).

C3 Steel Plate Measurements:

- ❒ Minimum thickness: 0.096 inch (2.44 mm)
- ❒ To determine warpage/coning, lay the disc on a flat surface. Measure between the flat surface and the disc. The maximum cone for each plate is 0.0157 inch (0.400 mm).
- ❒ C3 backing plate minimum thickness in the thickest areas is 0.04370 inch (11.10 mm). Dimension C is the thickest part of the backing plate, and the minimum thickness is 0.7165 inch (18.20 mm).
- ❒ The backing plate on this clutch has three cushion springs or thrust plates that must be checked for the proper thickness. Measure from the top of the thrust plate to the bottom of the backing plate (Dimension A). Measure from the top of the thrust plate inner rim to the bottom of the backing plate bore (Dimension B). Subtract the last measurement from the first measurement, which represents the thrust plate wear. Minimum thrust plate wear area thickness is 0.1150 inch (2.920 mm). Repeat this process for all three thrust plates.

C4 Friction Disc Measurements:

- ❒ Minimum disc thickness: 0.0659 inch (1.675 mm)

- ❒ To determine warpage/coning, lay the disc on a flat surface. Measure between the flat surface and the friction material. The maximum cone for each plate is 0.0089 inch (0.225 mm).

C4 Steel Plate Measurements:

- ❒ Minimum thickness: 0.096 inch (2.440 mm)
- ❒ To determine warpage/coning, lay the disc on a flat surface. Measure between the flat surface and the disc. The maximum cone for each plate is 0.015 inch (0.400 mm).
- ❒ The C4 backing plate minimum thickness is 0.4370 inch (11.10 mm).

C5 Friction Disc Measurements:

- ❒ Minimum disc thickness: 0.0935 inch (2.375 mm)
- ❒ Minimum oil groove depth: 0.0079 inch (0.200 mm)
- ❒ To determine warpage/coning, Lay the disc on a flat surface. Measure between the flat surface and the friction material. The maximum cone for each plate is 0.0089 inch (0.225 mm).

C5 Steel Plate Measurements:

- ❒ Minimum thickness: 0.096 inch (2.440 mm)
- ❒ To determine warpage/coning, lay the disc on a flat surface. Measure between the flat surface and the disc. The maximum cone for each plate is 0.015 inch (0.400 mm).
- ❒ C5 backing plate minimum thickness is 0.7047 inch (17.900 mm)

C5 Clutch Steel Selective Plates Available

C5 Selective Plate Measurement	Use Steel Plate Identification Number
1.393–1.412 inches (35.3–35.86 mm)	1
1.413–1.431 inches (35.87–36.36 mm)	2
1.432–1.467 inches (36.37–37.27 mm)	3

Disassembling and Removing the C4/2-6 Clutch and C5/Low and Reverse Clutch

1 *The output shaft/C3 ring gear, parking components, and C5 clutch/springs are shown.*

2 *Note the position of the parking pawl, pawl pin, and pawl spring.*

3 *Remove the pawl spring, pawl pin, and park pawl.*

4 *Remove the park cam and roller linkage.*

5 *Lift the output shaft spacer from the shaft.*

6 *Lift the output shaft/P3 ring gear out of the case.*

7 *Lift the C5 clutch return springs from the case.*

8 *Remove the P3 sun gear and bearing from the mainshaft.*

9 *Lift the sun gear spacer from the mainshaft.*

10 *Lift the mainshaft and P2 sun gear as an assembly from the case.*

11 *Lift the P3 ring/P2 carrier from the case. Some or all of the C5 clutches may lift out when the ring/carrier assembly is removed.*

12 *If not previously removed, lift out the C5 clutches. If planning to reuse the clutches, inspect and measure the parts as outlined in the text.*

13 *The C4 clutch is held into the case by two snap rings: a small-diameter ring and a large-diameter ring housed in the same groove.*

14 *Using a screwdriver, remove the C4 clutch outer snap/retaining ring.*

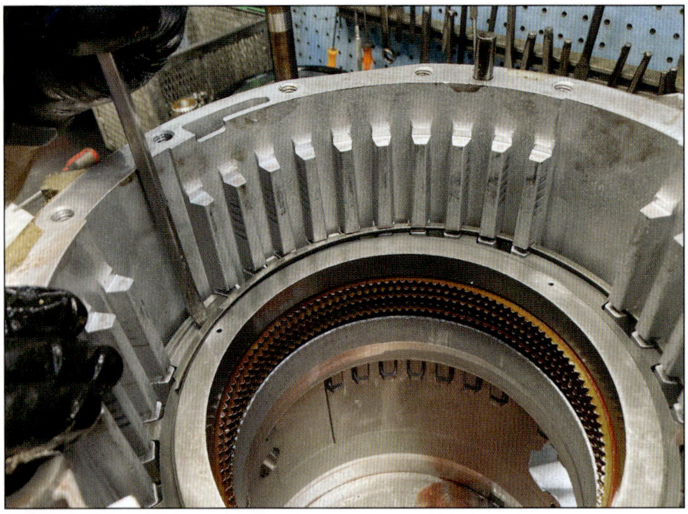

15 *Using a screwdriver, remove the C4 clutch inner snap/retaining ring.*

16 *If you plan to reuse the C4 clutches, inspect and measure the parts as outlined in the text.*

17 *The C5 piston is housed in the extension/4x4 adapter housing. Remove the piston, remove the seals, and clean and inspect the bearings and components.*

P1, P2, and P3 Planetary Service

Clean and inspect the gear teeth for damage. Inspect the P3 carrier parking lugs for wear and damage. Measure the pinion end play using a feeler gauge on each planetary pinion gear. Measure the bushing inside diameter with a dial caliper or a snap gauge. Measure the bearing race on the output shaft outside diameter with a dial caliper or a micrometer.

- The P1 carrier pinion end play maximum is 0.040 inch (1.00 mm).
- The P1 carrier bushing maximum diameter is 1.9957 inches (50.69 mm).
- The P1 carrier spacer plastic washer minimum thickness is 0.059 inch (1.49 mm).
- The P2 carrier pinion end play maximum is 0.040 inch (1.00 mm).
- The P2 carrier bushing maximum diameter is 1.440 inches (36.575 mm).
- The P3 carrier pinion end play maximum is 0.040 inch (1.00 mm).
- The output shaft bushing maximum inside diameter is 0.794 inch (20.07 mm).
- The output shaft bearing inner race surface minimum diameter is 1.77 inches (44.978 mm) for the early shaft.
- The 2WD output shaft yoke minimum seal surface area diameter is 2.562 inches (65.08 mm).
- The mainshaft small diameter shaft pilot minimum diameter is 0.7869 inch (19.987 mm).
- The mainshaft large diameter journal minimum diameter is 1.4333 inches (36.405 mm).

Bushing Replacement

The bushings in the planetary and shafts are replaceable. Remove the bushings by carefully splitting them with a chisel or by using a blind hole puller to remove the bushing.

Bushing	General Motors/Allison Tool Number
Output shaft	J44526-1
P2 carrier	J43785
P1 carrier	J43781

Case Inspection, Service, and Output Seal Replacement

The valve body and shift shaft components should have been previously removed. If not, remove them now as outlined. Clean the case. Clean the internal components previously removed.

Inspect the internal case lugs for damage. Inspect the case for cracks and damage. Clean and inspect all the threaded holes. On 4WD applications, the output shaft seal is located in the transfer case while 2WD applications have the seal located in the extension housing.

Clean the case and components that have not been previously cleaned. Install the shift-shaft seal, shift shaft, detent (rooster comb), and park rod into the case.

Planetary Layout and Component Inspection

1 *The planetary components are shown as they sit in the case.*

2 *Lay out all of the planetary components on the workbench for identification.*

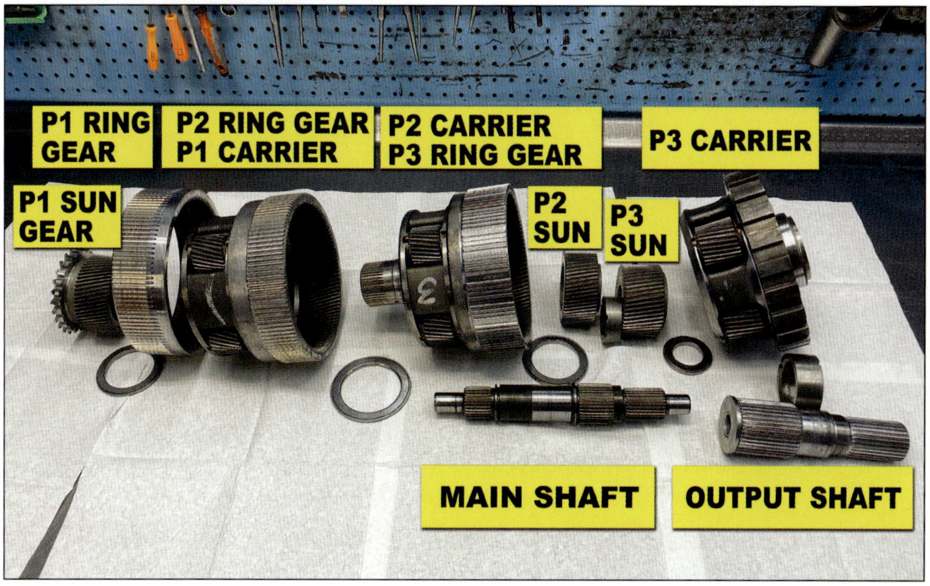

3 *Planetary components are shown as they are positioned in the case.*

4 Closely inspect all the bearings, as they are usually the cause of planetary damage.

5 Damaged teeth are usually caused by bearing failure that allows a piece of debris to become ingested by the gearset.

6 Inspect the pinion, sun, and ring teeth closely. Damage is usually caused by bearing failure, which allows a piece of debris to become ingested by the gearset.

7 Pinion washer wear can be checked with a feeler gauge between the pinion and the washer. Check all the planetary pinions end clearance, which has a maximum value of 0.040 inch (1 mm).

8 All of the bushings in an Allison application have wear measurements that can determine if the bushing is excessively worn. Measure each bushing's inside diameter and compare the value to the specifications listed in the text.

9 Inspect each bushing for damage (as shown). Many Allison bushings are Teflon coated (orange color). If the coating is worn, replace the bushing.

10 *Inspect the P3 carrier sleeve for damage and wear. Measure the diameter as outlined in the text.*

11 *Inspect all bushings, including the output shaft bushing for size and damage.*

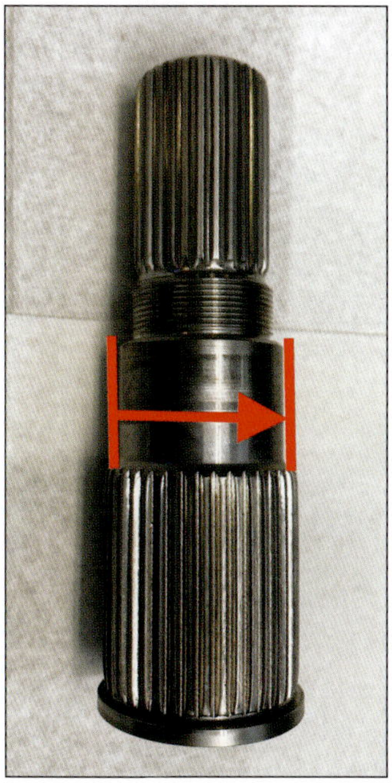

12 *Measure the output shaft contact area for wear.*

13 *The shafts used in the Allison applications have been updated as torque capacity changed. Make sure to order the correct parts for your application. The smaller shaft is used in the earlier-model lower-torque applications.*

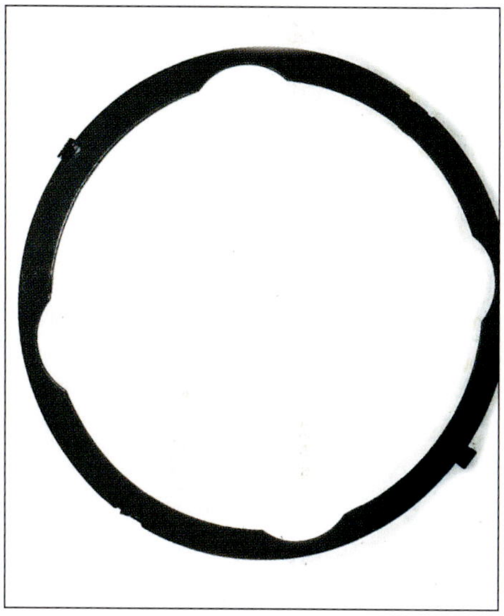

14 *A plastic spacer is used to separate some planetary components. Its thickness must be measured for wear, as described in the text.*

15 *As discussed earlier, the shafts have been updated. Some of those changes appear very minor, but they are actually major changes, and interchanging early- and late-model parts can create major issues. In this instance, it can create lubrication issues due to orifice changes.*

16 *Inspect the mainshaft journals for wear. Inspect the lube orifices and openings for restriction and contamination.*

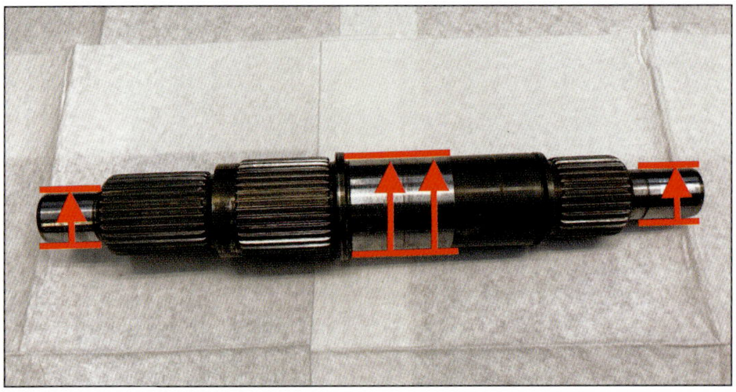

17 *Measure the mainshaft for wear in four locations: on each end and each journal in the middle of the shaft.*

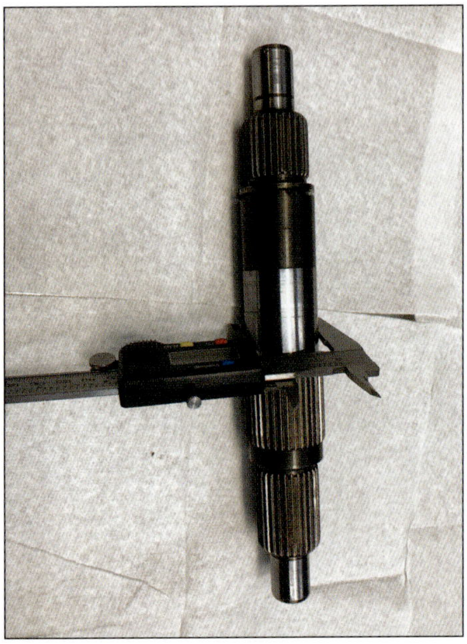

18 *Use a dial caliper or micrometer for your measurements.*

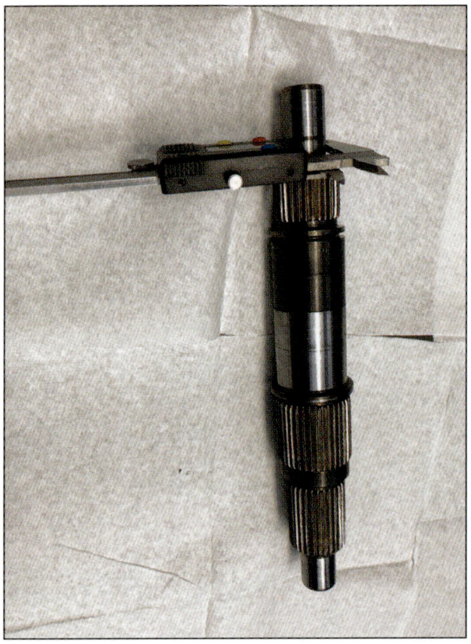

19 *Measure the small journals on each end of the shaft. Use a dial caliper or micrometer for your measurements.*

20 *Make sure the vent is not restricted.*

21 *Inspect the case lugs, bolt holes, and snap-ring grooves for wear and damage.*

22 *On 2WD applications, the seal is located in the extension housing and can be replaced without removing the extension housing.*

Assembly of C3/C4/C5 Clutches and Planetaries

Two methods can be used to assemble the unit. The direction taken will typically be determined by access to the planetary holding special tool. The process can be accomplished without the tool, but care must be taken and a slightly different process followed to ensure that all the components are properly aligned.

After inspecting the clutch components, including the C3 backing plate thrust plates (as outlined previously), the clutch and its components are ready to install. Two methods can be used to build the unit.

GM/Allison Factory Method

- Install the C3 clutch components.
- Install the shaft holding tool (J44587).
- Install the planetaries/shafts/bearings.
- Install the C4 and C5 clutch components.
- Install the extension/4x4 adapter housing.
- Install the C1/C2 drum and P1 sun gear bearing.
- Install the pump and bellhousing assembly.

GM/Allison Non-Factory Method

- Install the C3 clutch components.
- Rotate the case and install the C1/C2 clutch drum.
- Install the bellhousing and pump assembly.
- Rotate the case and install the P1 sun gear bearing.
- Install the planetaries/shafts/bearings.
- Install the C4 and C5 clutch components.
- Install the extension/4x4 adapter housing.

If you do not have access to the holding tool or do not wish to fabricate a tool, use the alternative method. The assembly of each subcomponent is the same, so the only difference is which components are installed in the case and when they are installed.

We will be using the GM/Allison process, so you will understand the process, as it is the most common. Either process will work; the unit is simply built from the opposite end of the case.

C3/3-5-R Clutch Assembly

Lubricate the C3 piston with transmission assembly lubricant or an equivalent. With the front of the case facing up, install the C3 piston. The C3 piston has an air bleed/clutch lube orifice that must be located at the top of the case (12 o'clock). Make sure the piston is fully seated.

Install the C3 return spring assembly into the case with the springs facing up. Install a C3 steel plate and then a presoaked friction plate. Alternate between steel and friction plates until all the plates are installed: four friction and four steel. Do not stack two frictions against each other. Otherwise, failure will occur. Lubricate the backing plate thrust plates with Transjel. Install the C3 backing plate with the thrust plates facing the clutch pack.

Using clutch compressor J44530 or an equivalent tool, lightly compress the return springs and install the clutch snap/retaining ring into the case. Make sure the tool is not pushing against the backing-plate thrust-plate pins.

Make sure the snap/retainer ring is fully installed in the groove. If a compressor was used, remove it.

Reassembling the C3/3-5-R Clutch Assembly

1 *The C3 and C4 pistons contain orifices that are used as air bleeds.*

2 *Lubricate and install the C3 piston. The orifice in the piston should be located toward the top of the case (12 o'clock). Make sure the piston is fully installed.*

3 *The number of steel and friction plates may vary with the application, so to make it easier, install the same plate counts as were removed.*

4 *Install the C3 clutch return spring with the springs facing up in the case. Install one steel plate.*

5 *Presoak in transmission fluid and install a C3 friction plate.*

6 *Install a C3 steel plate followed by a friction plate. Alternate friction/steel plate installation until all the plates are fully installed. Do not stack two frictions together.*

7 *Lubricate the C3 backing plate thrust plates with Transjel. Install the C3 backing plate and thrust plates toward the C3 clutches.*

8 *Using a clutch compressor, such as J44530 or your hands, lightly compress the C3 return springs. Install the C3 snap/retaining ring into the groove in the case. If using a compressor, be sure the tool is not contacting the backing plate rivets.*

9 *Check that the C3 snap/retaining ring is fully seated.*

C4/2-6 Clutch Assembly

Rotate the case so the rear is facing up. Lubricate the C4 piston with transmission assembly lubricant or an equivalent. Install the C4 piston. The C4 piston has an air bleed/clutch lube orifice that must be located at the top of the case (12 o'clock). Make sure the piston is fully seated.

Install the C4 return spring assembly into the case with the springs facing up. Install a C4 steel plate. Install the P1 ring gear in the case so that the splines are facing down and seated against the C3 backing-plate thrust plates.

Lubricate and install the plastic spacer onto the P1 carrier/P2 ring-gear assembly. Install the P1 carrier/P2 ring-gear assembly with the planetary pinions engaging the P1 ring gear. Rotate to engage the pinions with the P1 ring gear. A steel plate should have been previously installed. Install a presoaked friction plate. Alternate between steel and friction plates until all the plates are installed: five friction and five steel or six friction and six steel, depending on the year. Do not stack two frictions against each other. Otherwise, failure will occur. Install the C4 backing plate with the flattest side facing the friction discs.

Using clutch compressor J44530 or an equivalent tool, lightly compress the return springs and install the clutch snap/retaining ring into the case. Some technicians do not use the compression tool but rather use their free hand to force the backing plate down on one side while at the same time using a screwdriver to work the snap ring around and into the case groove.

The C4 clutch uses two snap/retaining rings. The lightest and largest in diameter ring is installed first. The heaviest is then installed into the same groove in the case last. Make sure the snap/retainer rings are fully installed in the groove. The ring end gaps should be installed 180 degrees apart from each other. Make sure they are fully seated.

If a compressor was used, remove it carefully. Otherwise, damage to the carrier bushing can occur. Install the P1 carrier/P2 ring-gear thrust bearing with the black side up and the race with the outer lip up away from the carrier.

Reassembling the C4/2-6 Clutch

1 *The C3 and C4 pistons use air bleed orifices. The orifices should be located at the top, 12 o'clock position in the case when the piston is fully installed.*

2 *Lubricate and install the C4 piston with the orifice at the 12 o'clock position toward the top of the case. Make sure the piston is fully seated.*

3 *Install the P1 ring gear. It should rest on the C3 backing plate thrust plates.*

4 *Make sure the P1 ring gear is fully seated, contacting the C3 thrust plates.*

5 *The number of steel and friction plates may vary with the application. To make it easier, install the same plate counts as were removed.*

6 *Install the C4 return springs with the springs facing up. Install a C4 steel plate.*

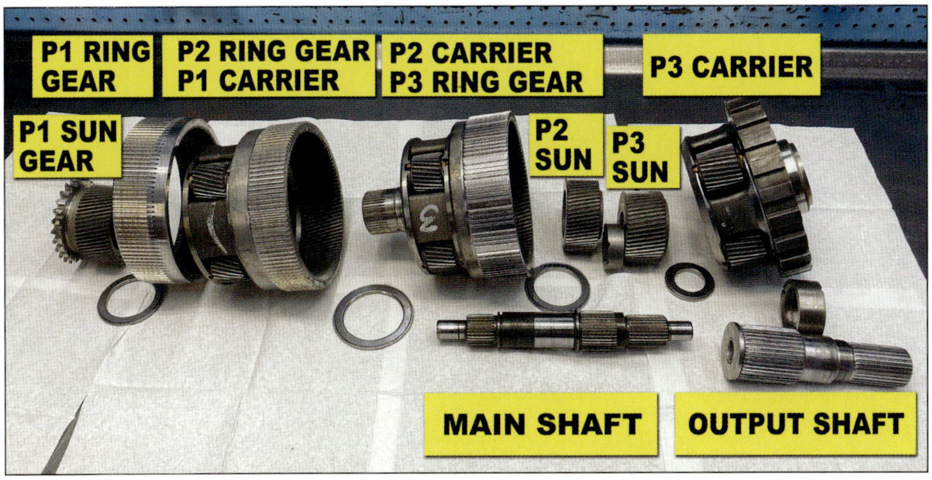

7 *The planetary stack up is very important, especially when it comes to the thrust bearings. The thrust bearings separate the various rotating components which then allows the components to rotate at different speeds and directions from one another.*

8 *Lubricate the area where the plastic spacer contacts the planetary.*

9 *Lubricate the spacer with Transjel. Install the spacer over the P1 carrier and onto the P2 ring gear.*

10 *Make sure the plastic spacer is fully installed.*

11 *The P1 sun/P2 carrier thrust bearing will be installed at a later time. Install the P1 carrier/P2 ring-gear planetary into the case with the carrier facing the P1 ring gear that was previously installed. Rotate the assembly to make sure it is fully engaged. The C4 return springs and one C4 steel clutch plate should have been previously installed.*

12 *Install a presoaked C4 friction disc. It should sit on the steel plate previously installed.*

13 *Install a C4 steel plate followed by a presoaked friction plate. Alternate friction and steel plate installation until all the plates are fully installed. Do not stack two friction plates together.*

14 *Install the C4 backing plate, lining it up with the case lugs.*

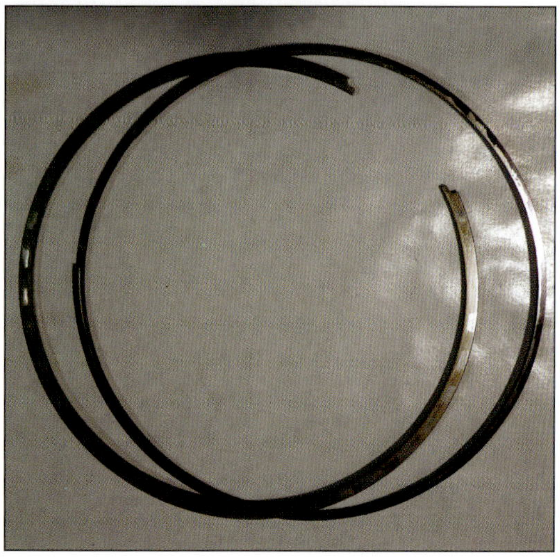

15 *Two snap/retaining rings are used to hold the C4 clutch in position in the case. One ring is thinner and larger in diameter, while the other is heavier and smaller in diameter.*

16 *Using a clutch compressor, such as J44530 or your hands, lightly compress the C4 return springs. Install the C4 large-diameter, thin snap/retaining ring into the groove in the case.*

17 *With the pack compressed, install the C4 smaller-diameter, heavier snap/retaining ring into the case with the opening 180 degrees from the outside ring. Make sure the rings are fully installed.*

18 *Look closely at the picture. Lubricate and install the P1 carrier thrust bearing. Install the bearing with the black race side up and the outer race side up. The inner-race side thrust bearing will face the planetary. Note that your bearing may not have a colored race.*

Depth Measurement	C5 Selective Plate Identification Number
1.393–1.412 inches (35.3–35.86 mm)	1
1.413–1.431 inches (35.87–36.36 mm)	2
1.432–1.467 inches (36.37–37.27 mm)	3

C5/Low-Reverse Clutch Assembly

Install the C5 backing plate into the case. The backing plate may have grooves in one side, both sides, or no grooves, depending on the build date. The C5 clutch is selective. Note that the C5 clutches and the P3 ring-gear design changes occurred starting with serial number 6310013648 (Indianapolis) or 6320002001(Baltimore), and the components are not designed for interchange.

If checking the clutch clearance on the C5 clutch, it is accomplished with a measurement. Make sure 0 coning is present in the plates or the pack will have to be compressed as part of the measurement. All of the steel plates have ID numbers, and the one that does not match all of the others is the selective plate. The selective plate is then removed from the stack up.

Install the C5 clutches into the case with two friction discs stacked together. This leaves a steel plate as the top plate. Compress the pack by using a weight or a compressor. Measure down from the rear of the case machined area to the top steel plate. Compare the depth measurement to the selective plate table and select the correct plate from the table.

Remove the C5 clutches from the case.

C5 Clutch Assembly

If the C5 backing plate is not installed, install it now. Install the P2 carrier/P3 ring gear and rotate the unit to engage the planetary teeth. Lubricate and install the P2 carrier/P3 ring-gear thrust bearing with the outside-diameter lip race side up. If the bearing has blue ink stamping, the blue stamping faces the carrier. Install a presoaked friction plate. Alternate between steel and friction plates until all the plates are installed (six friction plates and six steel plates). Do not stack two friction plates against each other. Otherwise, failure will occur. Typically, the selective plate will be the top steel plate.

Install the J44587 mainshaft holder or an equivalent tool into the PTO cover area. Rotate the P2 carrier/P3 ring gear so that it is fully engaged.

Mainshaft P2 and P3 Sun Gears

Install the P2 sun gear and sun-gear spacer onto the mainshaft. Install the completed mainshaft into the P2 carrier/P3 ring gear. Lubricate and align the P3 sun gear so that the flat side of the P3 sun gear is facing the spacer. Install it onto the mainshaft. Make sure the splines are fully engaged. Lubricate and install the P3 sun gear thrust bearing with the "blue ink" side up and the race with the inside-diameter lip facing up.

Reassembling the C5 Clutch

1 *The number of steel and friction plates may vary with the application. To make it easier, install the same plate counts as were removed.*

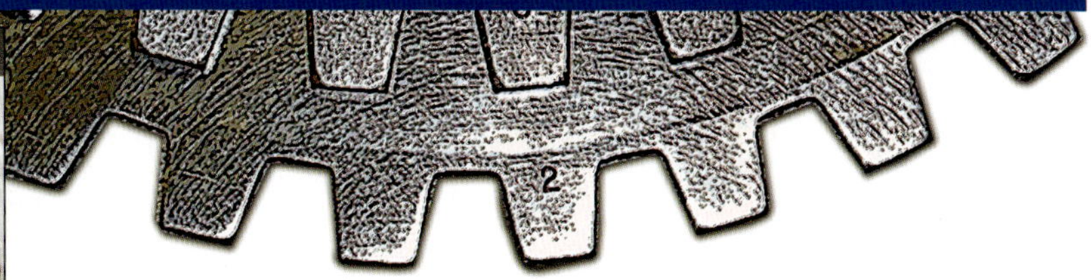

2 *The steel plates for the C5 clutch are stamped with number 1, 2, or 3, representing their thickness. Inspect all the steel plates. All of the plates will be stamped with the same number except one plate, which is the selective plate for that stack.*

3 *With the pack on the bench, stack two frictions together. This will ensure that a steel is on top for measuring purposes. Make sure the clutches have no warpage. Load the clutch pack by putting a weight across the pack, by using a clutch compressor, or by putting pressure with your free hand to take any clearance from the clutches. Measure to the top of the pack and compare the reading to the values in the text to determine which selective should be used. Remove the pack stack up and lay the clutch out with the selective chosen in order of assembly.*

4 *Install the C5 backing plate into the case.*

5 *Install the P2 carrier with the snout end down.*

6 *Rotate the carrier to engage it with the other planetary.*

7 *The P2 thrust bearing fits over a lip on the P2 carrier.*

8 *Look closely at the picture. Lubricate and install the P2 carrier thrust bearing with the side of the race with an outer lip facing up. If one race has a blue ink marking, the race side with the ink marking faces down.*

9 *Here, the P2 thrust bearing is properly installed.*

10 *If not previously installed, install the C5 backing plate. Install a presoaked C5 friction disc.*

11 *Install a C5 steel plate. Alternate the friction plate and steel plate installation until all the plates are fully installed. Do not stack two friction plates together.*

12 *Following the factory procedure, install J44587 or an equivalent to keep the mainshaft from falling out during installation. Keep in mind that if the order was reversed for component installation as described early in the chapter text, the tool will not be necessary, as the C1/C2 drum keeps the shaft from falling.*

13 *Install the P2 sun gear on the mainshaft.*

14 *Install the P2/P3 sun gear spacer on the mainshaft.*

15 *Install the mainshaft and rotate it to fully engage the components.*

16 *Install the P3 sun gear on the mainshaft with the flat side facing the spacer.*

17 *Lubricate and install the P3 sun gear thrust bearing into the P3 sun gear bearing pocket with the ink marks facing up and the race with the inner lip facing up.*

Install the Park Pawl and Linkage, C5 Return Springs, and Output Shaft

The park linkage, detent (rooster comb), shift seal, and shift shaft should have been previously installed. If not, install them now. Install the park linkage roller inside the linkage cam. Install the C5 clutch return springs with the springs facing up. Install the park pawl and pawl spring. Install the park pawl pin. Install the output shaft/P3 ring-gear assembly. Install the spacer and end-play shim if it is a 4x4.

Park Pawl and Related Components Installation

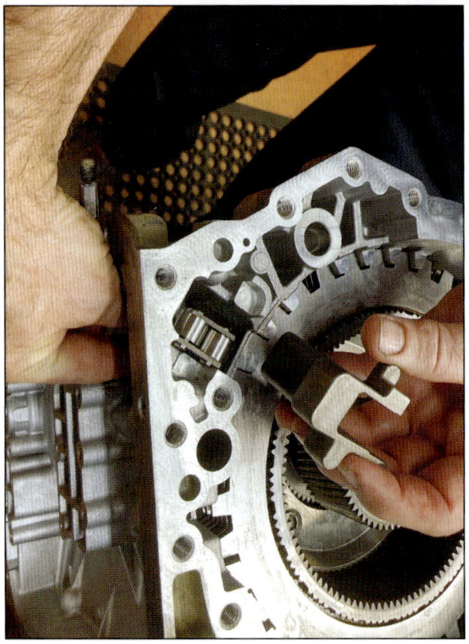

1 *Install the park cam and roller linkage.*

2 *The park linkage is shown here installed.*

3 *Install the C5 return springs with the springs facing up.*

4 *Install the pawl spring into the case and pawl.*

5 *Install the park pawl pin into the pawl and case.*

6 *Install the P3 carrier and output shaft. Rotate the components to fully engage them.*

7 *Install the spacer on the output shaft.*

8 *If the end play was correct during disassembly and no major components were replaced, it is likely safe to install the old end-play shim and finish assembling the unit. If major components were replaced, perform the end-play shim measurement prior to completing the assembly. On 2WD applications, the shim will be placed in the extension housing as outlined in the text.*

C5 Clutch Piston Installation

The C5 clutch piston is housed in the 4x4 adapter/extension housing. Prior to installing the piston, inspect the bearings and housing for wear, damage, and cracks, as outlined earlier. Replace any bearings that are damaged or worn. Replace the 4x4 adapter/extension housing if it is damaged or cracked. Cracks are common on 4x4 adapter applications.

If it is a 2WD application, inspect the speed-sensor tone ring for chips and damage, which are common on applications that have had bearing failure.

Install the two new seals on the C5 piston. The inner seal should be installed with the lip of the seal facing toward the 4x4 adapter/extension housing. Lubricate the seals and bore with transmission assembly lubricant or an equivalent. Install the piston into the bore.

Installing the C5 Clutch Piston

1 *The piston bore for the C5 clutch is located in the extension/4x4 adapter housing.*

2 *Make sure the seals are properly installed on the C5 piston. The inner seal is a lip design. The lip should face the direction of the piston housing bore when the piston is fully installed. Lubricate the seal with transmission assembly lube or an equivalent.*

3 *Install the C5 piston into the piston housing bore.*

4 *Make sure the piston is fully seated in the bore.*

Extension Housing and 4x4 Adapter Housing Installation

The bellhousing bolts are longer than the extension housing/adapter housing bolts. Intermixing bolts between the two locations can cause case damage.

4WD Applications

Install the housing gasket. Lubricate the bearings with transmission fluid. Install the output shaft spacer then the end-play shim onto the output shaft if not previously installed. Align the 4WD adapter housing with the case dowel pins and the park pawl pin. Install the 4WD adapter housing. Install 4 bolts and hand-tighten them evenly until the adapter housing is seated on the transmission case. Install the remaining 12 bolts and hand-tighten all the bolts. Tighten the bolts in a crossing pattern to 41 ft-lbs (56 Nm).

Install the output shaft ball bearing if it was previously removed. Install the bearing retaining ring with the beveled side facing up. Make sure the snap ring is fully seated.

Move the shift selector into Park. Install a new output-shaft nut onto the shaft using blue Loctite. Torque the 2009-and-earlier-design nut to 45–50 ft-lbs (61–68 Nm) and the late-design nut to 66 ft-lbs (90 Nm). Install the transmission vent if removed.

2WD Applications

Install the housing gasket. Lubricate the bearings with transmission fluid. Install the output speed-sensor tone wheel into the extension housing. The tone wheel lugs face the rear of the housing. Gently tap the housing needle bearing into the extension housing. Then, install the snap ring. Make sure the output shaft rotates. Install the extension housing over the output shaft. The housing will need to be aligned with the speed-sensor tone ring, case dowels, and park pawl pin. Install 4 bolts and hand-tighten the bolts evenly until the adapter housing is seated on the transmission case. Install the remaining 12 bolts and hand-tighten all the bolts. Tighten the bolts in a crossing pattern to 41 ft-lbs (56 Nm).

Install the end-play shim onto the output shaft. Install the output-shaft ball bearing onto the output shaft. Using the J24446 bearing driver or a piece of pipe, drive the bearing down into the housing until it is seated against the tone wheel. Install the output-bearing snap ring with the beveled side facing up. Make sure that the snap ring is fully seated. Install the output shaft seal into the extension housing using J43782 (without parking brake drum), J43783 (with parking brake drum), or equivalent tools. The seal should be installed to 0.179–0.211 inch (4.55–5.35 mm) or 1.222–1.256 inch (31.10–31.90 mm) with the parking brake drum below the face of the housing. Lubricate the seal surface with Transjel or automatic transmission fluid.

Lubricate and install the output-shaft yoke. Torque the retaining bolt to 91 ft-lbs (123 Nm).

Installing the Extension Housing/4x4 Adapter Housing

1 *Install the gasket followed by the adapter/extension housing. Carefully shift the housing to align the bearings, park pawl pin, and, on 2WD applications, the speed-sensor tone wheel. Make sure the housing is fully installed against the case and the gasket.*

2 *Install 4 outer bolts and hand-tighten. Install the other 12 bolts after the housing is fully seated. The extension/adapter housing bolts are a different length compared to the bellhousing bolts. Do not intermix the bolts from other locations. Otherwise, case damage can occur. Note the position of the bolts that use the copper washers.*

3 *Torque the adapter/extension housing bolts in a crossing pattern to 41 ft-lbs (56 Nm).*

4 *On the 4x4 application, install a new output shaft nut onto the shaft using blue Loctite. Torque the 2009-and-earlier-design nut to 45 to 50 ft-lbs (61–68 Nm) and the 2010-and-later-design nut to 66 ft-lbs (90 Nm).*

5 *Keep in mind that the socket required for the output shaft nut is based on the nut design.*

C1 and C2 Clutch Drum Installation

With the rear of the unit assembled, assembly of the front of the unit can begin. Rotate the case with the front of the unit facing up. Remove the J44587 holding tool. Install the P1 sun-gear thrust bearing into the P1 sun gear with the blue-inked side facing the P1 carrier race with the inside-diameter lip up. Retain the bearing with Transjel.

Install the C1/C2 clutch drum and input shaft into the transmission. Make sure the sun-gear bearing does not fall out of place. Rotate the shaft to make sure it is fully engaged. Make sure the PTO gear/speed-sensor tone wheel is visible through the speed-sensor hole.

Installing the C1/C2 Clutch Drum

1 *Rotate the case and remove the mainshaft holding tool.*

2 *Install the P1 sun-gear thrust bearing with the blue-inked side facing away from the P1 sun gear. The race with the inner lip is facing away from the sun gear. You can either install the bearing into the sun-gear pocket and retain it with Transjel or install it onto the carrier and retain it with Transjel.*

3 *As with all other thrust bearings, double-check the direction that the bearing is installed once it is in the sun-gear bearing pocket.*

4 *Double-check to make sure that all of the input shaft seal rings were installed. Rotate the C1/C2 clutch drum to make sure that it is fully installed.*

5 *Visually check for proper position by looking for the PTO gear/speed-sensor tone wheel, which should be visible through the speed-sensor case hole.*

Bellhousing and Pump Installation

Install the pump separator plate gasket onto the case. Lubricate the inside diameter of the stator support bore with Transjel. Make sure the three seal rings were previously installed into the seal ring grooves on the bottom of the stator support. Lubricate the stator support seal rings with Transjel. Install the previously completed pump and separator plate assembly onto the case. Make sure the separator plate is seated against the case gasket.

Install the bellhousing gasket onto the pump separator plate. Make sure the pump/bellhousing O-ring seal was previously installed. Installing two M10x1.5 guide pins will help with bellhousing alignment. Install the bellhousing and make sure it is fully seated. Install the 14 bellhousing bolts. The 2 bottom bellhousing-to-case bolts will use copper washers, while the 6 outside bellhousing bolts are different lengths than the other bolts. Install the 10 inner bolts that are equipped with rubber seals.

The bellhousing pump bolts and bellhousing bolts are longer than the extension-housing/adapter-housing bolts. Installing the incorrect bolts can cause case damage.

Torque the inner bellhousing-to-pump bolts to 42 ft-lbs (56 Nm) using a crossing pattern. Torque the bellhousing-to-case bolts to 42 ft-lbs (56 Nm) using a crossing pattern.

Install a new O-ring on the line-pressure plug located next to the spin-on oil filter. Torque the plug to 106 in-lbs (12 Nm).

Install new cooler-line coupler seals. Install/tighten the cooler-line coupler into the bellhousing threaded fitting.

TECH TIP

Check Alignment

If the parts are not fully seated, check for the P3 sun gear, P3 sun-gear spacer, sun-gear thrust bearings, or a seal ring that may be misaligned. Do not force the pump and support plate into position. ■

Installing the Bellhousing and Pump

1 *Lubricate the inside diameter of the pump/stator support as well as the needle bearing on the back of the support.*

2 *Install the case gasket. The rebuild should have been previously completed of the pump/channel plate assembly. Make sure the three seals were installed on the bottom of the stator support. Install the pump/channel plate assembly onto the case. Make sure it fully seats against the gasket. If not, something is out of position, such as a thrust bearing or seal ring. Do not force the assembly into position.*

3 *If not previously installed, install the stator support seals and lubricate them with Transjel.*

4 Make sure the two seals are properly installed in the grooves. Make sure the pump/bellhousing seal is properly installed. Lubricate all three seals with Transjel.

5 Install new seals on the pump bolts. Make sure all the bolts are cleaned and ready for installation.

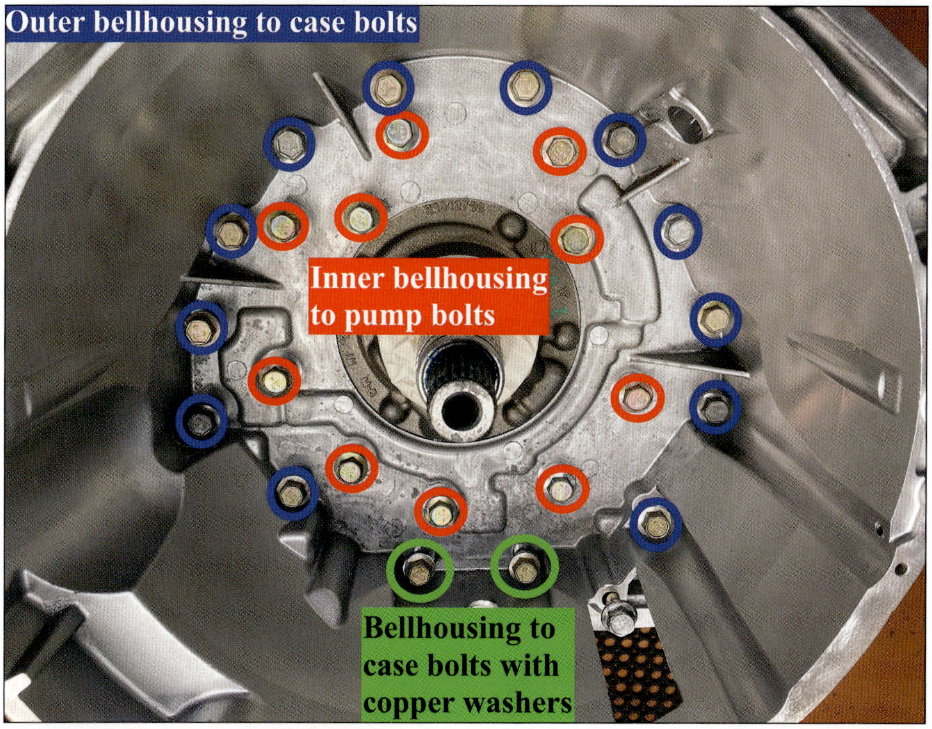

6 Install the bellhousing-to-pump/channel plate gasket onto the channel plate. Carefully lower the bellhousing into position on the pump. Make sure it is fully seated on the channel plate and the gasket. Install the bolts with seals into the inside-diameter row of holes. The other bolts fit into the outside-diameter row of holes. Install copper washers on the two bottom bolts. Hand-tighten the bolts.

7 An update was made due to leakage issues. The bottom two bolts should be equipped with copper washers.

8 Six bolts are used to clamp the outside of the bellhousing to the case. Install the bolts.

9 ***Torque all bellhousing-to-case and bellhousing bolts to 42 ft-lbs (56 Nm), using an inside-to-outside crossing pattern. Install a new seal on the line pressure plug and torque to 106 inch-pounds (12 Nm).***

10 ***Install the cooler-line fittings into the bellhousing.***

Aftermarket End Play Measurement

With the unit assembled, rotate the case so that the input/turbine shaft is facing up. Mount a dial indicator to the end of the input shaft. Using a long screwdriver placed at the base of the C1/C2 drum, pry the drum upward and read the indicator. Specifications should be 0.011–0.061 inch (0.279–1.549 mm).

Care must be taken not to damage the speed-sensor tone wheel. The aftermarket method of determining the correct shim is simple. Measure the end play with a dial indicator. Determine how far off from specifications the measured end play is. Install a shim that will address the amount of difference between the measured end play and the factory specifications. Recheck your end play.

Factory End Play Measurement to Determine Shim Thickness

If end play was checked and found to be within specifications (0.011–0.061 inch/0.279–1.549 mm), this process will not need to be performed. If the end play was incorrect, two methods can be used to select the correct shim: the factory method and the aftermarket method. If the end play needs to be changed, the adapter/extension housing will need to be taken back off to set the end play.

Perform the following steps to take the measurement for the 4x4 factory method:

- Remove the output-shaft ball bearing from the adapter housing. Remove the end-play shim. Install the 4x4 adapter housing and the gasket. With the rear of the case facing up, measure from the 4x4 adapter rear face (where the transfer case bolts on) to the output shaft spacer (Dimension A).
- Measure from the adapter rear face to the bottom snap/retaining ring in the housing (Dimension B).
- Subtract Dimension A from Dimension B; this value becomes Dimension C. Select the correct shim by using the Dimension C measurement from the table.

Perform the following steps to make the measurement for the 2WD factory method:

- Remove the output-shaft ball bearing from the extension housing. Remove the end-play shim. Install the extension housing and the gasket. With the rear of the case facing up, measure from the rear housing face to the speed-sensor tone ring (Dimension A).
- Measure from the rear housing face to the bottom snap/retaining ring in the housing (Dimension B).
- Subtract Dimension A from Dimension B. This value becomes Dimension C. Select the correct shim by using the Dimension C measurement from the table.

Dimension C (Inches)	Dimension C (mm)	Number of Holes in Shim for ID	Shim Thickness
0.0397–0.0466 inch	1.0081–1.184 mm	0	0.0096–0.0116 inch
0.0467–0.0557 inch	1.185–1.414 mm	1	0.0187–0.0207 inch
0.0557–0.0647 inch	1.415–1.644 mm	2	0.0278–0.0297 inch
0.0648–0.0738 inch	1.645–1.874 mm	3	0.0368–0.0388 inch
0.0738–0.0828 inch	1.875–2.104 mm	4	0.0459–0.0478 inch
0.0829–0.0919 inch	2.105–2.334 mm	5	0.0549–0.0569 inch
0.0919–0.0988 inch	2.335–2.5015 mm	6	0.0640–0.0659 inch

Mount a dial indicator to the end of the input shaft. Using a screwdriver, pry the C1/C2 drum vertically. Do not push against the speed-sensor tone wheel or the PTO gear.

End-play reading specifications are 0.011–0.061 inches (0.279–1.549 mm).

Air Testing

Once the transmission has been completed, prior to installing the valve body, the clutches can be air tested to make sure that a seal was not damaged during installation. Using shop air pressure regulated to 50 psi, apply air pressure to the case passages for the clutch to be tested. If air testing a clutch, the clutch should make a "thump" type of noise. If testing a compensator/clutch dam circuit, simply listen for an excessive air leak. If the clutches and compensator circuits appear to be working, it is now ready for the valve body installation, which is covered in Chapter 4.

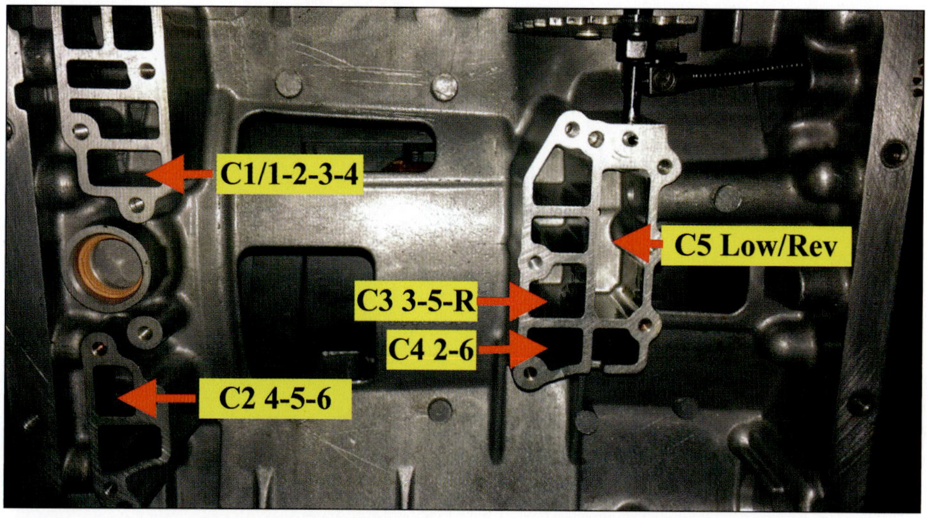

Clutches can be air tested via the passages listed. Using 50 psi of air pressure, apply air to the clutch and listen for the clutch thump as it applies. On early-model applications, do not air test the C1 1-2-3-4 clutch, as it can be misleading due to the backflow valve.

If working with an early pump with a C1/1-2-3-4 backfill valve, General Motors/Allison recommend against air testing the C1/1-2-3-4 clutch, as the results can easily be misconstrued.

Once the air test is complete, the valve body can be installed as outlined in Chapter 4.

Lubricate the seal and install each of the speed sensors.

Speed Sensor Installation

After testing/inspection or replacing the speed sensors, they can now be installed. Lubricate the sensor O-ring seal and install the sensors. The sensor retaining bolts are torqued to 106 in-lbs (12 Nm).

Do not rotate the sensors in their brackets. Otherwise, sensor operation may be affected.

Install the filter magnet, lubricate the filter seal with transmission fluid, and install the spin-on filter.

Spin-on Oil Filter Installation

Install the spin-on filter magnet. Lubricate the new filter seal with transmission fluid. Install the spin-on filter.

PTO Cover Installation

Install new gaskets and the PTO cover. Torque the bolts to 29–33 ft-lbs (40–45 Nm).

Range Sensor Installation

If used, refer to the range sensor installation procedure in Chapter 2.

Install the gaskets and PTO covers. Torque the bolts to 29–33 ft-lbs (40–45 Nm).

Electronic Control System

The electronic control system is the heart of the Allison transmission. Issues with the vehicle's electrical system or the transmission electronic control system can and will cause issues with transmission operation.

Thoroughly checking the battery, TCM, transmission power, and grounds are critical to isolating a transmission issue on these applications. Testing of the transmission components can help to isolate transmission component electrical issues.

Scan testing the components to check their operation prior to condemning the transmission is always wise. If issues are found during the scan testing, bench testing of the component may help to isolate an electrical component failure.

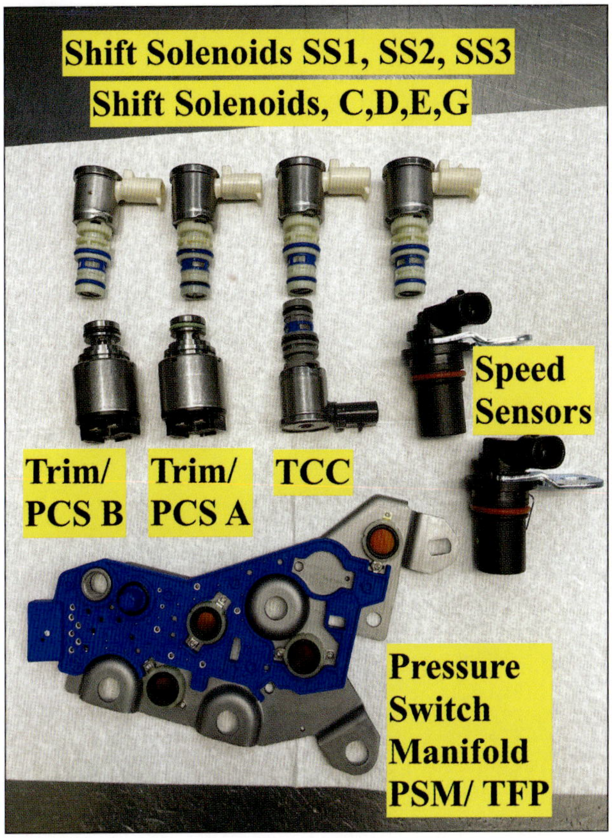

Bench Testing Components

Bench testing of the electrical components is simply another way to confirm a diagnosis that was made with the scan tool. Bench testing is generally conducted with a digital volt ohmmeter (DVOM).

The Allison applications use multiple electrical components. The number of solenoids and speed sensors will depend on the year and the application. Components for a 2005 application are shown.

Speed Sensors

Many technicians choose to install new speed sensors as part of the overhaul process. Allison applications use two different speed-sensor designs, depending on the year: variable reluctance magnetic

Two types of speed-sensor designs have been used in the Allison applications: the magnetic style and the magneto resistive Hall-effect type. If you are replacing the sensor, it is important to replace it with the same design. Otherwise, the vehicle harness connector will not connect to the sensor because they are not interchangeable. In addition, it is important that the bracket not be rotated in relation to the sensor. Otherwise, sensor operational issues can occur.

Magnetic speed sensors can be bench tested with an ohmmeter. Value should measure between 1,930 and 4,260 ohms, depending on temperature.

IMS Pin and Circuit Layout		
IMS Pin	**Wire Color, Circuit #**	**Scan Tool IMS Range Pin Display**
A	BK/WH, 1995	P/N
B	TN/WH, 776	P
C	YE/BK, 771	A
D	PK/BK, 772	B
E	YE/BK, 773	C
F	BK, 407	Ground

sensors or magneto resistive/Hall effect sensors. A magnetic sensor produces an AC voltage/sine wave output, whereas the Hall sensors produce a square wave as their output. This means the sensor designs cannot be interchanged. Either sensor can be tested with a lab scope prior to the transmission being removed from the vehicle.

Magnetic-type sensor resistance can be bench tested using an ohmmeter. The sensors have two terminals. Connect the meter leads to the terminals and read the resistance. It should be 1,930 to 4,260 ohms, depending on temperature.

The speed sensors have a mounting bracket attached to the sensor. Do not rotate the bracket in relation to the sensor. Changing the bracket position may affect the sensor operation.

The speed-sensor wiring has twisted pairs for EMI protection. If a wiring repair is performed, the wiring must be twisted at a rate of nine revolutions per foot. If a connector or a terminal issue is present, GM sells both harness terminals as well as harness pigtails.

2006-and-Later Applications

Diagnosis of the IMS can be accomplished with a scan tool prior to transmission disassembly by monitoring the IMS values outlined in Chapter 2. If the values do not match the table, either the IMS or the TCM is likely defective. The IMS can be bench tested using an ohmmeter, but that takes a lot more effort.

To bench test the IMS, use an ohmmeter. Bench testing should be conducted with the IMS and valve body/detent system fully installed in the transmission. Disconnect the sensor connector from the harness. Using a terminal probing tool or a paper clip, touch the ohmmeter to the appropriate IMS pins. Move the shift lever located on the driver's side of the transmission through the ranges. As the shifter is moved, the meter should display a resistance reading of less than 10 ohms (grounded) or OL (open circuit), depending on which range was selected.

While moving through the ranges, the reading will show some ranges with continuity while other ranges will indicate and open circuit (OL). All we are looking for is that the switch is capable of closing and opening. If the meter stays locked on OL or if it shows continuity in every range, the IMS is faulty. If the first circuit tests good, move to the other circuits and repeat the process.

- Connect one meter lead to Pin C and the other to Pin F on the IMS.
- Connect one meter lead to Pin D and the other to Pin F on the IMS.
- Connect one meter lead to Pin E and the other to Pin F on the IMS.
- Connect one meter lead to Pin B and the other to Pin A on the IMS.

IMS Typical Scan Tool Values				
Range	**A**	**B**	**C**	**P**
P	Ground	Open	Open	Ground
R Transitional	Ground	Ground	Open	Ground
R	Ground	Ground	Open	Open
N	Open	Open	Open	Ground
D Transitional	Open	Ground	Ground	Ground
D	Open	Ground	Ground	Open
*M	Ground	Ground	Ground	Ground
D1 Transitional	Ground	Open	Ground	Ground
1	Ground	Open	Ground	Open

For 2006-and-later applications, use an internal mode switch (IMS). Prior to valve body installation, the IMS needs to be installed.

The shift shaft holds the IMS in position. The IMS is retained with a bolt and a dowel pin. Prior to installation, the shift-shaft seal should have been replaced, which is outlined in Chapter 3.

Bench testing should be conducted prior to removal of the valve body and detent spring with the IMS installed in the transmission. Using an ohmmeter, connect between the appropriate pins and rotate the shift shaft through each range. The value should indicate either continuity or an open circuit, depending on the range and the pins selected for testing. Testing the IMS with a scan tool prior to transmission removal as outlined in Chapter 2 is simpler and faster.

To replace the IMS, remove the electrical connector and remove the valve body. Remove the IMS Torx 27 bolt. Remove the spherical pin from the case using a pair of pliers while being careful not to damage the case. Remove the shift shaft and IMS. For installation, reverse the removal process. The Torx bolt is coated with Loctite, so the bolt either needs to be recoated or replaced with a new bolt, which is included in some gasket kits.

PSM Switch and TFT Testing and Replacement

The pressure switch manifold (PSM), also known as a PSA or TFP, and transmission fluid temperature (TFT) sensor are one assembly. A scan tool can be used to test the PSM and TFT operation prior to transmission removal or after the transmission is back in the vehicle.

An ohmmeter can be used to bench test the PSM and the TFT. Remove the PSM/TFT assembly from the transmission valve body. Disconnect the wiring connector. Connect the ohmmeter to the following pins:

- Connect one meter lead to PSM Pin A and the other to the metal body of the PSM.
- Connect one meter lead to PSM Pin B and the other to the metal body of the PSM.
- Connect one meter lead to PSM Pin C and the other to the metal body of the PSM.
- Connect one meter lead to PSM Pin D and the other to the metal body of the PSM.

Using a pencil eraser, press on the switch membrane. The meter should measure less than 10 ohms or OL as the membrane is pressed/released if the switch is good. Repeat for each switch. If a switch is found to be faulty, the PSM will require replacement.

Connect one meter lead to PSM Pin E and the other to Pin F of the PSM to test the TFT.

PSM Pin and Circuit Layout

PSM Pin	Pin, Function	Wire Color, Circuit Number
A	Sw1, Shift valve 1	Org, 1224
B	Sw2, Shift valve 2	WH, 1225
C	Sw3, Shift valve 3	GY, 1226
D	Sw4, Reverse	BN, 1530
E	TFT Signal	TN, 1227
F	Ref Low, Ground	BK, 407

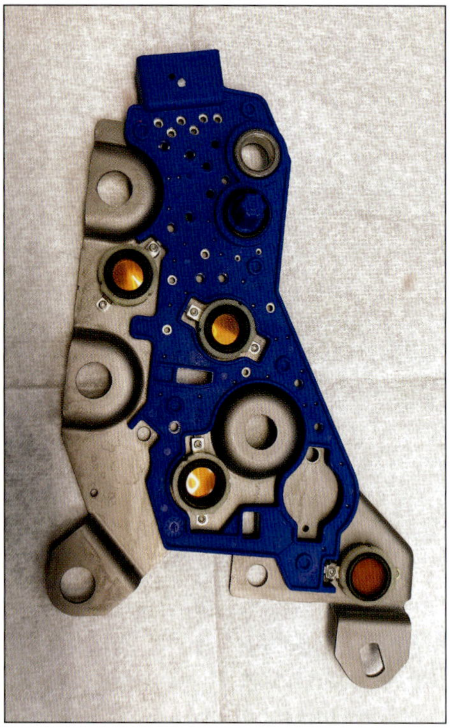

The PSM is bolted to the valve body and uses a series of hydraulic switches to monitor the operation of the shift valves and solenoids. The PSM can be bench tested if one desires by using an ohmmeter and a pencil with an eraser on its end. With the ohmmeter probing the appropriate pins as outlined in the text, press and release the switch membranes with the pencil eraser. Each switch should indicate continuity or open, depending on the switch position. The PSM also houses the TFT. With the ohmmeter connected across the appropriate pins, check the resistance of the sensor, which will vary based on ambient temperature. Testing the PSM with a scan tool prior to transmission removal as outlined in Chapter 2 is simpler and faster.

The reading will depend on the ambient temperature. At 70°F, the sensor will register between 3,360 and 3,600 ohms. If the sensor has an issue, the PSM will need to be replaced.

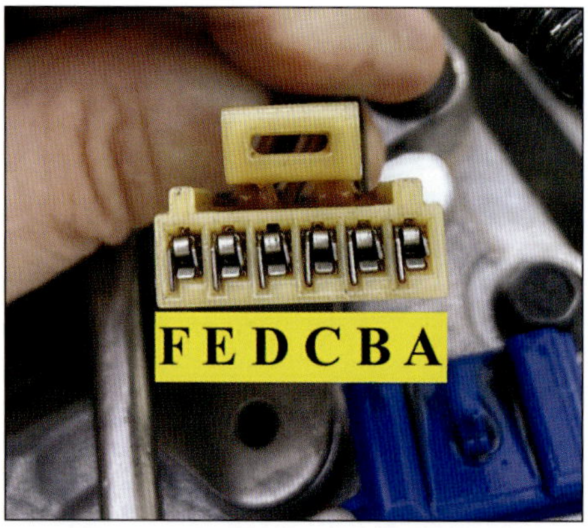

The PSM is connected to the TCM via the transmission electrical harness. The pins of the harness should be inspected for the proper pin tension. If a pin is found to be loose, it is suggested to simply update the harness.

Valve Body Service

The valve body is the brains of the hydraulic system on all Allison transmissions. The valve body houses the solenoids and the valves that are used to control the clutches within the transmission. A properly operating valve body is critical to a properly operating transmission.

Valve Body Identification

When servicing or replacing the valve body, it is important to understand that there are several valve body designs.

Valve Body Designs	
Year Range	**Design**
1999–2003	5-speed, one tube on the bottom and six solenoids
2004–2005	5-speed, one tube on the bottom and seven solenoids
2006–2009	6-speed, two tubes on the bottom
2010–2019	6-speed, no tubes on the bottom

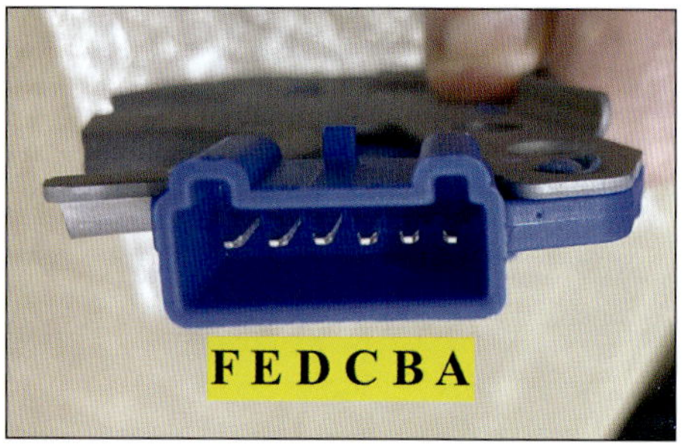

Connect the ohmmeter to the appropriate pins as is outlined in the text.

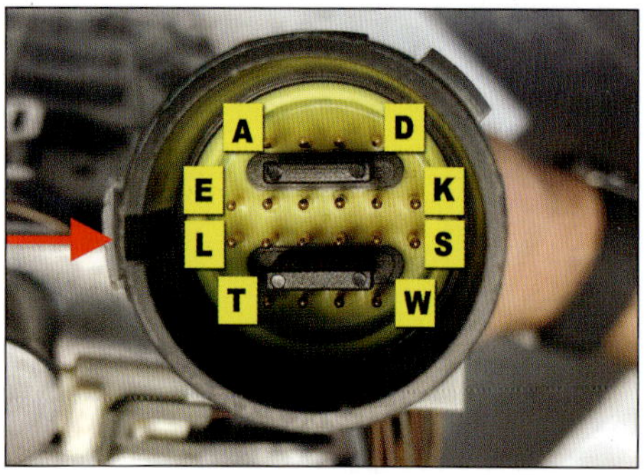

These are the case harness pass-through connector pin locations. Keep in mind that the harness part number varies based on the year of the transmission because the number of pins used and their function varies based on the year and application.

The vehicle side of the harness pin locations show the positioning lug location, which needs to be aligned with the harness side connector slot to allow the harness to be connected. Keep in mind that the vehicle harness connector varies based on the year of the transmission because of the pins used. Their use varies based on the year and application.

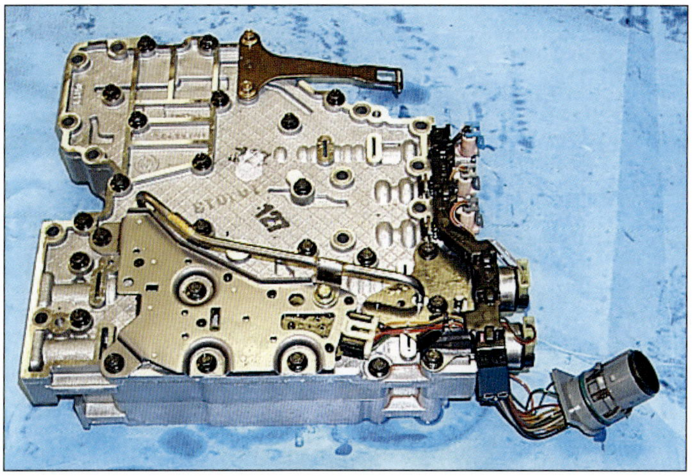

This valve body has six solenoids and one pipe on the bottom side. It is used on the 1999–2003 5-speed applications.

This valve body uses an additional solenoid located in a bolt-on auxiliary valve body for line pressure control: solenoid G. This application has seven solenoids and one pipe on the bottom side. It is used on the 2004–2005 5-speed applications.

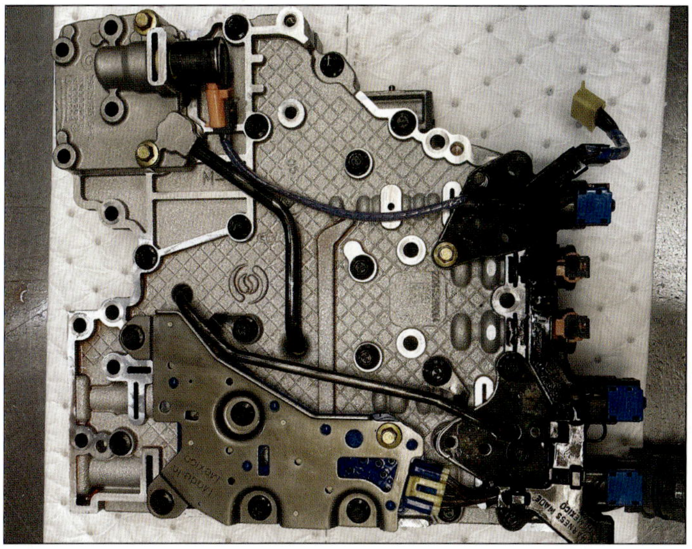

This valve body was introduced for the 2006–2009 6-speed application. It uses seven solenoids and two pipes on the bottom side.

Used with the late-model 6-speed applications, the 2010–2019 valve body uses seven solenoids. They are housed in the valve body. The pressure-control solenoid is a true PCS-design solenoid, providing variable line pressure control. The line pressure PCS was moved into the valve body and the auxiliary valve body was eliminated. No pipes are used.

Valve Body Disassembly

Cleanliness is the most important attribute to have when it comes to servicing the valving in the valve body and pump. Flip the valve body over and allow the fluid to drain.

Using brake cleaner or solvent, spray off the valve-body castings. Air dry the castings. This will make the valve body/pump valve service much more pleasant.

The valves are held in position with retainers and clips, so a small screwdriver, picks, and a small pair of needle-nose pliers are needed to help with disassembly and reassembly of the valve body. Make sure to wear safety glasses. Prepare a clean surface

Common Valve Body Issues

The 2009-and-earlier applications have issues with Shift Valve E, which is also called Shift Valve 3 on some model years. The valve-sticking problem is generally intermittent, leading to a lot of frustration, as the TCM typically sets a PSM DTC of P0872, forcing the transmission into limp mode for the duration of the key cycle.

All of the shift valves are very long, which leads to issues with the valves sticking. Many times, the symptom is temperature sensitive, which means the concern will only happen when the transmission is operating within a specific temperature range. Keep the fluid and filters changed, as any type of contamination can cause shift-valve issues.

Shift valve F/TCC wear can lead to TCC-related issues on 2002–2004 applications. TCC slip/shudder/surge issues and the possible P0741 TCC slippage DTC can set. This can lead to the transmission to overheat, as TCC operation is critical for fluid temperature control.

Warped valve-body castings can lead to cross leakage between circuits. The symptom varies, depending on the location of the leakage.

Sticking solenoids can be an issue. On high-mileage units, it is common to have DTCs set that relate directly to solenoid operation. Many times, this is due to mechanical issues within the solenoid.

TECH TIP — Safety

Just like when working on the other portions of the transmission, wear disposable gloves, safety glasses, and a mask for protection from the solvents used to clean the parts. ■

on your workbench where the components can be laid out in the order they were removed.

Depress the valve to remove, remove the retainer holding the valve in, and remove the valvetrain (valve, spring, and end plug). Tipping the valve body on end and lightly tapping it on the workbench may help to get the valves to move in the bore. If needed, use a pick to lightly push on the edge of a valve land to get the valve to move. In some instances, small needle-nose pliers can be used to grab the end of a valve plunger to remove the valve. Do not grab the valve land, as damage can occur. Be really careful not to damage a valve land or the valve bore when removing the valves.

The valve body and its valves are the heart of the hydraulic system in today's automatic transmissions. Valves are used to control how much pressure each component receives as well as when and where that pressure will travel within the transmission. To operate correctly, the valves need to have a specific clearance between the valve and its bore. Typically, the manufacturer will run a valve-to-bore clearance between 0.0006 and 0.0016 inch (0.0127 and 0.040 mm). In comparison, a human hair is approximately 0.0034 inch (0.086 mm), and a sheet of paper is about 0.0045 inch (0.114 mm).

If the clearance is too tight, the valve may stick. If the clearance is too loose, valve leakage may occur. Valve issues can result in symptoms that include a transmission failing to make a shift, flares, bumps, slippage, tie-up, and clutch-damage issues.

Inspect the valves for burrs/nicks and wear. Valve wear is typically due to valve side loading, which occurs on many valve bodies due to the valve body pressures exerting more force on one side of a land than on the other side of the land. This is generally due to the design of the castings. Spring pressure also has an effect on valve side loading, as the spring may be exerting side load pressure rather than just fore and aft pressure on the valve. The use of PWM-design solenoids as well as poor-quality casting materials also lead to accelerated valve and bore wear in today's transmissions.

In addition to valve wear, the valve bores can also wear. This is typically due to the same forces that can cause valve wear. Beyond visual inspection, the valves and bores can be inspected by using any of the following methods:

- Vacuum testing
- Light testing
- Air testing
- Wiggle testing
- Bore/valve measurements
- Sag/deflection measurements

Vacuum testing is the most effective form of valve-wear testing, but it requires a vacuum-test tool that is not generally used except by a transmission repair shop. Light and wiggle testing are the most common processes used by the average technician.

Light testing typically uses a small flashlight. The clean valve is installed into the clean bore with the valves in their normal resting position. Place the light onto the valve body casting with light facing the side of the valve land you want to inspect. Look at the other side of the valve land for any light escaping the land. If light can be seen, the valve/bore are worn.

The wiggle test is just as the name indicates. The valve is placed into the bore in the position it normally rides. Wiggle the valve sideways and up/down and note the amount of movement.

Measure the valve-body castings for flatness using a straightedge. Flat sanding an Allison valve body is a common service procedure, as 2009-and-earlier OEM applications do not use spacer-plate gaskets.

1000 and 2000 Valve Function

The key to diagnosing the Allison hydraulic operation is to understand that unlike many other transmissions, most solenoids and valves serve multiple functions. In other words, when we are talking about the apply or release of a clutch, more than one solenoid and more than one valve are typically responsible for clutch operation. In some gears, the pressure for a clutch is controlled by as many as three shift solenoids, three shift valves, and a trim/pressure-control solenoid.

Multiple component names are listed below for the same valves and solenoids, depending on the year of the transmission.

Oil-Pump Valves

The oil pump acts as the heart of the transmission's hydraulic system. Multiple valves are housed within the oil-pump assembly, and they are used to control various functions, such as the pressure and torque converter clutch (TCC).

Pressure Regulator

The pressure regulator is responsible for controlling the transmission pressures. The regulator valve receives supply oil from the oil pump. The valve regulates that flow, and its output becomes the transmission line pressure. Line pressure is used to apply the clutches as well as to feed other regulator valves within the transmission, which then reregulates the pressure for several functions, including the torque converter and cooler.

C1 1-2-3-4 Clutch Backfill

This provides a rapid release of the C1 clutch. This valve is no longer used on late-model applications.

Converter Relief and Lubrication Regulator

The converter relief valve regulates the torque converter pressure when the TCC is off. This prevents damage to the converter and cooler.

The lubrication-regulator valve regulates the flow/pressure entering the transmission lubrication system.

Converter Flow Control

This valve is controlled by the SSF/TCC solenoid. When the solenoid is turned off, the valve allows fluid to travel to the front side of the TCC pressure plate, releasing the TCC. When the solenoid is turned on, the valve will reverse flow, allowing the pressure plate to make contact with the torque converter cover, applying the TCC.

Keep in mind the solenoid is PWM controlled, so TCC apply should be smooth. Unlike GM EC3 converter designs, the 1000 and 2000 TCC should fully lock up when the TCC is applied.

In addition to applying and releasing the TCC, the valve also controls cooler flow.

Valve Body Valves

The valve body is the "brains" of the transmission hydraulic system. The majority of the valves used in the Allison applications are housed in the valve body. Issues with valve or solenoid operation affect the operation of the transmission.

PCS1, PCS A, and Trim A

The trim/PCS valves control how aggressive the clutch apply and release are. The Trim A valves control the flow to Shift Valve D. Trim A is controlled by a normally closed PCS/Trim A solenoid. As the TCM changes the solenoid duty cycle, the solenoid changes the position of the valve, which affects the hydraulic pressure in the circuit.

PCS2, PCS B, and Trim B

The trim/PCS valves control how aggressive the clutch apply and release are. The Trim B valves control the flow to Shift Valve C. Trim B is controlled by a normally open PCS/Trim B solenoid. As the TCM changes the solenoid duty cycle, the solenoid changes the position of the valve that affects the hydraulic pressure in the circuit.

Shift Valve C and Shift Valve 1

The shift valve controls the flow of fluid to the clutch, which controls the apply or release of the clutch. Shift Valve C controls the pressure to the C5 and C2 clutches. Shift Valve C is controlled by Shift Solenoid C (SSC/SS1).

Shift Valve D and Shift Valve 2

The shift valve controls the flow of fluid to the clutch, which controls the apply or release of the clutch. Shift Valve D controls the pressure to the C2, C3, C4, and C5 clutches.

Shift Valve D is controlled by Shift Solenoid D (SSD/SS2).

Shift Valve E and Shift Valve 3

The shift valve controls the flow of fluid to the clutch, which controls the apply or release of the clutch. Shift Valve E controls the pressure to the C1, C2, and C4 clutches. Shift Valve E is controlled by Shift Solenoid E (SSE/SS3).

TCC Flow Control

The TCC valve operates the torque converter and torque-converter clutch. It also controls the flow to the cooler and lubrication circuit. The TCC valve is controlled by the TCC solenoid and SSF/TCC solenoid.

TECH TIP

SVE/SV3 Valve

The SVE/SV3 valve is a major problem in the 1000- and 2000-series applications. The valve tends to intermittently stick, leading to DTCs and transmission operational issues. ■

Control Main Relief and Control Main

These valves regulate the pressure available to feed the Trim/PCS solenoids and shift valves. If issues occur with either of these valves, shifts and shift feel will be affected.

Exhaust Backfill

Also called an exhaust pressure regulator on early applications, this valve controls the release rate of several clutches during shifts.

Manual Valve

The manual valve is controlled by the driver through the use of the shift lever. Unlike many other transmissions, the manual valve routes pressure for some clutches through the valve.

Valve Body Assembly

The assembly of the valve body is the reverse of the disassembly. Once the valve body has been cleaned and inspected, the valves/springs can be lubricated and reinstalled into their correct bores. Lubricate the bores and valves with clean transmission fluid. Insert the valves/springs in their

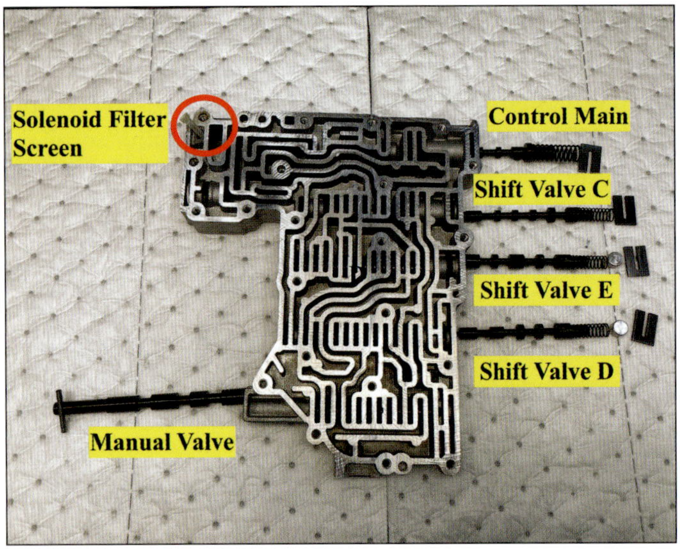

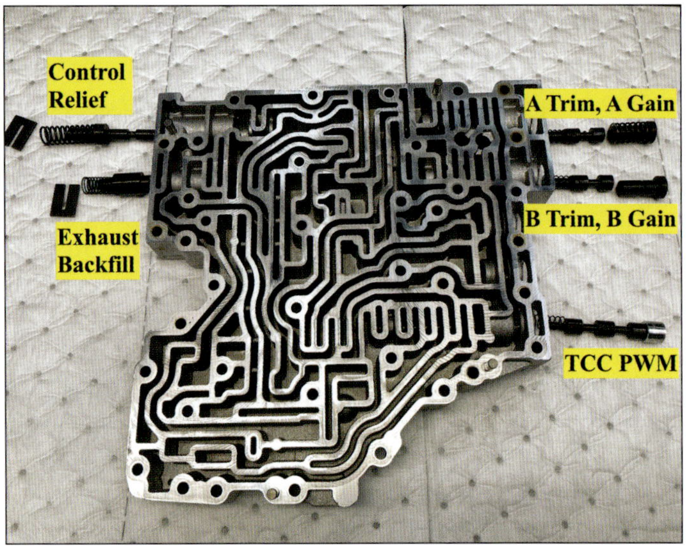

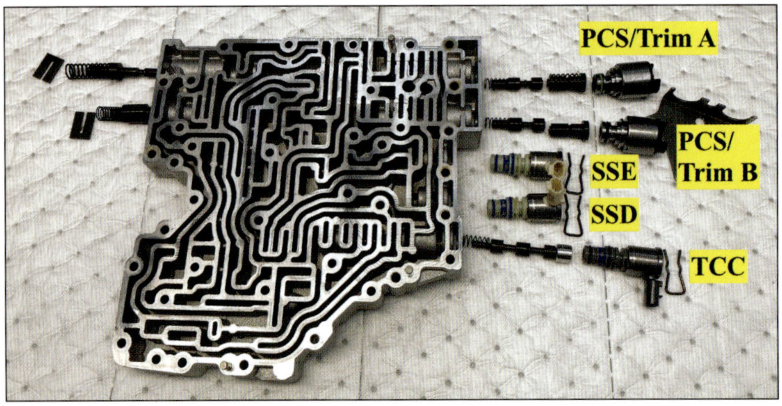

This is a 2005 shift valve body valve, which is a 5-speed with one transfer tube on the bottom and seven solenoids. The seventh solenoid is housed in the auxiliary valve body that is bolted onto the main valve body assembly.

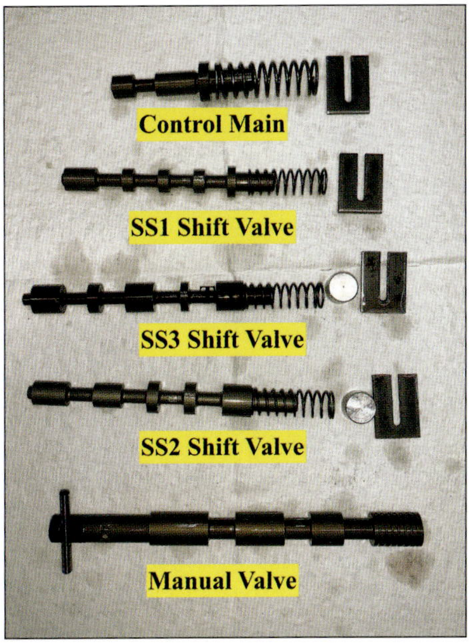

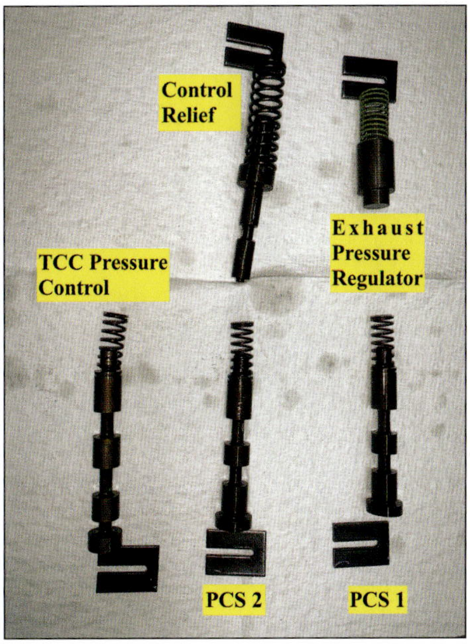

The 2010–2019 shift valve body components have a 6-speed application and no transfer tubes used on the valve body. A 2014 application is shown.

Solenoid accumulators level out the pressure pulsations coming from the solenoids. Solenoid accumulator and accumulator bore wear is common and must be checked whenever the valve body is apart. The number of accumulators vary with the valve-body design. A 2014 application is shown.

Multiple design spacer plates have been used. Early-model plates did not use gaskets, while later applications used them. If the spacer plate requires replacement, it must be replaced with the correct plate. Otherwise, operational issues will occur. A 2005 plate is shown.

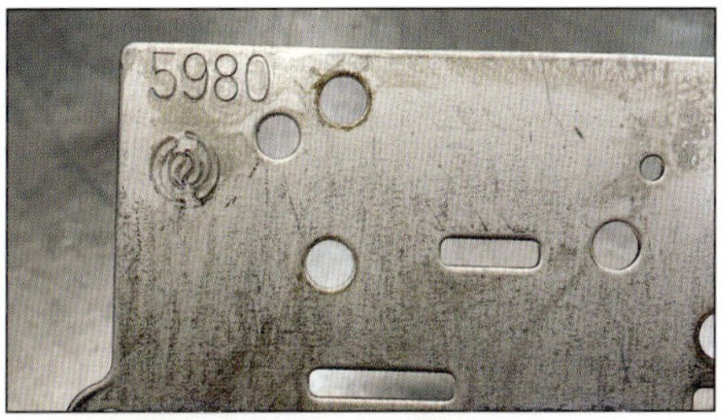

The spacer plate has a number stamped into the corner of the plate for identification purposes. A 2014 plate is shown.

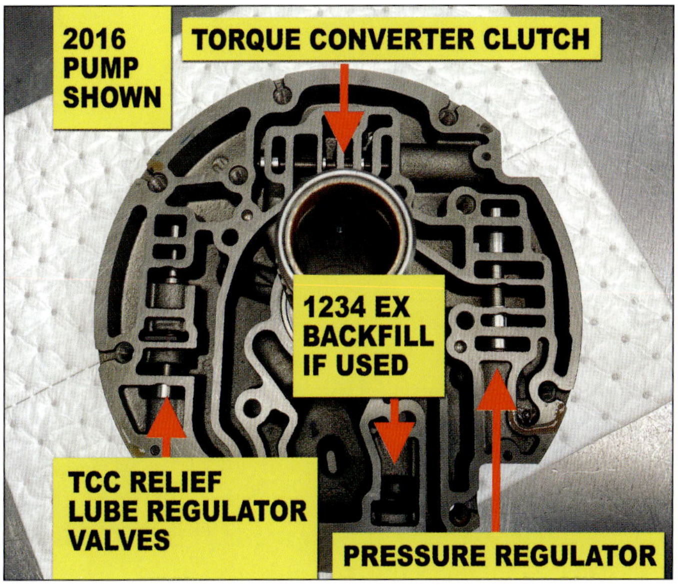

The pump houses three or four valves, depending on the year of the transmission. Some transmission performance modifications will make changes to the pressure-regulator valve and spring. Pump service should be performed as part of the overhaul, as covered in Chapter 3.

If you do not have access to the GM/Allison pump-valve removal tools, make a homemade tool to do the job, which is outlined in Chapter 3. Using a socket or a piece of pipe, grind notches in the tool 180 degrees from each other.

Remove the pressure regulator valve by compressing the spring and removing the pin as outlined in Chapter 3.

correct orientation into the bores. Install the end plug (if used) and the retainer/clip for the valve being serviced. Caution: always wear safety glasses and disposable gloves.

The valve-body spacer plate fits between the two valve-body halves. Early-model spacer plates do not use gaskets. General Motors bonds the gaskets to its spacer plates on late-model applications, so if you reuse the spacer plate, the old gaskets need to be removed from the spacer plate. The new gaskets can be held in place on the spacer plate by using a thin layer of Transjel.

Several methods can be used to remove the gaskets, such as chemical treatments like TranTec's Gasket Wizard, CRC, or Permatex Gasket Removers. A new plate with the bonded gasket already installed can be purchased from General Motors.

Solenoid Service

Many technicians simply choose to replace the solenoids, as hydraulically testing the solenoids is not possible on this application unless you have access to a valve body/solenoid test machine. If reusing a solenoid, resistance and current flow testing can be performed. Make sure to take into account the resistance of the meter leads when taking the resistance measurements.

To test the solenoid winding resistance, connect an ohmmeter between the two terminals on the solenoid. Resistance should measure between the following:

- C/D/E/G or SS1, SS2, SS3 solenoids: 19–30 ohms (depending on temperature)
- F/TCC solenoid: 9–13 ohms (depending on temperature)
- Trim A/PCS A, Trim B/PCS B solenoids: 4–9 ohms (depending on temperature)

To test the solenoid winding for being shorted to ground, connect an ohmmeter test lead to one of the solenoid terminals. Connect the other meter test lead to the metal can of the solenoid. The meter should read OL, indicating no continuity between the solenoid winding and the solenoid metal can.

To check the solenoid winding current flow, connect the meter to one of the solenoids leads. Connect the other meter to a battery ground. Position the meter leads in the correct position to measure amperage. Connect a fused jumper wire between the other solenoid terminal and B+. The meter should now display the current flowing through the solenoid. Do not leave the solenoid energized longer than 1 second. Resistance should measure between the following:

- C/D/E/G or SS1, SS2, SS3 solenoids: 0.4–0.7 amps (depending on temperature and supply voltage)
- F/TCC solenoid: 1–1.4 amps (depending on temperature and supply voltage)
- Trim A/PCS A, Trim B/PCS B solenoids: 1.4–3.1 amps (depending on temperature and supply voltage)

Solenoid Installation

Replace the solenoid O-rings if not replacing the solenoids. Lubricate the seals and install the solenoids. Keep in mind that Trim A/PCS A uses a green seal and is a normally closed (N/C) design solenoid, while Trim B/PCS B is a normally open (N/O)

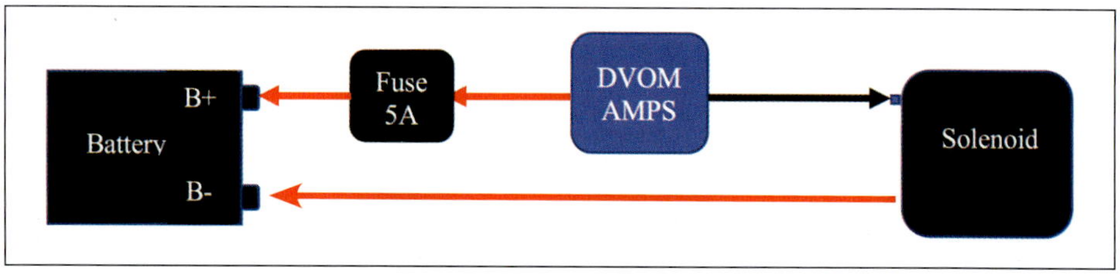

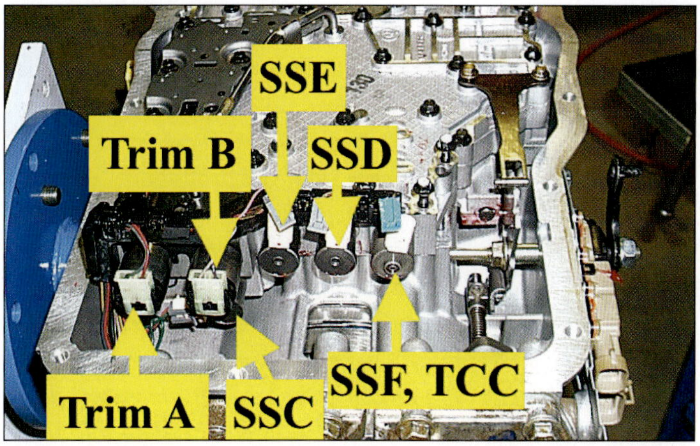

The 1999–2003 5-speed applications can be identified by the one transfer tube and six solenoids that are used. This application does not use any type of line pressure control solenoid, so the trim solenoids are used to control the shift feel.

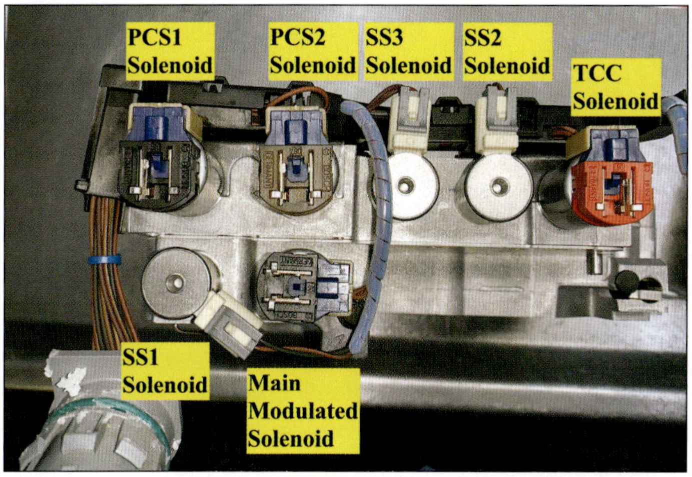

The 2010–2019 solenoid layout and solenoid part numbers were updated with this design change. A true PCS provides variable line pressure control. These applications no longer use solenoid G or the auxiliary valve body. This is a 2014.

With the redesign of the valve body, a new retaining clip was used in 2010–2019. It must be installed (as shown).

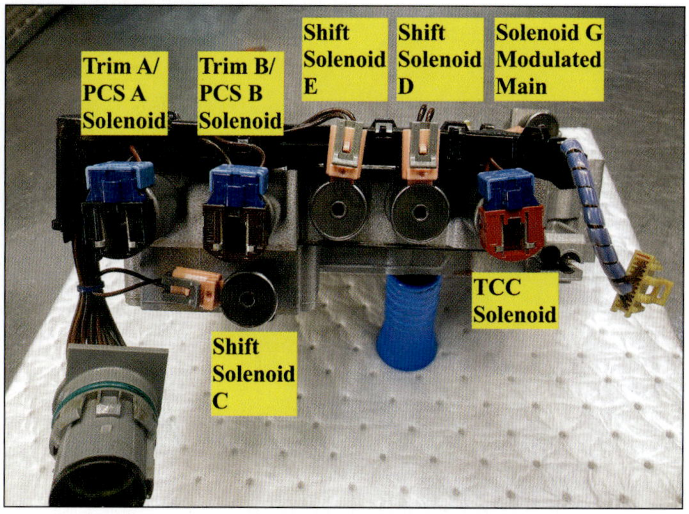

The solenoid layout for a 2004–2009 is the same, although the valve body for the 2004/2005 and the 2006–2009 have different part numbers. As the 2006–2009 applications are 6-speed units. This is a 2005.

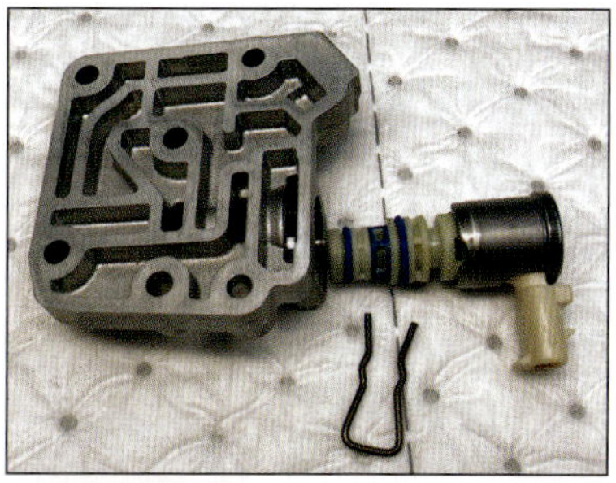

The 2004–2009 applications use a modulated main auxiliary valve body and solenoid G to vary main line pressure. The auxiliary valve body is bolted onto the main valve body.

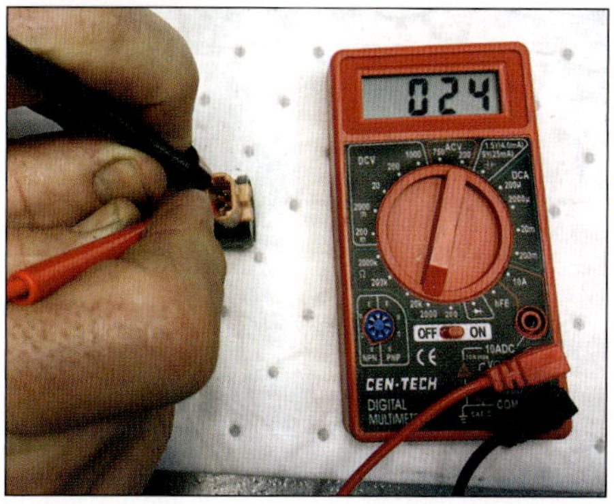

The solenoids can be tested for proper resistance. Connect the ohmmeter between the solenoid pins. Resistance should measure between 9 and 13 ohms (TCC solenoid) and 19 and 30 ohms (shift solenoids), depending on the temperature. Make sure to take into account the resistance of the meter leads. The solenoid winding should also be tested for a short to the solenoid housing. Connect one meter lead to a solenoid pin and the other lead to the solenoid housing metal can. The meter should read OL. Resistance testing can be done as a bench test of the solenoid or with the solenoid installed in the valve body, so do not be concerned if you failed to test the solenoids when you had the valve body apart.

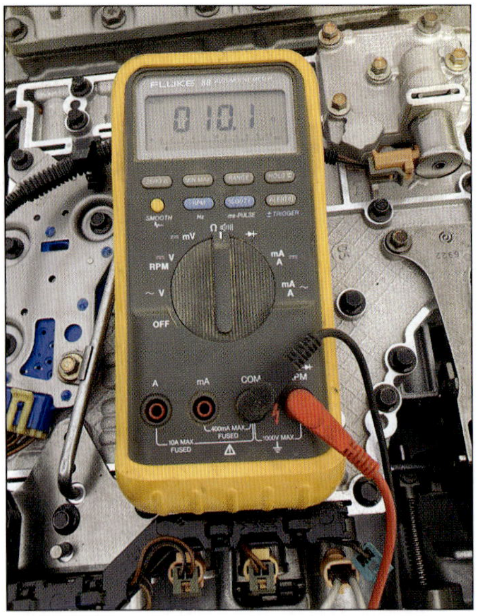

The shift solenoids can be tested for proper resistance. Connect the ohmmeter between the solenoid pins. Resistance should measure between 9 and 13 ohms, depending on the temperature. Make sure to take into account the resistance of the meter leads. The solenoid winding should also be tested for a short to the solenoid housing. Connect one meter lead to a solenoid pin and the other lead to the solenoid housing metal can. The meter should read OL.

The TCC, the shift solenoids, and the trim solenoids can be tested for proper current flow using an amp meter, even though it is not a method listed by GM or Allison as a test procedure. Remember the amp meter must be connected in series with one of the solenoid pins and B+. The other solenoid pin is connected to ground, which will energize the solenoid. Do not leave the circuit connected for longer than 1 second. The TCC solenoid should flow between 1 and 1.4 amps while the shift solenoids will flow between 0.4 and 0.7 amps and trim A/B solenoids will typically flow between 1.4 and 3.1 amps. TCC solenoid current flow is shown at 1.22 amps, 1,224 milliamps in the picture.

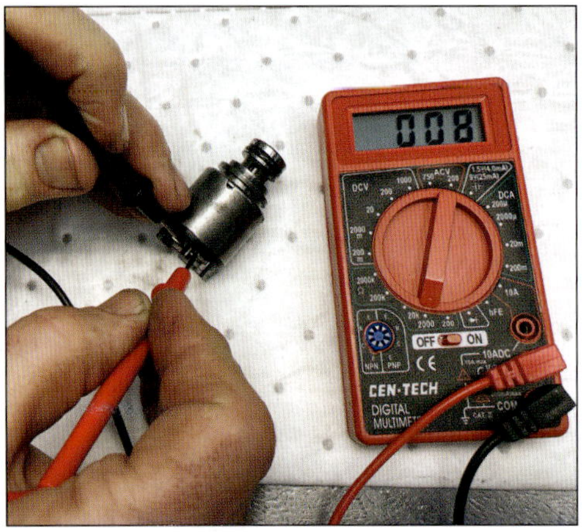

Connect the ohmmeter between the solenoid pins. Resistance should measure between 4 and 9 ohms, depending on the temperature. Make sure to take into account the resistance of the meter leads. The solenoid winding should also be tested for a short to the solenoid housing. Connect one meter lead to a solenoid pin and the other lead to the solenoid housing metal can. The meter should read OL.

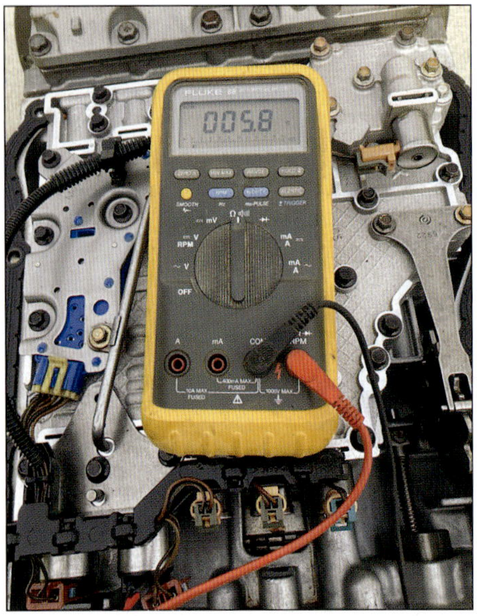

This is what a good trim solenoid resistance value looks like.

The TCC, shift solenoids, and the trim solenoids can be tested for proper current flow using an amp meter even though it is not a method listed by GM or Allison as a test procedure. Remember the amp meter must be connected in series with one of the solenoid pins and B+. The other solenoid pin is connected to ground that will energize the solenoid. Do not leave the circuit connected for longer than 1 second. Trim A and B solenoids typically flow between 1.4 and 3.1 amps. In this example, the solenoid is flowing 2.23 amps, or 2,235 milliamps, which indicates a good solenoid electrically.

solenoid and uses a black seal. The solenoids cannot be interchanged. Install the Trim A/PCS A solenoid in the bore to the outside of the valve body. Trim B/PCS B fits into the bore inboard of Trim A/PCS B. Install the solenoids with the electrical connector facing up.

The shift solenoids' plastic bodies are white in color for C/D/E/G, and SS1, SS2, SS3 solenoids are the same solenoid part numbers. The C/D/E/F solenoids should be installed with the connector facing up. A clip holds the solenoid in place. Insert the solenoid into the valve body and install the clips. On 2010, 2011, and later applications, solenoid G was moved, and its design was changed to a PWM variable line pressure design. The new design solenoid is located directly under the PCS2 solenoid, which is next to the SS1 solenoid.

The TCC/F solenoid plastic body is grey. Insert this solenoid into the valve-body TCC bore and install the clip. The TCC/F solenoid should be installed with the connector facing up.

Make sure the valve body dowel pins are installed. Install the accumulators and springs (two or three, depending on year) into the valve body. Install the bracket to retain the accumulators and trim solenoids in position and torque the three bolts to 108 in-lbs (12 Nm). Install the separator/spacer plate or spacer plate and gaskets (depending on year) between the valve-body halves. Install the upper valve body onto the lower valve body and secure the halves of the valve bodies by attaching 24 valve-body bolts, which hold the halves together.

Install the pressure switch manifold (PSM/PSA) and any fluid pipes if used. Note that the PSM bolt closest to the PSM electrical connector and the center of the valve body is slightly longer than the other bolts. Seven bolts retain the PSM and the reverse pipe (if used) to the valve body. Evenly tighten the valve body bolts to 108 in-lbs (12 Nm), working from the inside to outside bolts.

Install the solenoid G valve body (if used). Install the two retaining bolts and tighten them to 108 in-lbs (12 Nm).

Service Kits and Other Components

The 1000- and 2000-series transmissions are quite popular, so several companies have repair kits to address issues with valve wear as well as other problems. Some companies offer updates for stock applications as well as performance upgrades. The most popular companies are TransGo (transgo.com), Ratio Teck (ratiotek.com), and Sonnax (sonnax.com).

Most of the TransGo and Ratio Teck products are designed to be a drop-in component. Some of the Sonnax repairs will require valve body reaming for updated valve installation, while other Sonnax parts are drop-in components.

TransGo Valve Body Repair Products	Part Number
Allison SK 5-speed VB repair kit	Allison SK
SK Allison JR shift kit 2006–2010	SK Allison JR
A1 shift valves 2001–2010	A1-shift-valves
A1 Lockup boost valve kit 2002–2003	A1-LU-BST
A1 Lockup boost valve kit 2004–2010	A1-LU-BST-04
Cooler bypass valve kit 2017–2019 Allison	6L80-CLR-Bypass

Sonnax Products	Part Number
C1 clutch valve and seal kit 2004 and earlier	37000-05K
Lube regulator converter relief spring 2001–2003	37000-01K
E shift valve spring 2000–2009	37000-02
Exhaust backfill valve kit 2000–2015	37000-17K
Manual valve pin 2000–2015	37000-29K
Oversize control main relief 2000–2015	37000-15K
Oversize E shift valve 2000–2009	37000-15K
Oversize F Trim valve kit 2000–2005	37000-30K
Oversize gain valve kit 2000–2009	37000-24K
Oversize manual valve kit 2000–2015	37000-28K
Trim valve and spring kit 2000–2009	37000-12K

TECH TIP

Bracket Installation

It is imperative that the bracket holding the 2010-and-later modulated main line pressure solenoid be installed correctly. The end of the bracket must face the top (up) of the valve body. ■

Ratio Teck	Part Number
Valve body kit	RT-A01-PR
Valve body kit	RT-A10-PR
Valve body kit	RT-A10L-PRX
Valve body kit	RT-A11-PR
Valve body kit	RT-A11-PRX

Remanufactured Valve Bodies

If you feel more comfortable, GM and several aftermarket valve body remanufacturers offer valve bodies for the Allison applications. Keep in mind that there are several valve body versions available, depending on the production date of the transmission. The following are remanufacturing companies:

- Valve Body Pros (valvebodypros.com)
- Suncoast Transmission Products (suncoastdiesel.com)
- RevMax (revmaxconverters.com)
- Central Valve Bodies (centralvalvebodies.com)
- Sonnax (sonnax.com)

Shift kits and valve body pump performance kits are available from various suppliers. The main manufacturers of these products include TransGo, Ratio Teck, and Sonnax.

Repair kits for the valve body and pump valvetrains are also available. Some are drop-in components, while others require that the bore be reamed oversize, as the replacement valve is oversize.

Valve Body Installation

Once the valve body has been reassembled, it is ready for installation. Install the electrical harness pass-through connector into the opening in the case and lock it into position. Fold the harness out of the way.

Make sure the manual valve is installed in the valve body and that the shift-selector pin is installed into the manual valve. Install the valve body into the case, making sure that the selector pin for the manual valve is installed into the detent (rooster comb). The valve body must be aligned with the case dowel pins. Seat the valve body in the case and install the remaining case bolts. Install the detent spring and the two bolts. Evenly torque all the valve-body bolts to 108 in-lbs (12 Nm).

Attach the electrical harness to the valve-body components.

Some Sonnax repair kits require that the worn bore be reamed, as the replacement valve is oversized. If you choose to go in this direction, find a shop that has the holding fixture and the correct reamer for the valve you wish to replace.

Installing the Valve Body

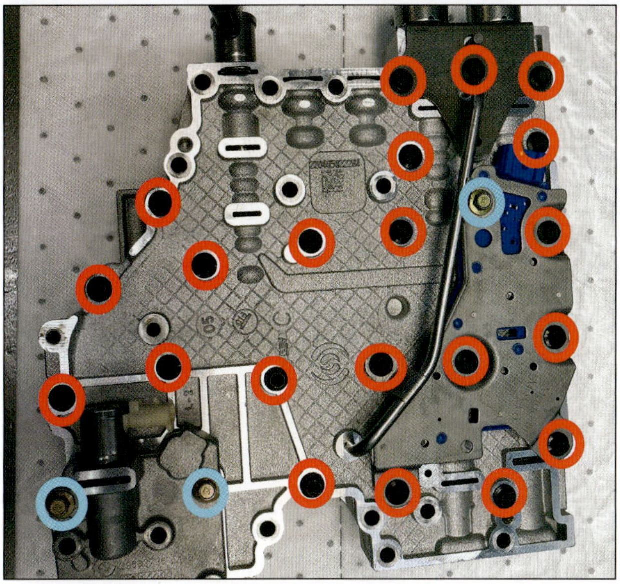

1 *Install the spacer plate between the valve-body halves and install the correct-length bolts in the holes shown. The bolts are torqued to 108 inch-pounds (12 Nm) in a crossing pattern working from the inside to the outside. This is a 2005.*

2 *Position the manual valve so that it can be aligned with the detent (rooster comb) and position the valve body in the case so that it sits flat.*

3 *Align the valve body and insert it into position in the case. Be sure to properly align the manual valve pin with the detent (rooster comb). The valve body should sit flat on the case.*

4 *The valve body bolts need to be torqued once the valve body has been installed into the case.*

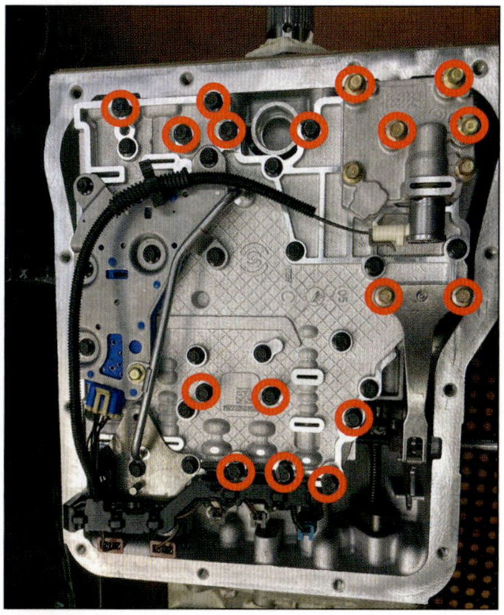

5 *Lay the harness into the case and push the pass-through connector into place in the case. Fold the harness out of the way. Install the valve body-to-case attaching bolts and torque the bolts to 108 inch-pounds (12 Nm) using a crossing pattern. This is a 2005.*

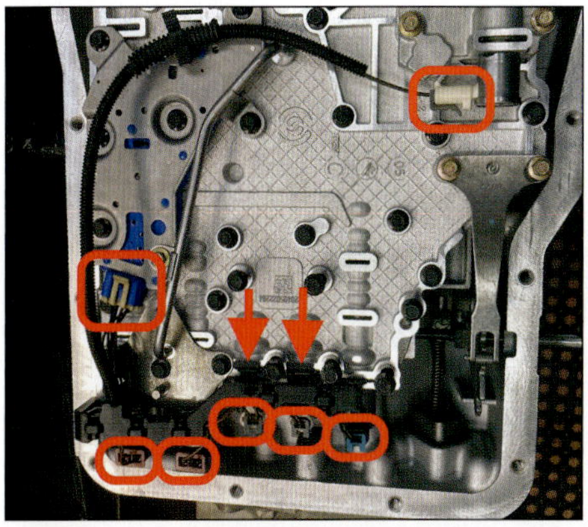

6 *Install the harness connectors and retainers. This is a 2005.*

7 *Install the harness retaining clips. This is a 2005.*

Lubricate and install the filter seal onto the neck of the filter. Carefully install the filter into the pump inlet opening.

Oil Filter and Oil Pan Installation

Install the filter seal onto the filter neck. Lubricate the filter seal and filter neck with transmission fluid. Install the filter. Install the gasket/pan and tighten the 10 bolts to 20 ft-lbs (27 Nm) using a crossing pattern.

Fill with Dexron VI or Allison TranSynd fluid. Follow the fluid-level-checking procedures. Check for leaks. Test drive the vehicle to make sure no issues are present.

Fluid Capacity, Initial Fill, Checks, and Operation

Using the correct fluid and having the transmission properly filled with fluid is critical to proper transmission operation. Something as simple as putting in the wrong transmission fluid can lead to transmission issues and failure.

Fluid

General Motors recommends the use of Dexron VI transmission fluid. Dexron VI is far superior to Dexron III, which it replaced. Major improvements in wear control, film strength, friction durability, and oxidation stability were achieved. Clutch-to-clutch-shift transmissions, such as the LCT 1000 and 2000 series, require a much more robust fluid compared to previous automatic transmission designs. Companies currently licensed to produce Dexron VI include Mobil, Chevron, Shell, SK Lubricants, and Valvoline.

Allison recommends the use of

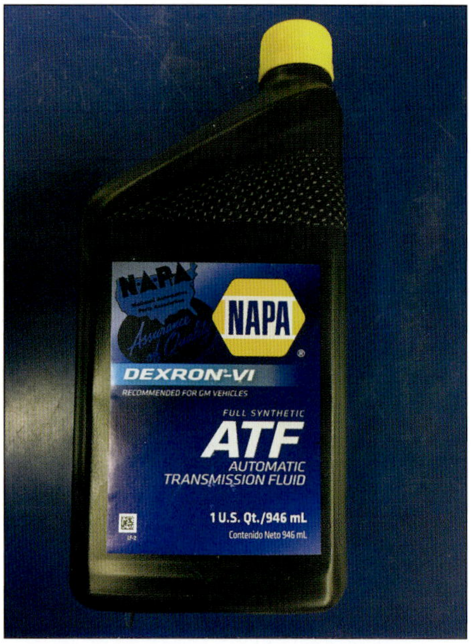

Dexron VI and Allison TranSynd are the only approved fluids for the 1000 and 2000 applications. Do not use Dexron III or other fluids in this application. Dexron VI made major improvements in oxidation resistance, lubrication capabilities, and temperature ranges compared to Dexron III. Dexron VI is licensed by several manufacturers including Valvoline, which manufactures the NAPA fluid shown.

Install the pan gasket.

Install the oil pan. The bolts are torqued to 20 ft-lbs (27 Nm) using a crossing pattern.

Allison TES 668, TES 295, and TES 389 are approved for the 1000- and 2000-series units.

Allison TranSynd. TranSynd is available as TES 668, TES 295, or TES 389, which are acceptable in the GM and Allison 1000- and 2000-series units. Companies currently licensed to produce TranSynd fluid include Volvo, John Deere, Castrol, BP, International, Exxon Mobil, Case/New Holland, and Shell.

Fluid Level

All 1000- and 2000-series units are equipped with a dipstick. The dipstick can be located on either side of the transmission, depending on application.

Before checking the fluid level, perform the following:

- Start the engine and park the vehicle on a level surface and block the wheels.
- Apply the parking brake and vehicle brake. Place the shift lever in Park. Move the shifter to each forward gear range as well as Reverse, pausing for 3 seconds in each range. Place the vehicle in Park.
- Allow the engine to idle for a few minutes.

Fluid Capacity

- Dry (12.7 quarts/12 liters) shallow pan
- Filter change (7.4 quarts/7 liters) shallow pan
- Dry (14.8 quarts/14 liters) deep pan
- Filter change (10.6 quarts/10 liters) deep pan

Observe the transmission fluid temperature (TFT) using the Driver Information Center (DIC) scan tool or by using a temperature gun to measure the oil-pan temperature.

Cold Fluid Checking Procedure

Use the cold-check procedure to check fluid level when the transmission fluid temperature is between 80°F and 90°F (27°C and 32°C).

- ❒ Locate the dipstick, flip the handle, pull out the dipstick, and wipe it with a clean rag.
- ❒ Install the dipstick, pushing it back in all the way, wait a few seconds, and then pull it back out again.
- ❒ Check both sides of the dipstick and use the lower level.
- ❒ Inspect the color of the fluid and its condition.
- ❒ If the fluid level is below the cold mark (lower), add only enough fluid through the dipstick tube as needed to bring the level into the mark.
- ❒ If the fluid level is correct, push the dipstick back in all the way, then flip the handle down to lock the dipstick in place.
- ❒ Perform a hot check once the transmission has reached operating temperature.

Hot Fluid Checking Procedure

Use this procedure to check the transmission fluid level when the transmission fluid temperature is between 165°F and 185°F (74°C and 85°C).

- ❒ Locate the dipstick, flip the handle, pull out the dipstick, and wipe it with a clean rag.
- ❒ Install the dipstick by pushing it back in all the way, wait a few seconds, and then pull it back out again.
- ❒ Check both sides of the dipstick and use the lower level.
- ❒ Inspect the color of the fluid and its condition.
- ❒ If the fluid level is below the hot mark (upper), add only enough fluid through the dipstick tube as needed to bring the level into the mark.
- ❒ If the fluid level is correct, push the dipstick back in all the way and then flip the handle down to lock the dipstick in place.

Initial Fluid Fill

Install 6 to 7 quarts of fluid. Once the engine is started, move the shifter through all the ranges, pausing as the transmission engages in each range. The fluid level should then be checked. Add fluid as required to get the fluid level to the correct level.

On-Vehicle Repairs and Adjustments and Range Selector Cable Adjustments

Shifter Cable Adjustments and New Cable

- ❒ The steering-column shift lever should be placed in the Park position with the wheels blocked.

The 1999–2005 applications all used an external range sensor. Due to durability issues, it is recommended that the sensor be replaced. Early applications used a two-connector-design sensor. Moisture intrusion with this design was common, which can lead to issues from the transmission defaulting to Neutral to a flashing or a blank PRNDL display in the instrument panel.

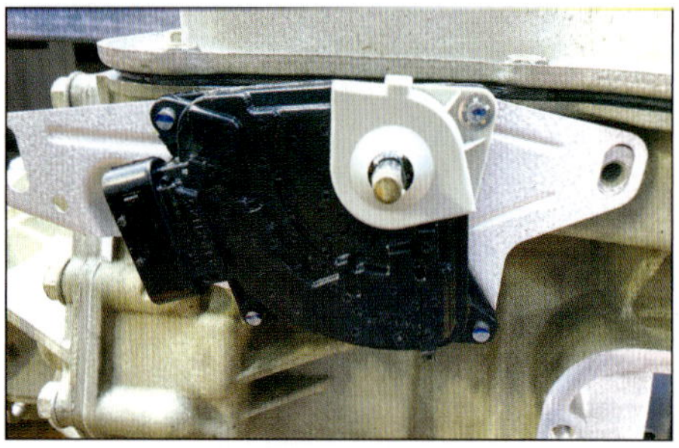

Later applications used a signal-wire connector. As with the two-connector design, it is recommended that the sensor be replaced any time the transmission is replaced or overhauled.

- ❒ The transmission manual shaft lever should be placed in the Park position.
- ❒ Open the cable white cover, using a screwdriver to unlock the cable locking teeth. Grasp the shift-cable shifter end in your left hand and the shift-cable transmission end in your right hand. For a new cable, align the two ends and slide them together. Once the two-piece cable is slid together, it will no longer come apart, as it locks permanently into position.
- ❒ Release the transmission end. This will allow the spring to apply tension to the cable.
- ❒ Open the white cover on the shifter end of the cable. Push the natural-colored lock button down. This will engage the locking teeth on the transmission end of the cable.

Adaptive Learning, Clearing Adapts, and Relearning Adapts

The 1000 and 2000 software is equipped with a feature known as adaptive learning. The adaptive learning feature is designed to ensure that the transmission shifts and operates the same at 100,000 miles as it does at 100 miles. Adaptive operation is covered in Chapter 2.

The shift-adapt pressure offset pressure values are learned and stored in the TCM memory for each shift at specific loads and temperatures. If repairs are performed on the transmission that can affect shift times, it is important that the stored values be reset and relearned using a scan tool.

Clearing Adapts and Relearning Adapts

The shift adapts should be cleared and relearned if any of the following occur:

- The transmission was replaced.
- The transmission was rebuilt.
- The valve body was replaced or repaired.
- Any repair that could impact shift times was performed, including replacing or reprograming the TCM.

Clearing the adapts on all 1000 and 2000 applications will not result in all the values resetting to 0. The values will reset to predetermined software values which may or may not be 0.

Clearing the adapts clears all the adaptive memories. Clear all DTCs prior to clearing the adapts. Follow the instructions on the scan tool to clear the adapts. Once the adapts are cleared, new transmission adapts need to be relearned. This means both upshift and downshift adapts for each gear change as well as garage shift adapts (Neutral to Reverse and Neutral to Drive) need to be learned.

Some scan tools have the ability to perform a "fast learn," shortening the length of time it takes to relearn the adapts. This typically occurs when the adaptive values are cleared on an Allison and fast-learn mode is selected. Following the scan tools instructions, fast learn will move through three modes of learning: Park, Drive, and Reverse. After the adaptive shift values have been "roughed in," the TCM will switch to slow-learn mode. This process is repeated for each shift and gear. Typically, this process is referred to as "shift convergence."

Once all the shifts have converged, the relearn process is complete. Relearning the adapts involves operating the vehicle as instructed by the scan tool and monitoring the adaptive parameters to be sure the process is complete.

Once the adaptive relearn process has been performed, a complete road test should be performed, upshifting and downshifting through all gears at various throttle openings. If the scan tool does not have the ability to perform a fast learn, then a very extensive road test needs to be performed, operating the vehicle through all the upshifts and downshifts at various throttle openings and temperatures.

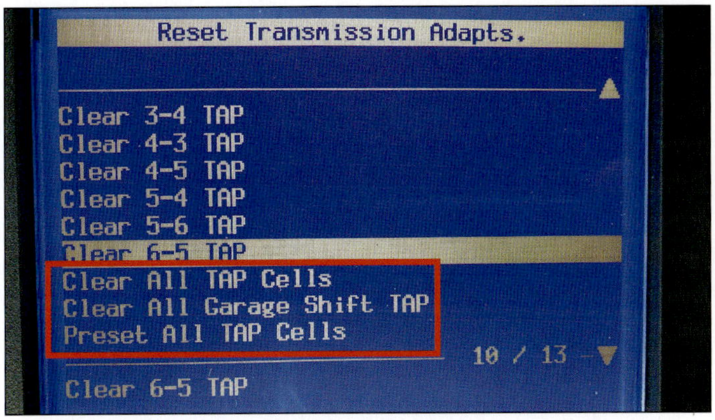

The adapts must be reset any time the transmission is replaced, the transmission is overhauled, the TCM is replaced, the TCM calibration is updated, or any changes are made to the transmission that may affect shift quality. Reset the adapts with a scan tool. Many tools allow the resetting of individual adapts, such as the upshift and downshift (TAP) adapts and garage shift adapts, or all of the adapts can be reset at one time. The TCM can also be forced into fast-learn mode by clearing the adapts on some applications or presetting all the TAP shift cells.

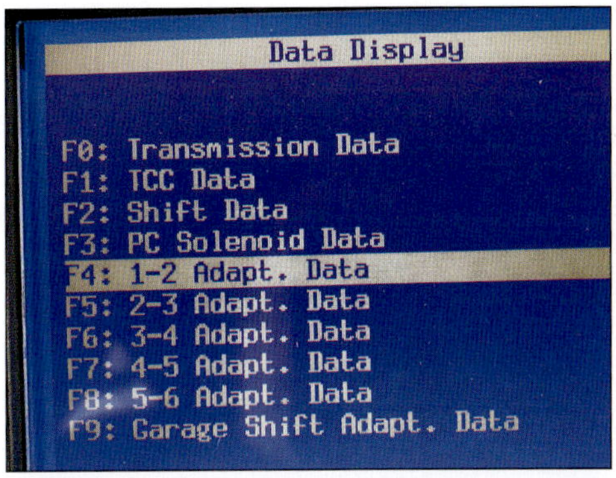

With the scan tool, monitor adaptive data for each gear and shift.

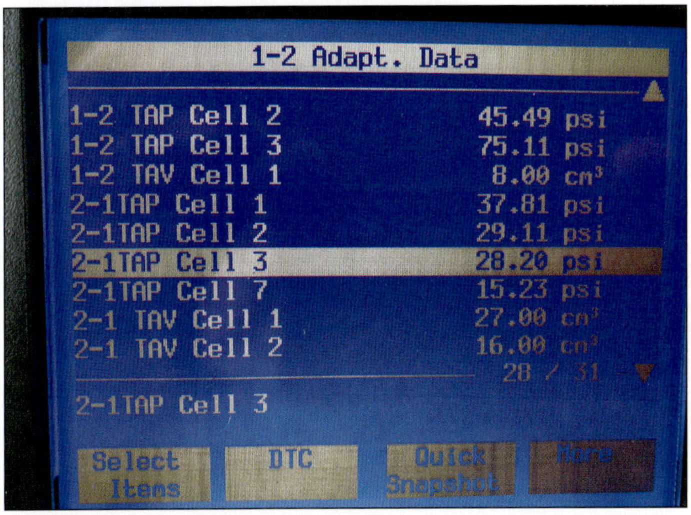

This is LCT 1000 2009 adapt data.

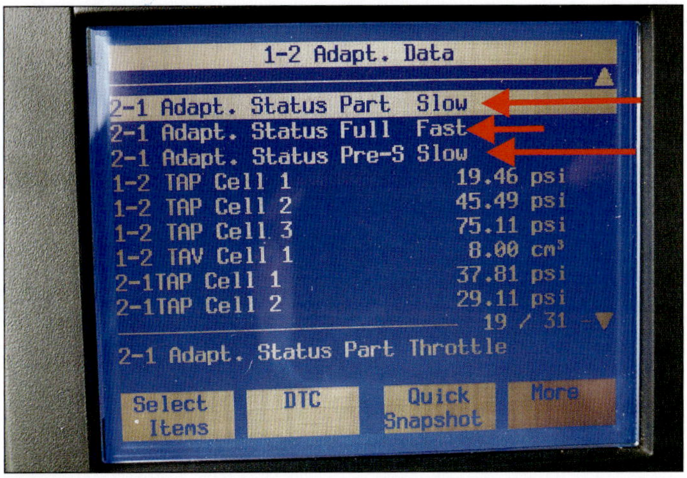

With the scan tool, monitor which mode the adaptive relearn has entered: fast learn or slow learn.

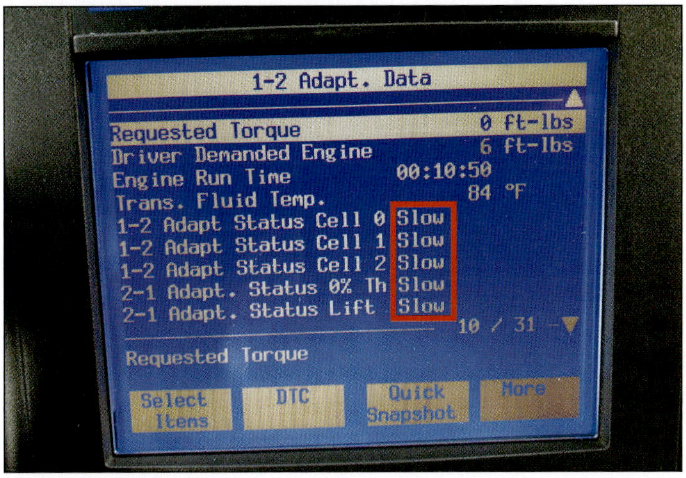

When the adapts have changed from "fast to slow," the relearn for that shift is complete, and the shift is considered "converged."

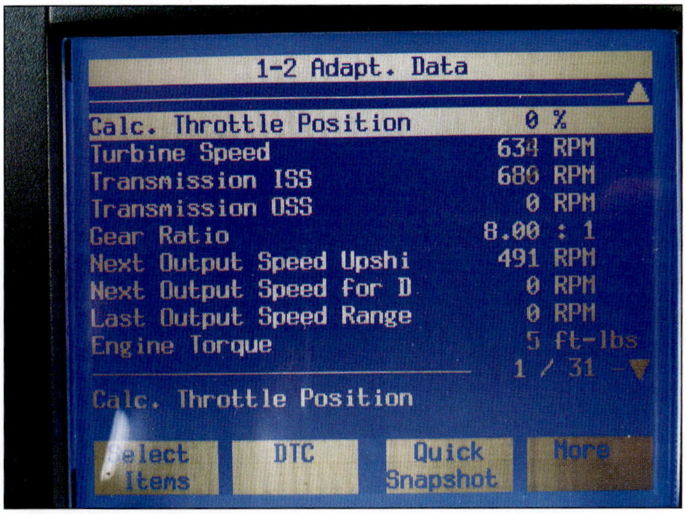

This is LCT 1000 adapt data that has typical values.

Allison 1000 in a Non-OEM Application

Numerous companies handle parts for Allison applications:

- Allison to Dodge Cummins Conversion: Howards Allison conversions, transfer-case adapter AD-TA-01, Allison output shaft to Dodge spline AD-OS-03, bellhousing adapter AC-TE-01
- G Force Conversions: GF-A-S 1989–2002 Dodge Conversion and a 2003–2017 Dodge Conversion
- GA-A-SL (crossmembers.com)
- Extreme Diesel Conversion kits (xtremediesel.com)
- ATS Diesel sells components to convert an Allison to fit behind a diesel, including the transfer-case adapter, shift-linkage kit, cooler lines, transmission mount, bellhousing adapter, and aftermarket TCM (atsdiesel.com/allison-conversion)

Tuners

Aftermarket tuners are available for the Duramax-Allison applications. If installing an aggressive tune, upgrade the transmission's internal components (clutches, shafts, planetaries, and the torque converter), as damage can occur. Note that GM invalidates a vehicle warranty if it finds out that tuning software or hardware has been added to a vehicle. In addition, the federal government is currently applying pressure to the tuning companies to limit their abilities for making software changes.

Tuner features vary, depending on the company. Some offer performance-tuned ECMs, TCMs, and upgraded turbos, which can simply be installed on a vehicle. Some offer software that allows selection of a specific horsepower range, and the tuner simply takes care of the software update. Others allow adjustment of specific parameters, such as turbo boost, fuel pressure, injector operation, tire size, and transmission pressure. Some brands sell remote controls that allow tuning on the fly, while others make Wi-Fi updates available. Many of the products available also allow clearing of DTCs, resetting shift adapts, and monitoring engine and transmission parameters while driving.

Popular tuning products include:

- Bully Dog (bullydog.com)
- Duramax Tuner (duramaxtuner.com)
- EFI Live (efilive.com)
- Edge (edgeproducts.com)
- Hypertech (hypertech-inc.myshopify.com)
- Diablo Sport (diablosport.com)

Internal Component Upgrades

Upgraded internal components are also available to increase the torque and horsepower capacity of the units. Components include the torque converter, shafts, clutch hubs, planetaries, and clutch plates. Some of the manufacturers/distributors include Suncoast Transmission and Converter Products (suncoastdiesel.com), RevMax (revmaxconverters.com), Goerend transmissions (goerend.com), and TCS (tcsproducts.com).

Always discuss the performance components you are considering purchasing with the manufacturer prior to ordering the parts, as there are many variables based on application, option content (RPO), and horsepower/torque requirements.

Internal Transmission Component Upgraded Parts

Component	Suncoast	RevMax	Goerend	TCS
Input Shaft	A1-109600	A1000-500	A100-2 TCS, A-24281105-X, A-29539506-X, A-29548947	109600, 109602
Mainshaft	A1-109700	–	A-29546284-X	109700
Output Shaft	A1-109100, A1-109102	A1000-501	A139-12 Early TCS, A139-12 Late TCS, A-29531252-X	–
–	109102, 109100	–	–	–
Planetary P2	A1-P2K-6 6-speed, A1-P2K 5-speed	–	A139-10 5-speed	–
P1 Sun Gear	A1-P1B	–	–	–
C2 Clutch Hub	A1-BC2, A1-C2S	–	A101-32C2BILLET	109300
C3 Oiling Cover	–	A1000-911 and A1000-912 tool	A-GT BILLET PTO COVER-LOGO, Tool needed also	–
Oil Pan	MAG-A1000	A1000-900	A-GTPANA1000	–
Flexplate	A1-BFP-ZB, A1-BFP-AZB, A1-BFP-1, A1-BFP-2, A1-BFP-3	A1000-901	–	–
Torque Converter	Various available	Various available	Various available	–

Raybestos and Alto manufacture performance clutches for the Allison applications.

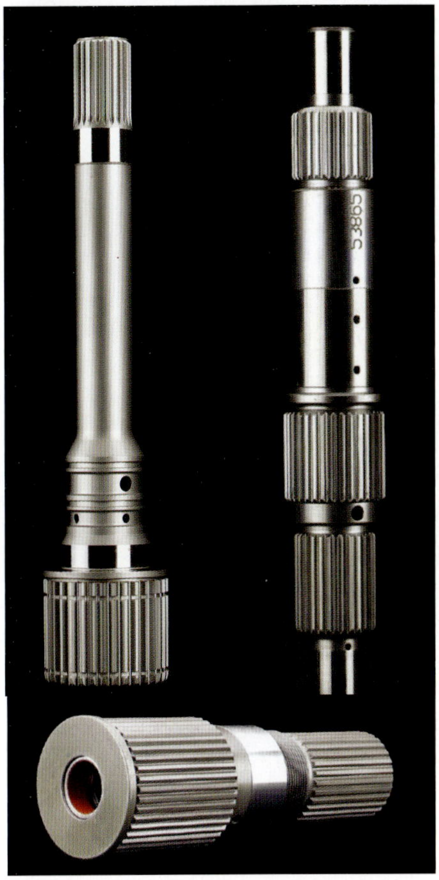

High-horsepower and high-torque applications require upgrades to the shafts. (Photo Courtesy Suncoast Transmission and Torque Converter Products)

The C2 hub is a weak link for high-horsepower and high-torque applications. (Photo Courtesy Suncoast Transmission and Torque Converter Products)

Performance Clutch Manufacturers

Performance clutches can be purchased through Raybestos Powertrain (raybestospowertrain.com) or Alto Clutch Products (altousa.com). Suncoast also sells special Raybestos pre-compressed friction plates for ultra-high-torque applications.

Diagnostic Pointers

Always start a diagnosis by inspecting the battery, power, and ground circuits for issues. In addition, check for engine, fuel system, and sensor issues that may be present. Engine operational issues will cause transmission-related issues, so they must be addressed prior to condemning the transmission.

Using a scan tool, check for any DTCs that are stored in the various controllers. DTC default actions may be causing the complaint, so they need to be addressed prior to condemning the transmission.

Keep in mind that slippage issues are typically due to low clutch-apply pressure, while hard engagement issues are typically due to high clutch-apply pressures. If you have slippage or hard/slipping shift issues, always verify that the line pressure is correct as a starting point. Again, many hard shift–related issues and other operational issues are created by the default actions that the TCM takes when some DTCs are set.

The most common issues that you are likely to experience include a "range/shift inhibited" message or light, the PRNDL may flash, or the transmission may default to Neutral. Multiple things can cause these issues, including the following:

- Moving the shift lever between forward and reverse prior to the vehicle being fully stopped
- High engine speed when a range is selected
- The throttle not being at 0 percent when shifting into gear
- Erratic input or output speed-sensor reading
- A faulty range sensor
- A misadjusted range sensor/cable
- A faulty IMS
- A faulty pressure switch manifold
- Ultra-low fluid temperature or transmission overheating
- Transfer case in Neutral when changing transmission range
- Transmission slippage
- Faulty ignition switch (loss of B+)
- Loss of ground
- Low fluid level or restricted filter
- A clutch failure
- A faulty solenoid
- Low or no pressure at startup

Performance planetary components are available. (Photo Courtesy Suncoast Transmission and Torque Converter Products)

- DTCs set and default action is Neutral
- A faulty TCM

The flexplate is a weak link in the Allison application. Performance flexplates are available. The part is courtesy of RevMax converters and products.

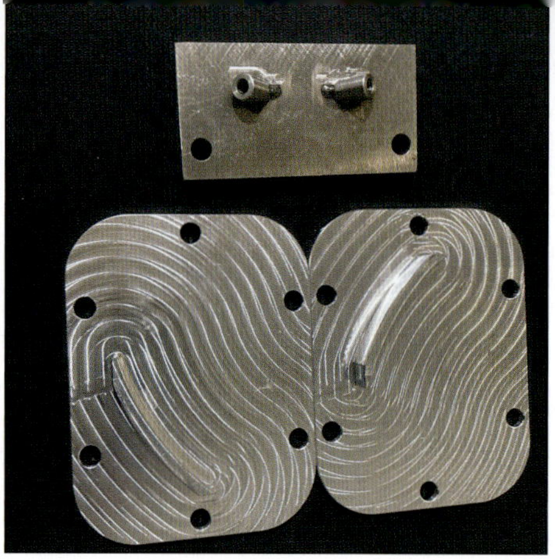

Additional lubrication for the C3 clutch can be accomplished by using a modified PTO cover. To use the cover, drill holes in the case. The cover suppliers can sell or rent the tool so you can properly install the updated cover. The part is courtesy of RevMax converters and products.

When Third and Reverse are available but there are no shifts, DTCs set and default action results in limp mode. This can be caused by a failed solenoid, stuck valve, failed/leaking C1 clutch, B+ or ground issues, transmission overheating, or a faulty TCM.

A vibration or noise that changes with speed can be caused by torque converter bolts, the torque converter position on the flexplate, engine thrust bearing damage, planetary carrier teeth damage, TCC shudder, engine misfire, a faulty engine or transmission mount, a worn U-joint, or a damaged driveshaft.

Worn transfer case shift forks may cause the transmission to pop out of gear or make a popping noise under load. This condition could also cause a DTC.

If the transmission will not shift into a higher gear, there could be low engine power, a fuel system issue, a fuel filter issue, high fluid temperature or a faulty temperature sensor/circuit, a faulty speed sensor or circuit, loose/damaged speed-sensor tone ring, a faulty throttle position/MAF/MAP input, a misadjusted shift cable, faulty shift solenoid, a stuck shift valve, B+ or ground issues, DTCs set and default actions resulting in shift issues, or a faulty TCM.

Overheating of thc transmission can be caused by low fluid level, using the wrong fluid, restricted airflow through the oil cooler, a restricted transmission cooler or cooler lines, engine overheating and radiator issues, a defective cooler flow valve (if used), cooler lines reversed, the use of an incorrect torque converter, a faulty transmission fluid temperature sensor, a damaged clutch, or an inoperative TCC.

Hard shifts may occur for several reasons, including when the adapts have not been reset and have not been relearned, lending to high line pressure. There may be sticking valves, faulty solenoids, engine input–related concerns (MAF/MAP/TP), a faulty pressure regulator valve, B+ and ground issues, or a faulty TCM.

Slipping or flaring can occur when adapts have not reset and been relearned or with sticking valves, faulty solenoids, incorrect clutch clearance, engine input–related concerns (MAF, MAP, or TP), a faulty pressure regulator valve, B+ and ground issues, or a faulty TCM.

There can be buzzing because of

Clutch	Raybestos GPZ Performance Clutches	Alto Performance Clutches
C1	RTK-1001 1999 and later	152755B 1999–2009, 152755C 2010 and later
C2	RTK-1002 1999 and later	152756B 1999 and later
C3	RTK-1034 1999 and later	152757B 1999 and later
C4	RTK-1017 1999–2010, RTK-1044 2011 and later	152758B 1999 and later
C5	RCPS-07 1999 and later	152759B 1999 and later
All Clutch Kit	RCPTK-1000 or RCPS-142 1999–2010, RCPTK-1001 2011 and later	–

low fluid levels, air leaking into the pump inlet circuit (filter or seal), a faulty pressure regulator valve, or DTCs set resulting in high line pressure.

Low mainline pressure can be caused by low fluid level, a restricted filter, a filter seal leak, a sticking pressure-regulator valve, a faulty solenoid, a worn/damaged pump, or a worn/damaged valve body.

There can be high mainline pressure when DTCs set and default actions lead to high line pressure or there is an issue with the pressure-regulator valve.

The clutch can slip due to low fluid level, adapts not being reset or relearned, low mainline pressure, the TCC not being fully applied, clutch piston seals leaking, shaft seals leaking, stuck valves, faulty solenoids, incorrect speed-sensor readings, B+ or ground issues, or a faulty TCM.

APPENDIX

ALLISON DIAGNOSTIC TROUBLE CODES AND DIAGRAMS

Allison Diagnostic Trouble Codes

ode	Problem
:1312	Retarder Request Signal Failed Low
:1313	Retarder Request Signal Failed High
0121	Pedal Position Sensor Performance
0122	Pedal Position Sensor Circuit Low Voltage
0123	Pedal Position Sensor Circuit High Voltage
0218	Transmission Fluid Over Temperature
0500	Output Speed Sensor Lower/Higher than Desired Value
0562	System Voltage Low
0561	Ignition Voltage Lower/Higher than Desired Value
0563	System Voltage High
0601	Control Module Read-Only Memory Performance
0602	TCM Not Programmed
0603	Control Module Long-Term Memory Performance
0604	Control Module Random Access Memory Performance
0606	Controller Internal Performance
062F	Control Module Long-Term Memory Performance
0610	TCM Vehicle Option Error
0613	TCM Processor
0614	Torque Mismatch ECM to TCM
0634	TCM Internal Temperature High
063E	Auto Configuration Error TP Sensor
063F	Auto Configuration Error ECT Sensor
0657	High Side Driver 1
0658	High Side Driver 1 Low Voltage
0659	High Side Driver 1 High Voltage
0700	Transmission-Related Issue Reported to the ECM
P0701	Transmission Control System Performance at Key Up
P0702	Transmission ID Issue
P0703	Brake Switch Circuit
P0705	Transmission Range Sensor Circuit (PRNDL Input)
P0706	Transmission Range Sensor Circuit Performance
P0708	Transmission Range Sensor Circuit High
P0710	Transmission Fluid Temperature Sensor Malfunction
P0711	Transmission Fluid Temperature Sensor Circuit Performance
P0712	Transmission Fluid Temperature Sensor Circuit (High Temperature)
P0713	Transmission Fluid Temperature Sensor Circuit (Low Temperature)
P0716	Turbine Speed Sensor Circuit Performance
P0717	Turbine Speed Sensor Circuit No Signal
P07BF	Input Speed Sensor Circuit Low Voltage
P07C0	Input Speed Sensor Circuit High Voltage
P0719	Brake Switch Input Low
P071A	RELS Input Failed On
P071D	General Input Fault
P0721	Output Speed Sensor Circuit Performance
P0722	Output Speed Sensor Circuit No Signal
P077C	Output Speed Sensor Circuit Low Voltage
P077D	Output Speed Sensor Circuit High Voltage
P0726	Engine Speed Input Circuit Performance
P0727	Engine Speed Sensor Circuit No Signal
P0729	Incorrect 6th Gear Ratio
P0731	Incorrect 1st Gear Ratio
P0732	Incorrect 2nd Gear Ratio
P0733	Incorrect 3rd Gear Ratio
P0734	Incorrect 4th Gear Ratio
P0735	Incorrect 5th Gear Ratio
P0736	Incorrect Reverse Ratio
P0741	Torque Converter Clutch System Stuck Off
P0742	Torque Converter Clutch System Stuck On
P0743	TCC Solenoid or Circuit Open or Short to Power
P0746	PCS 1, "Trim A" Solenoid Stuck Off
P0747	PCS 1, "Trim A" Solenoid Stuck On
P0748	Pressure Control Solenoid Electrical Circuit Open or Shorted to Ground or Power
P0751	Shift Solenoid Valve 1 Performance – Stuck Off
P0752	Shift Solenoid Valve 1 Performance – Stuck On
P0756	Shift Solenoid Valve 2 Performance – Stuck Off
P0757	Shift Solenoid Valve 2 Performance – Stuck On
P0761	Shift Solenoid Valve 3 Performance – Stuck Off
P0762	Shift Solenoid Valve 3 Performance – Stuck On
P0763	Shift Solenoid C Electrical Circuit Open or Shorted to Ground or Power
P0768	Shift Solenoid D Electrical Circuit Open or Shorted to Ground or Power
P0773	Shift Solenoid E Electrical Circuit Open or Shorted to Ground or Power
P0776	PCS 2, "Trim B" Solenoid Stuck Off

Allison Diagnostic Trouble Codes

Code	Problem
P0777	PCS 2 "Trim B" Solenoid Stuck On
P0778	Pressure Control Solenoid B Electrical
P0796	PCS 3 Stuck Off
P0797	PCS 3 Stuck On
P0815	Shifter TAP UP Switch Circuit Shorted to Ground
P0816	Shifter TAP DOWN Switch Circuit Shorted to Ground
P0826	Shifter TAP Switch Circuit Fault
P0836	4x4 Low Signal Active
P0840	Transmission Pressure Switch C (1) Circuit
P0841	Transmission Pressure Switch C (1) Circuit Open
P0842	Transmission Pressure Switch C (1) Circuit Low Voltage
P0843	Transmission Pressure Switch C (1) Circuit High Voltage
P0845	Transmission Pressure Switch D (2) Circuit
P0846	Transmission Pressure Switch D (2) Circuit
P0847	Transmission Pressure Switch D (2) Circuit Low Voltage
P0848	Transmission Pressure Switch D (2) Circuit High Voltage
P0851	Park/Neutral (IMS) Position Switch Circuit Low Voltage
P0852	Park/Neutral (IMS) Position Switch Circuit High Voltage
P0870	Transmission Pressure Switch E (3) Circuit
P0871	Transmission Pressure Switch E (3) Circuit Stuck Open
P0872	Transmission Pressure Switch E (3) Circuit Low Voltage
P0873	Transmission Pressure Switch E (3) Circuit High Voltage
P0875	Transmission Pressure Switch R Circuit
P0876	Transmission Pressure Switch R Circuit Open
P0877	Transmission Fluid Pressure Switch 4 Circuit Low Voltage
P0878	Transmission Fluid Pressure Switch 4 Circuit High Voltage
P0880	TCM Power Loss
P0881	TCM Power Performance
P0882	TCM Power Signal Low
P0883	TCM Power Signal High
P0894	Clutch Slippage
P0960	PCS Main Mod Solenoid Circuit Open
P0962	PCS Main Mod Solenoid Circuit Low
P0963	PCS Main Mod Solenoid Circuit High
P0964	PCS Main Mod Solenoid Circuit Open
P0965	Pressure Control Solenoid Valve 2 Performance
P0966	PCS 2 Control Circuit Low Voltage
P0967	PCS 2 Control Circuit High Voltage
P0968	PCS 2 Control Circuit Open
P0970	PCS 3 Control Circuit Low
P0971	PCS 3 Control Circuit High
P0972	Shift Solenoid Open
P0973	Shift Solenoid 1 Control Circuit Low Voltage
P0974	Shift Solenoid 1 Control Circuit High Voltage
P0975	Shift Solenoid 2 Control Circuit Open
P0976	Shift Solenoid 2 Control Circuit Low Voltage
P0977	Shift Solenoid 2 Control Circuit High Voltage
P0979	Shift Solenoid Valve 3 Control Circuit Low Voltage
P0980	Shift Solenoid Valve 3 Control Circuit High Voltage
P0989	Retarder Pressure Sensor Failed Low
P0990	Retarder Pressure Sensor Failed High
P1571	Torque Signal Request Shorted to Ground, Open or Shorted to Voltage
P1688	Unmanaged Engine Torque Delivered to TCM
P1709	Transmission Pressure Switch E Circuit
P1710	Transmission Pressure Switch E Circuit Stuck Open
P1711	Transmission Pressure Switch E Circuit Stuck Closed
P1712	Transmission Pressure Switch E Circuit High
P1713	Transmission Pressure Switch Reverse Circuit
P1714	Transmission Pressure Switch Reverse Circuit Stuck On
P1716	Transmission Pressure Switch Reverse Circuit High
P1718	Incorrect Neutral Gear Ratio
P1720	Solenoid A Controlled Clutch Not Engaged
P1721	Solenoid B Controlled Clutch Not Engaged
P1723	Solenoid A Controlled Clutch Engaged
P1724	Solenoid B Controlled Clutch Engaged
P1726	Shift Solenoid D Controlled Clutch Engaged
P1727	Shift Controlled E Clutch Engaged
P1739	Incorrect Low Gear Ratio
P1760	TCM Supply Voltage
P1779	Engine Torque Delivered to ECM Incorrect
P1835	Kickdown Circuit
P1860	Torque Converter Clutch PWM Solenoid Circuit
P1875	4WD Low Switch Circuit
P1891	TPS PWM Signal Low Input
P1892	TPS PWM Signal High Input
P2184	ECT Sensor Low
P2185	ECT Sensor High
P2637	Torque Management Signal
P2641	Torque Management Signal
P2669	High Side Driver 2 Issue
P2670	High Side Driver 2 Low
P2671	High Side Driver 2 High
P2685	High Side Driver 3 Low
P2686	High Side Driver 3 High
P2714	PCS 4 Stuck Off
P2715	PCS 4 Stuck On
P2718	PCS 4 Control Circuit Open
P2720	PCS 4 Control Circuit Low
P2721	PCS 4 Control Circuit High
P2723	PCS 1 Stuck Off
P2724	PCS 1 Stuck On
P2727	PCS 1 Control Circuit Open
P2728	Pressure Control Solenoid Valve 1 Performance
P2729	PCS 1 Control Circuit Low Voltage
P2730	PCS 1 Control Circuit High Voltage
P2736	PCS 5 Control Circuit Open
P2738	PCS 5 Control Circuit Low Voltage
P2739	PCS 5 Control Circuit High Voltage
P2761	TCC PCS Circuit Open
P2771	4x4 Low Circuit Fault
P2762	TCC PCS Circuit High Voltage
P2763	TCC PCS Circuit Low Voltage
P2793	Gear Shift Detection Circuit
P2808	PCS 6 Stuck Off
P2809	PCS 6 Stuck On
P2812	PCS 6 Control Circuit Open
P2814	PCS 6 Control Circuit Low
P2815	PCS 6 Control Circuit High
U0001	High Speed CAN Bus Counter Overr
U0010	CAN Bus Reset Counter Overrun
U0103	Lost Communication with Shifter Modu
U0105	Lost Communication with ECM
U0291	Lost Communication with Shifter Modu
U0304	Incompatible Shift Module 1
U0333	Incompatible Shift Module 2
U0404	Invalid Data from the Shift Module 1
U0592	Invalid Data from the Shift Module 2
U1000	Serial Data Communication Link Malfunction
U1016	Class 2 Powertrain Controller State Health
U1041	Class 2 ABS Controller State of Healt
U1064	Class 2 TBC Controller State of Hea
U1096	Class 2 IPC Controller State of Heal
U1300	Serial Data Communication Link Low (Class2)
U1301	Serial Data Communication Link Hig (Class2)
U2104	CAN Bus Rest Counter Overrun
U2105	CAN Bus Error No Engine or TP Valu Received by the TCM

Inputs (LCT1000, Gen 5)

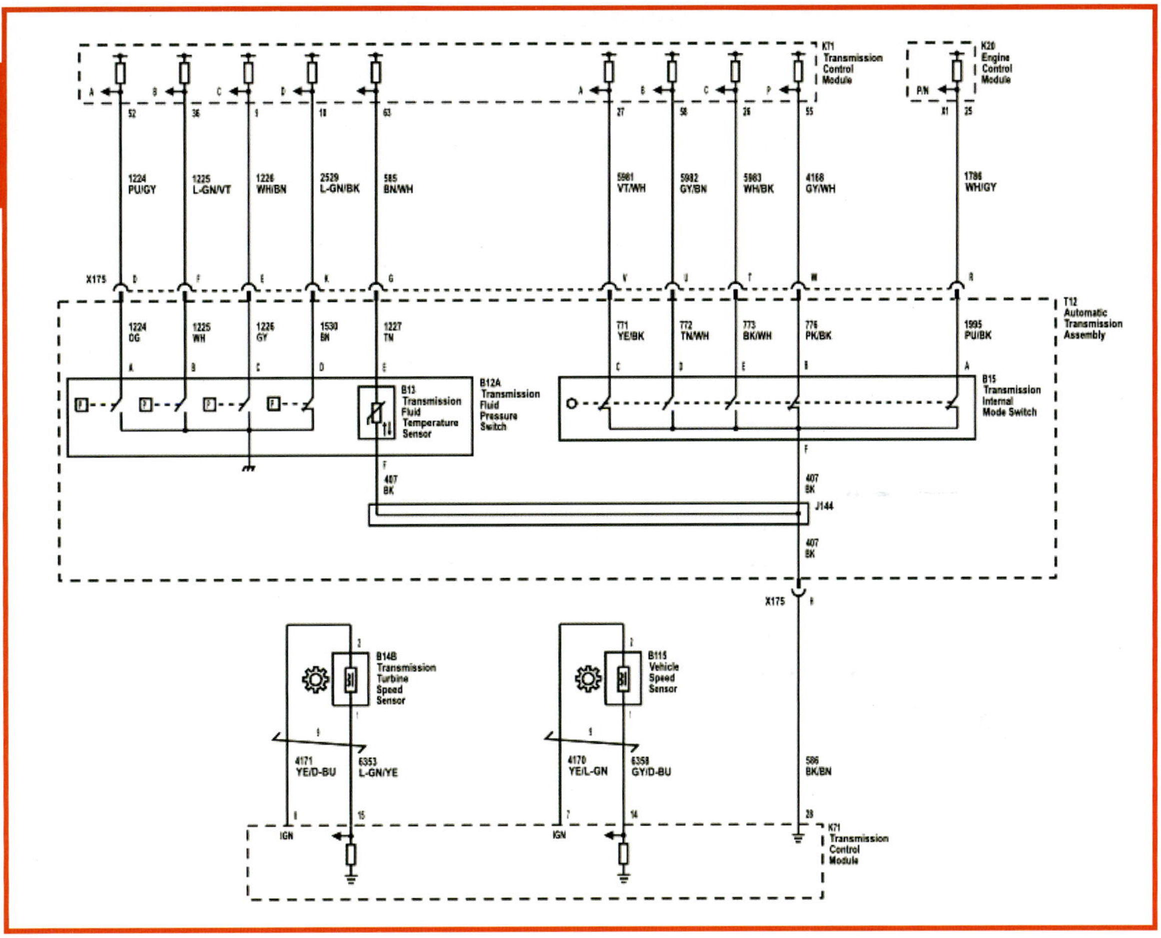

Outputs (LCT 1000, Gen 5)

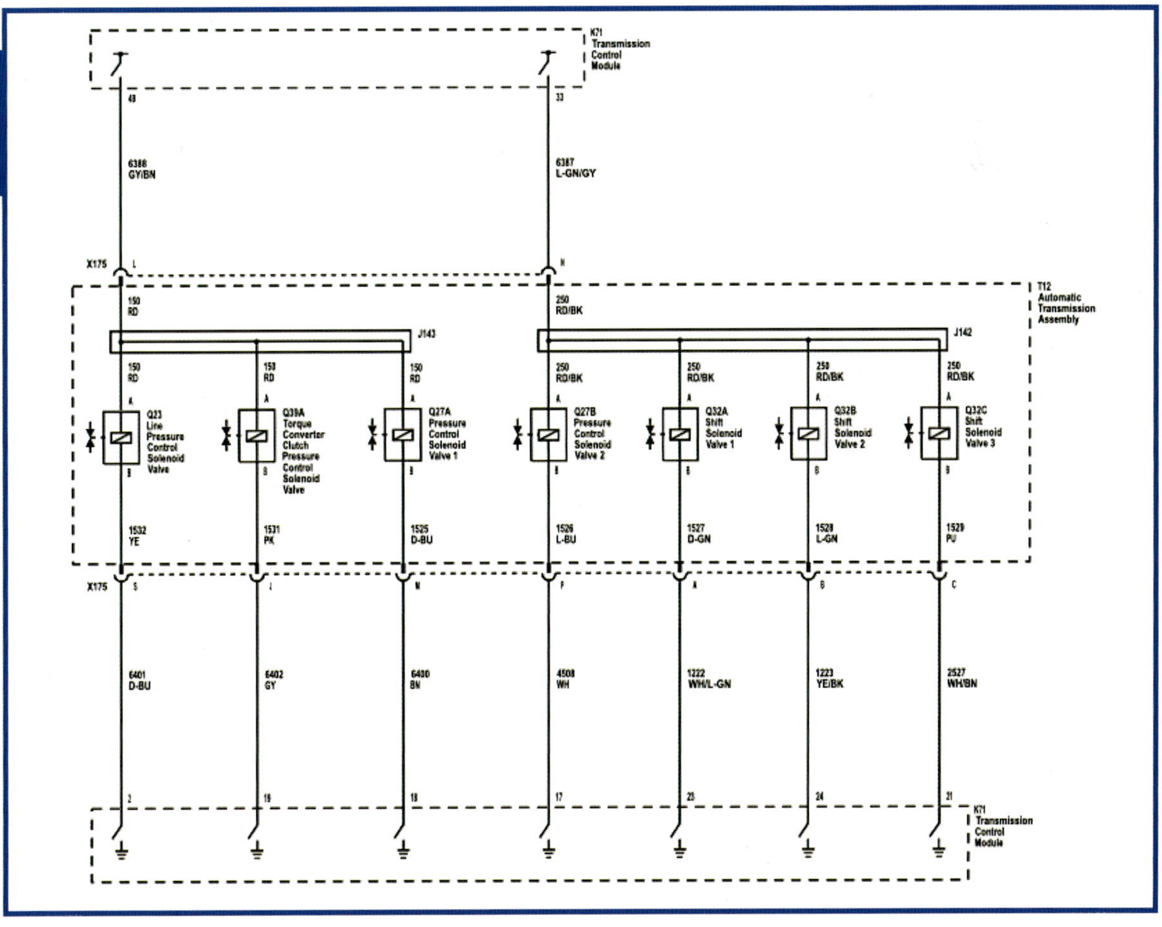

Power Ground, Shift-Lever Switches (LCT 1000, Gen 5)

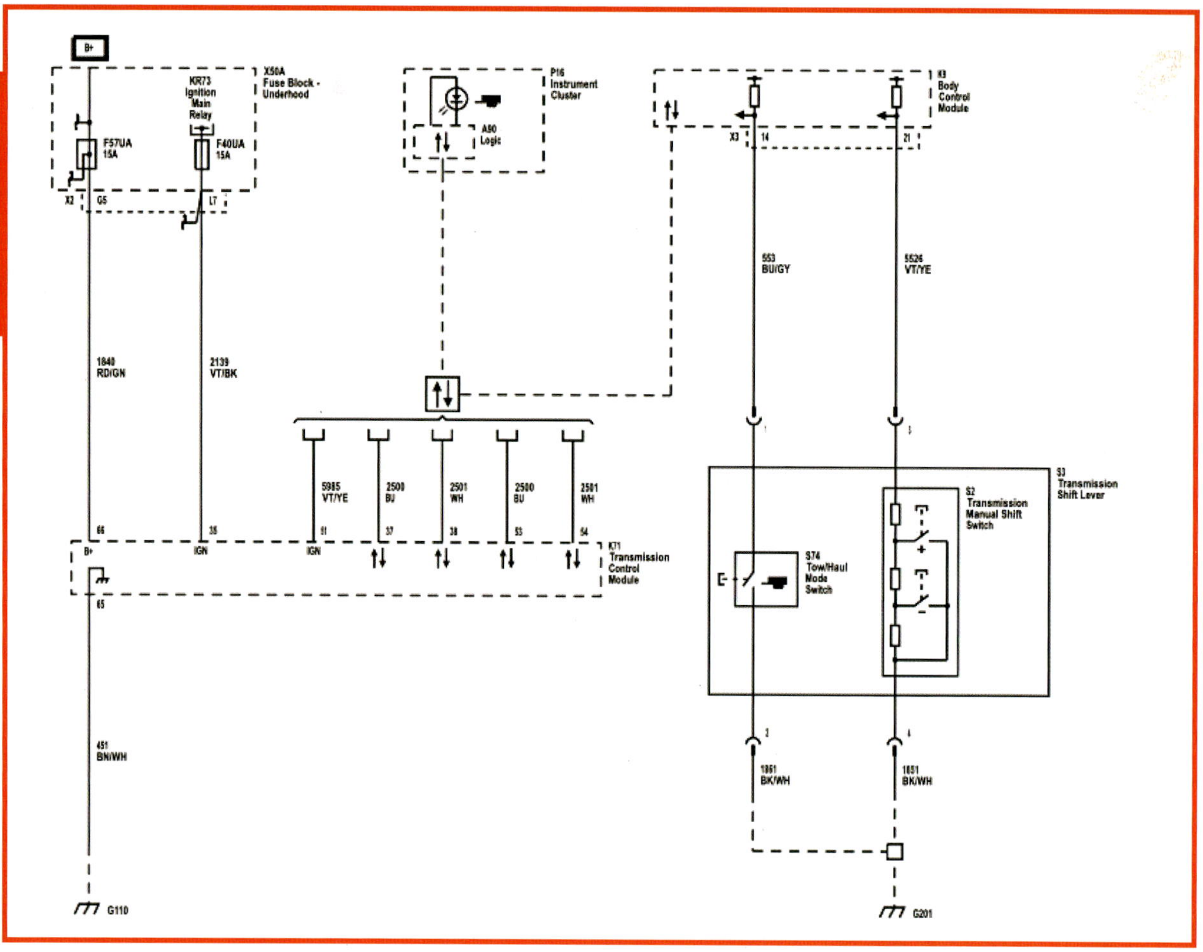

Serial Data Tow/Haul Switch, and Torque Signals (LCT 1000, Gen 1–3)

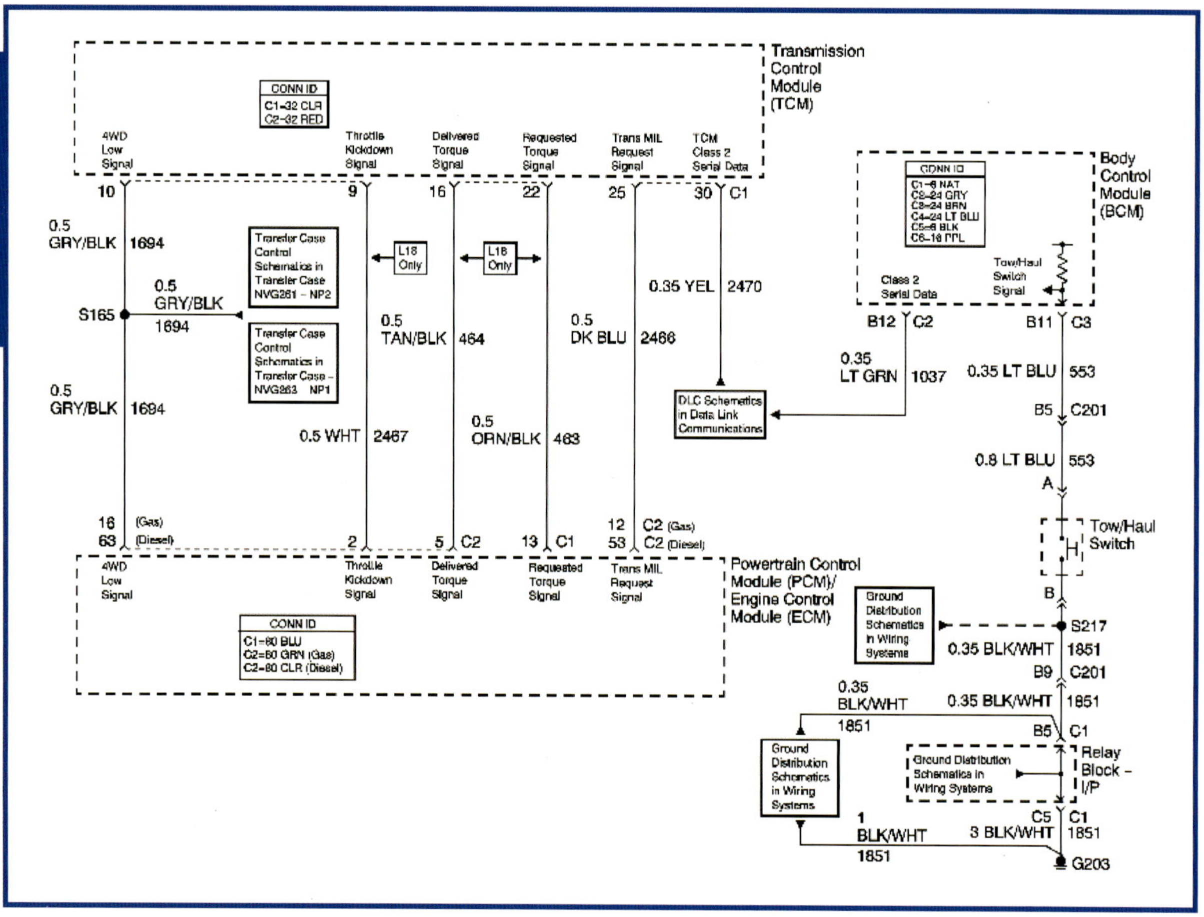

CAN Serial Data, VSS, and PNP Switch (LCT 1000, Gen 1–3)

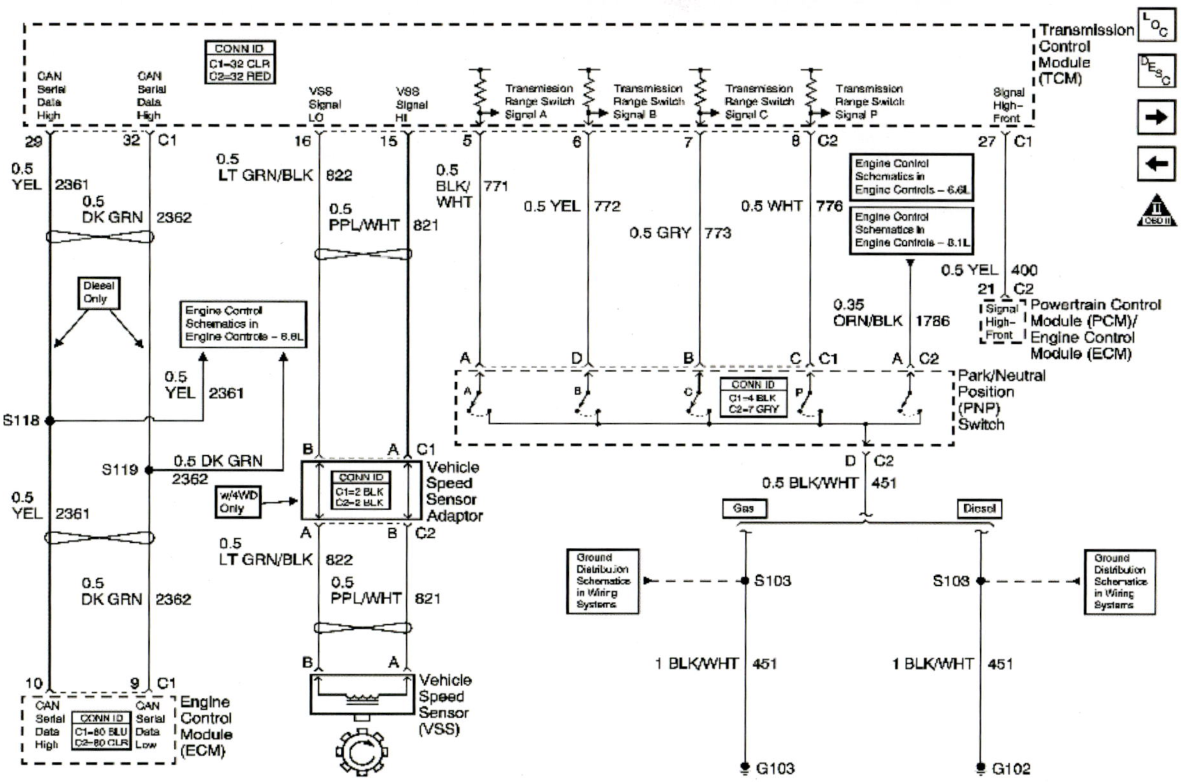

Power Ground (LCT 1000, Gen 1–3)

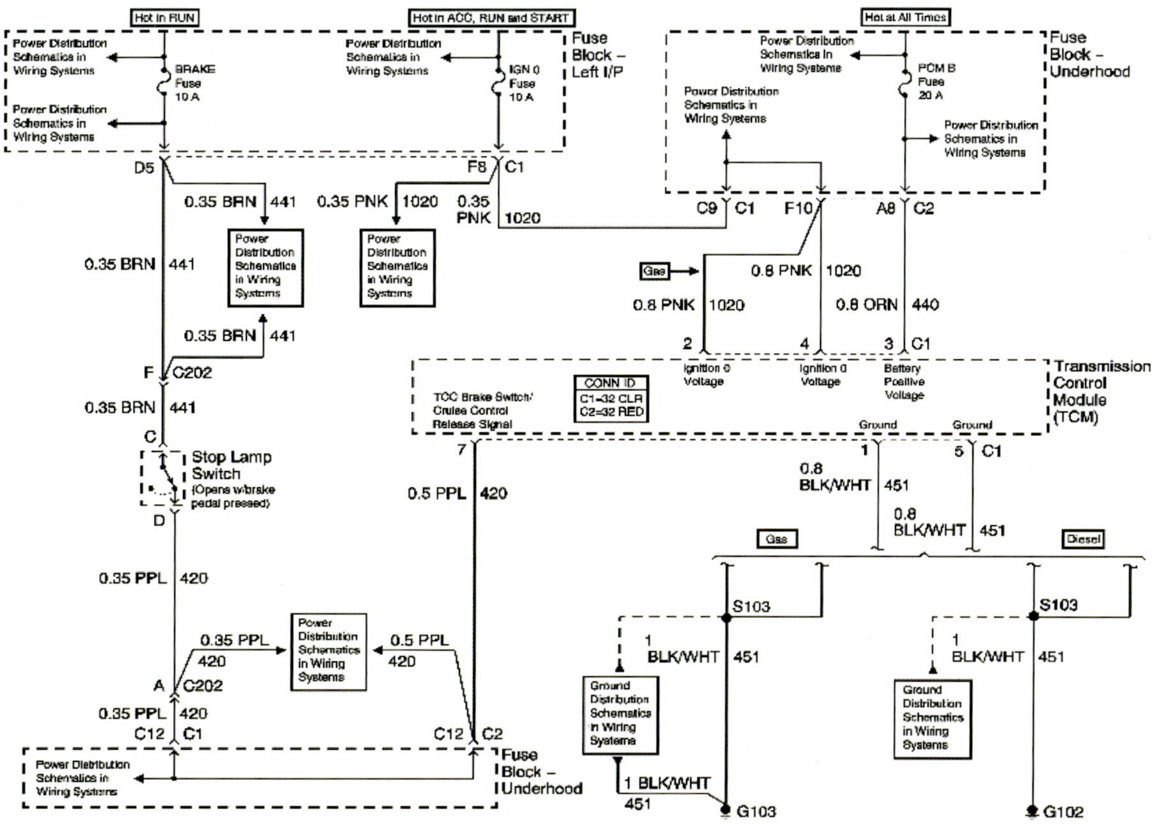

Speed Sensors, Trim B, and Shift Solenoids (LCT 1000, Gen 1–3)

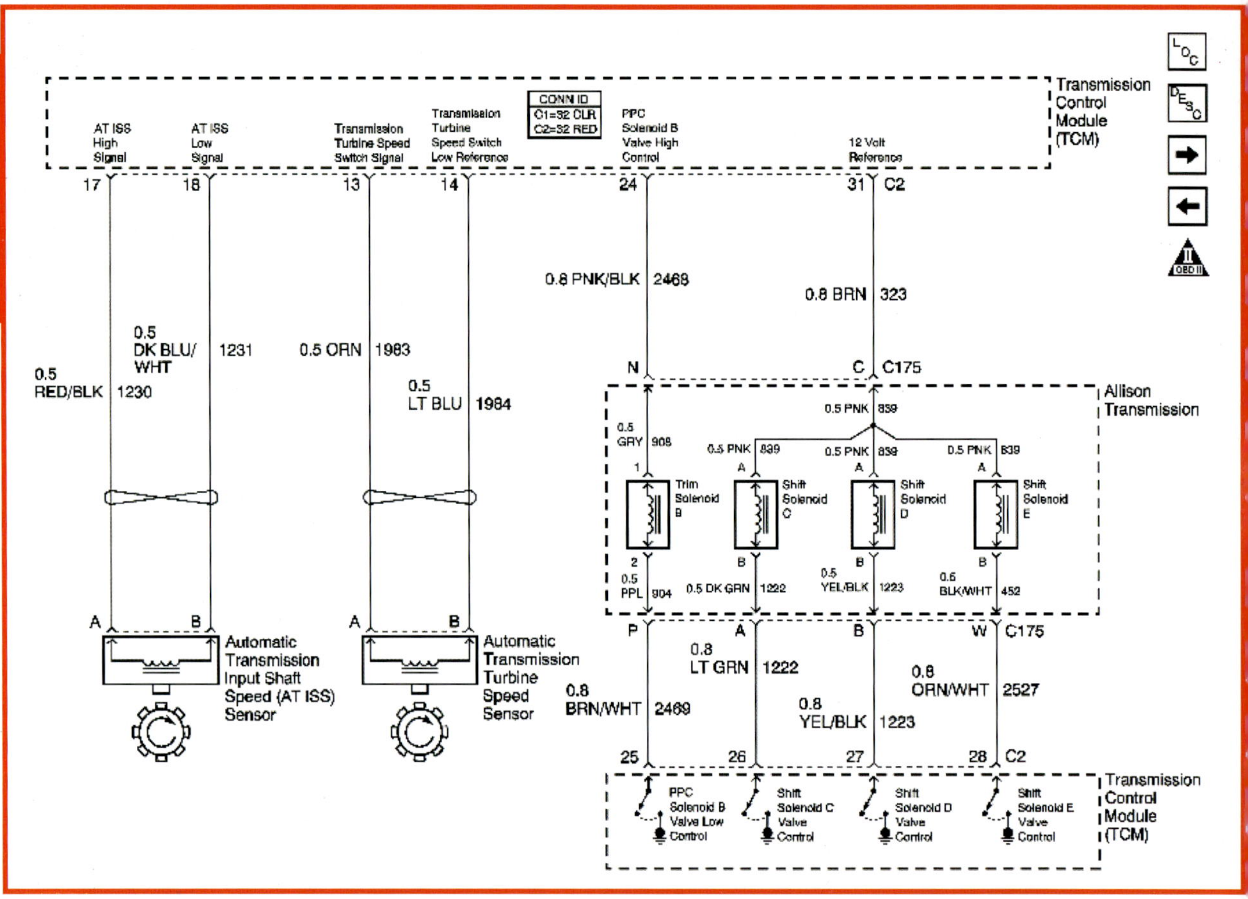

TCC PWM and Trim A Solenoids, Pressure Switches, and TFT Sensor (LCT 1000, Gen 1–3)

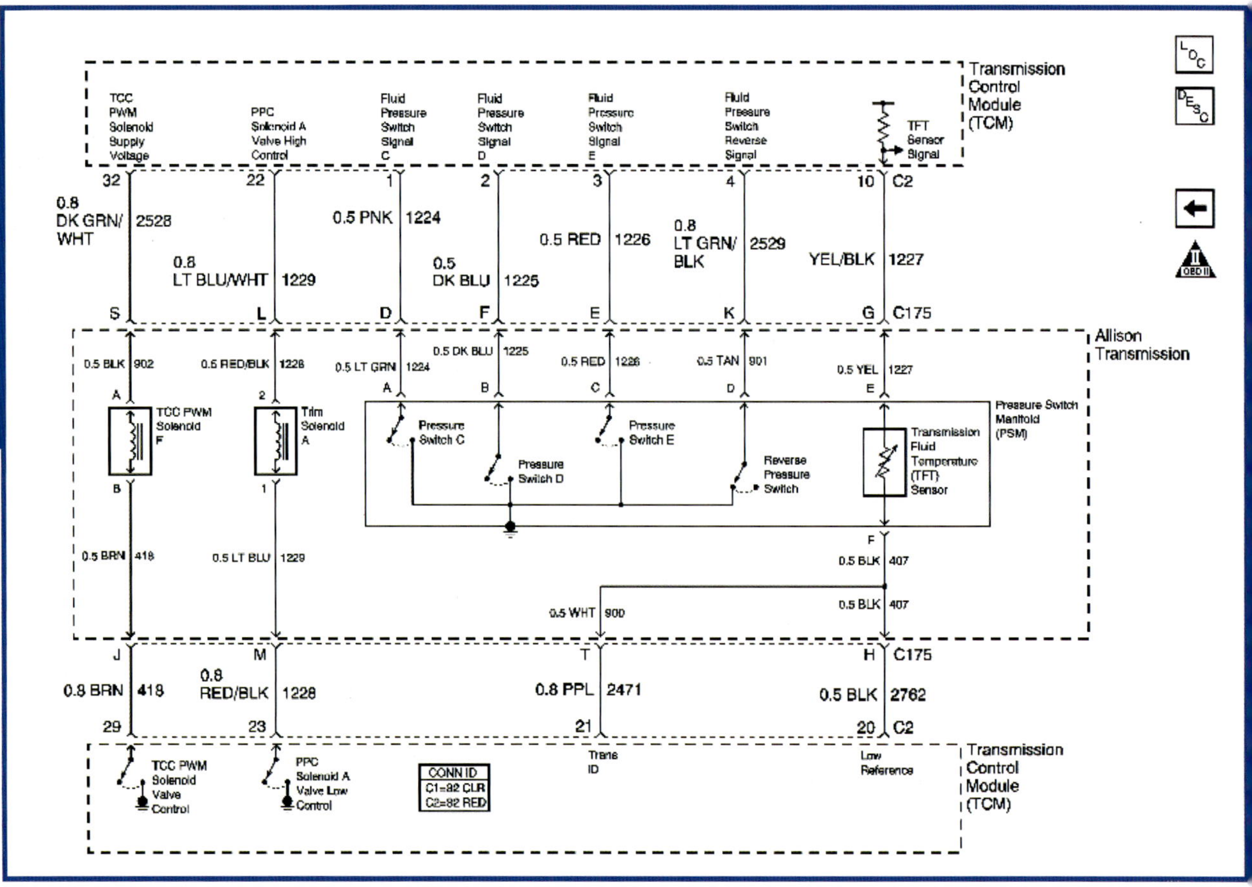